1,000,000 Books

are available to read at

Forgotten Books

www.ForgottenBooks.com

Read online
Download PDF
Purchase in print

ISBN 978-0-282-93253-4
PIBN 10873456

This book is a reproduction of an important historical work. Forgotten Books uses state-of-the-art technology to digitally reconstruct the work, preserving the original format whilst repairing imperfections present in the aged copy. In rare cases, an imperfection in the original, such as a blemish or missing page, may be replicated in our edition. We do, however, repair the vast majority of imperfections successfully; any imperfections that remain are intentionally left to preserve the state of such historical works.

Forgotten Books is a registered trademark of FB &c Ltd.
Copyright © 2018 FB &c Ltd.
FB &c Ltd, Dalton House, 60 Windsor Avenue, London, SW19 2RR.
Company number 08720141. Registered in England and Wales.

For support please visit www.forgottenbooks.com

1 MONTH OF FREE READING

at

www.ForgottenBooks.com

By purchasing this book you are eligible for one month membership to ForgottenBooks.com, giving you unlimited access to our entire collection of over 1,000,000 titles via our web site and mobile apps.

To claim your free month visit:

www.forgottenbooks.com/free873456

* Offer is valid for 45 days from date of purchase. Terms and conditions apply.

English
Français
Deutsche
Italiano
Español
Português

www.forgottenbooks.com

Mythology Photography **Fiction** Fishing Christianity **Art** Cooking Essays Buddhism Freemasonry Medicine **Biology** Music **Ancient Egypt** Evolution Carpentry Physics Dance Geology **Mathematics** Fitness Shakespeare **Folklore** Yoga Marketing **Confidence** Immortality Biographies Poetry **Psychology** Witchcraft Electronics Chemistry History **Law** Accounting **Philosophy** Anthropology Alchemy Drama Quantum Mechanics Atheism Sexual Health **Ancient History** **Entrepreneurship** Languages Sport Paleontology Needlework Islam **Metaphysics** Investment Archaeology Parenting Statistics Criminology **Motivational**

The Story of
Our English Towns

Told by
P. H. Ditchfield, F.S.A.

With Introduction by
Augustus Jessopp, D.D.

Second Edition

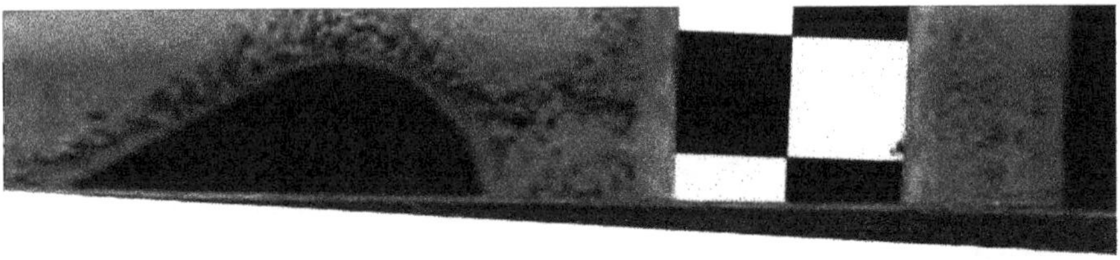

THE history of the origin, the growth, and the constitutional development of our English towns has been investigated so carefully and illustrated by such an immense expenditure of acumen and erudition during the last few years, that it is to be wondered at that no book has as yet appeared which has attempted to summarise, in a popular form, the main results which the labours of experts have arrived at.

The truth is that the literature of the subject has grown to somewhat bewildering proportions, and the questions involved, along with the complex historical problems discussed, and still unsolved, are so numerous that the task of presenting to the general reader—other than the professional student of history—a digest of the views put forward, the facts accumulated and the conclusions arrived at, is a task that few are qualified to undertake, and fewer still would venture to enter upon.

Nevertheless the time has come when the attempt should be made, and it may safely be prophesied that such a volume as this, by an antiquary who has won his spurs, has read widely and has not spared himself the requisite pains, will be accepted as a welcome boon by many who cannot hope to devote years of study to laborious historical research. It was the late John Richard Green who first taught us how much was to be learnt by looking into the past of town life, and how important it was to get an insight into the growth of the town communities. Before the appearance of his "Short History of the English People," few among us had realised that the prowess of heroes and the clash of arms do not make nations. We had been almost taught to believe that institutions can be turned out to order by Acts of Parliaments, by paper constitutions, or by the fiats of conquerors. So they can be up to a certain point, but that point is soon reached. Institutions are living organisms that must grow if they are to thrive and last, and though the gardener's shears may do a great deal in the way of stunting or of shaping the growth, there are limits beyond which he cannot pass in determining how the plant will submit to training. If we desire to know the nature of the organism, we must watch its development from the first appearance of life in it, and we must note its slow or rapid changes, through every successive step from the bud of promise to the branching of the tree that serves to shelter or to shade, or, it may be, to become a mere mischievous and poisonous growth, harmful and deadly.

When Julius Cæsar about half a century before Christ paid his first visit to our island, he took some care to collect information concerning the people he had set himself to conquer. If that information was not all quite correct, and if Cæsar's half-dozen pages are not all that could be desired, yet the wonder is, not that he did not tell us more that we can rely on, but that so much that he does tell us turns out to be true in the main.

There were no towns — as we now understand the word—in our island before the Roman times. Of communities associated under recognised Headmen, whether Provosts, or Mayors, or

Bailiffs, or by whatever other name they came to be known—communities occupying a certain definite area, enjoying a certain measure of authority, possessing a certain corporate existence, and rejoicing in their own laws and customs, having their own police, and taxing themselves to provide a revenue which was spent upon themselves and for the behoof of all—of such communities, I say, our remote ancestors knew little or nothing. In times of peril, Cæsar tells us, the Britons resorted to certain rallying-places which were centres of union, for defence against a common enemy; but of civic life—of city life—they had hardly a notion. Looking back through the dim past, London and Bristol come out of the haze as great trading-places very early. Very early it seems the carrying trade of the West was shared by the Veneti of the mainland and the Britons of the islands. There was commerce in Britain, and that implies association and a much higher civilisation than Cæsar's sketch of Britain would lead us to expect. But it is almost certain that town life among our ancestors began under our Roman masters, who were at the same time our Roman protectors, and the bringers in of new things for those whom they ruled. The Roman occupation of Britain lasted just four hundred years, dating from the first serious and successful invasion by Aulus Plautius, with an army of at least 50,000 men, in A.D. 43, down to the final abandonment of the island in A.D. 446. During all this long period the work of *civilisation* of the subject people went on continuously. That is to say, the Britons were being taught to see the advantages conferred upon a people by the *civil* institutions which town life inevitably brings with it. When Britain was left to defend itself against the hordes of German invaders which poured in upon the island from across the sea, there were at least fifty walled towns in England, exclusive of the military stations with their attendant suburbs, which may be looked upon as fortresses capable of defence by disciplined troops against any assaults which might be made upon them by rude warriors imperfectly organised.

The Teutonic hordes who poured in upon our forefathers, and whom it is usual to call Anglo-Saxons, found themselves more than a match for the Romano-Britons, and they conceived a not unnatural contempt for the islanders, who under their Roman masters had never learnt the art of war, and had found the lessons of military tactics hard to learn. The Saxons in the open probably carried all before them. They had an inbred dislike for cities; they associated gates and walls, and streets and rows of houses, with the notion of slavery. A town with them seemed to be little better than a huge prison, which the sooner it was pillaged and destroyed the better. Nor was this all, the Roman cities proved strong places of resistance for the Britons in the long conflict. As one after another they were stormed or reduced to submission by starvation, they were deliberately destroyed or dismantled. Under the Saxon occupation the towns up and down the land ceased to exist, and though it seems that here and there a Roman town in a dwindled and dilapidated condition managed to keep up the miserable semblance of the old civic organisation, it is hardly too much to say that during the two hundred years which followed the departure of the Romans, town life actually died out in our island, leaving only a few scarcely recognisable vestiges of its old self to testify to the ancient grandeur.

With the beginning of the seventh century a new and mighty force began to work its beneficent influence among the Saxon invaders. Up to this time they had been fierce pagans, and, from all that appears, pagans with no religious faith or religious observances maintained by the teaching or ritual services of an organised priesthood.

The Christian clergy during the long conflict had been driven further and further to the west of the island, and were animated by little or no missionary zeal, but rather by a fierce—if patriotic —hatred of the Teutonic invaders, from whom they and their fathers had suffered so much. But when it pleased God to send the first missionaries from Rome to England in 597, and when the long warfare began to draw to an end, and the fierce Anglo-Saxons began to be weary of battles, and to taste the first sweets of security and peace, the Gospel of Christ gained wonderful acceptance among them. It is true that the mission of St. Augustine produced very much less effect than used, till recently, to be claimed for it; but it certainly was a powerful factor in awakening the best and holiest of those who were still to be found in the old British Church to a sense of their responsibilities and their duties; and so great an awakening came about among the clergy of the older communion, that when sixty years after Augustine's death another band of missionaries arrived from Rome, Theodore, appointed to the Archbishopric of Canterbury, found that Britain was almost a Christian land, and his own work was confined to organising the English Church. Other men had been labouring, and he and his entered into their labours.

It was the influence of the gospel, preached by devoted men—for the most part working in societies bound together by the bands of a discipline which was immensely potent to give cohesion to the society itself, and to secure effectual co-operation and unity of purpose to the members—which brought about the astonishingly rapid conversion of the Anglo-Saxons, and which resulted, too, in the multiplication of those *Religious Fortresses* which the early monasteries became in the centuries that followed.

The Saxon monasteries were slowly contributing to the growth of the new towns, when another stream of invaders burst in upon Britain during the ninth century. What is usually called the Danish invasion was only not as devastating and overwhelming as the Teutonic invasion proved, because there was in the ninth century less to destroy and obliterate than there had been in the sixth. But the struggle with the Danes under the great Alfred and his house could not be a time for peace to bring her blessings to us; there could be no quiet town life then. In the main, during the ninth century *civilisation* was going back; and though there was a grand revival in more ways than one in the tenth century, it was not till the Norman Conquest that our English towns began, as we may say, to rise from the dead, or, if we may vary the metaphor, to raise up their heads above-ground, and to start upon a new growth.

When the great survey was made in 1087, commonly known as the Domesday Book, there were undoubtedly many *towns* to be found through the length and breadth of the land. Some few, as Chester, Lincoln, and York, were survivals of the old Roman cities. They retained certain fragments of their ancient privileges and their ancient importance, and may be said to have *belonged to nobody*, except so far as the mighty conqueror claimed them as his own by right of conquest, and claimed to do with them as he would.

Some again, as St. Albans, Bury St. Edmunds, and Abingdon, were towns that had grown up as suburbs round a great religious house, and which in the lapse of ages had developed into aggregates of traders, craftsmen, agriculturists, and labourers, who were in all cases tenants of the monastery and subject to considerable exactions at the hands of their lords and masters, the abbot and his monks.

Other towns again belonged to a lord temporal or spiritual—a bishop or baron—almost precisely in the same way as, in our own time, an agricultural parish, with every yard of land and every dwelling in it, belongs to the squire or lord of the manor. In these towns the *tenants* were bound to render certain services and to pay certain annual rents—exactly as the tenants of many large estates at the present day are required not only to pay money rents, but to cart a specified number of loads of coal every year to the capital mansion of the landlord. If the lord of the town were grasping, or the tenants were found to be growing rich too fast at the expense of the lord, the relations between the two would tend to become "strained," and each of the contending parties would be trying to get some advantage out of the other; the lord trying to increase his exactions, the tenants endeavouring to secure to themselves more privileges, more security of tenure, more liberty of action for themselves, and more freedom to manage their own affairs and to govern themselves. In all cases the lord of the town, whether he were abbot or earl or bishop, or the king himself, was in the first instance represented by the bailiff, whose business it was to get all he could from the townsmen for his master. It was inevitable that these bailiffs should tend to become the objects of dislike and suspicion to the community over which they exercised a jurisdiction, oppressive in so far as it was a fiscal jurisdiction, and irritating in so far as it was judicial and resulted in the exaction of amercements from the tenants for offences committed against the *customs* of the town or manor, such customs being of the nature of bye-laws, partly of survivals of ancient conditions of tenure imposed in the first instance by the lord, and partly accretions that had grown up under circumstances favourable to usurpations by the lord.

Gradually the townsmen chafed more and more against the pressure brought to bear upon them by the bailiffs, and against the unequal incidence of the dues levied by the lord and exacted by his official. The townsmen clamoured for deliverance from what we should call unfair rating, and everywhere the feeling grew that the lord's dues should be compounded for by a fixed annual payment by the whole body of the townsmen, such annual payment to be adjusted by a new assessment of the *rates*. Obviously this involved that the townsmen should take the management of their finances into their own hands, and be delivered from the presence of the lord's bailiff, who, under the new arrangement, would be left without any *locus standi*. But the old bailiffs had been officials of considerable power, and vested with a considerable measure of authority. To get rid of such an official without any magisterial functions, and to leave the townsmen without any one to take his place, would clearly be impossible. This would have been to reduce the old government to mere anarchy. When the transition came about, the place of the lord's bailiff was supplied by a new bailiff, who was the nominee of the townsmen themselves, an officer elected by themselves —holding his position as chief magistrate by no means necessarily for life — strengthened and to some measure controlled by certain assessors, who acted as a council for carrying on the government of the town, which by this time had begun to be a self-governing community. *Pari passu* with this organic change in the constitution of the towns there was growing up another development of town life. The towns freed from the domination of the old lords stood in very favourable contrast with those other towns which had not yet been able to win autonomy for themselves. It followed that those favoured communities became objects of envy to others. They were desirable places to settle in; they were gradually made *free* of many vexatious imposts; they gradually acquired many trade privileges, and by reason of these they grew in wealth and importance. But the new townsmen were most jealously and fiercely exclusive; they

B

were by no means ready to admit "foreigners" to share in the good things which they or their fathers had won for themselves. The spirit of selfishness, and of very short-sighted selfishness, displayed itself in all the history of town life during the Middle Ages.

Very soon, however, there came a pressure from without which proved irresistible. The towns could look for no growth and no rapid expansion of their trade if only the burgesses or owners of houses within the area of the town, or within the circuit of the city walls, were allowed to engage in commercial operations. Some of the privileges (not all) which the townsmen were so proud of, and guarded with stubborn intolerance of outsiders, were granted to merchants and wholesale dealers who were associated in a new union known as the "Merchant Guild." The "Merchant Guild" brought new capital into the towns, and in the end extended itself step by step to important dimensions. Next came those trade unions which had apparently borrowed their name from the older merchant guilds, but which were, as far as can be made out, mere associations of artificers who banded themselves together for the protection of their several crafts, and whose determined and obstinate tactics had in view simply the keeping up of wages, the keeping down of competition, and the restriction of the output of such manufactures as, but for the efforts of these early protectionists, could have been increased indefinitely, especially in the case of articles of general use. All these checks and fetters upon liberty of trade, all this artificial interference with production, which modern economists are almost unanimous in condemning as merely mischievous and indefensible, did nevertheless result in bringing about one benefit to the community at large, which has been too much overlooked. If the *volume* of English manufactures was kept down, and the consequent expansion of the trade seriously retarded, the *quality* of the work done by the limited number of the artificers could not help being improved. The craftsman could without much difficulty earn a livelihood; he had a great deal of spare time upon his hands, and, if he loved his art, he could pursue it for the mere love of it, with a genuine enthusiasm and a certain large-hearted rivalry, and endeavour to surpass in excellence and artistic finish the work turned out by his brother craftsmen. An artist could afford to throw his soul into his work, because he was not always toiling for mere pay.

But as the mediæval craftsman had, as I have expressed it, a great deal of spare time upon his hands, so he had an abundance of holidays, and he threw himself into his amusements with a determination to get enjoyment out of them. Hence town life in the days with which this volume deals was in the main a much gayer life than ours. The personal element then was much more apparent than it is among ourselves. The "individual" had not yet begun to "wither," and in the towns, not yet grown to monstrous aggregates of population, every man knew every one else within the limits of the civic boundaries. To be quite lost in a mediæval English town was by no means easy. A man who desired to be in hiding never felt safe in the streets; a stranger attracted the eyes of all. The habits of the townsman were eminently social; he was strictly drilled in his religious duties, and these obliged his attendance at the pomps and ceremonies of processions and functions in which every citizen was expected to bear his part. The Parish Church was the place of resort for the whole population, and in the repair and support and ornamentation of this the common home and, in some sense, the palace of the community, all alike took a pride. Things were not done in a corner.

But—

> "The old order changeth, yielding place to new,
> And God fulfils himself in many ways,
> Lest one good custom should corrupt the world."

Things could not go on for ever as they once did among the old burghers. The great break-up came. The suppression—which means the brutal and savage pillage—of the religious houses throughout England brought about incalculable changes in the sentiments, the beliefs, and the habits of Englishmen in town and country. If the townsman did not suffer as cruelly as the countryman did, yet he did suffer sadly—town life could never again be what it had been. English town life, such as it was, passed away for ever. Reading about it now-a-days, we find ourselves reading ancient history indeed. But it is ancient history which has more than one side to it, and these many sides are presented to us in an attractive way in the following pages. There is a bright and hopeful side, when the townsmen are seen at their best, each interested in, and each cheerfully working for, the welfare and the glorification of the community of which they were members; there is a dark and repulsive side, when we see the sordid greed of gain making men mean and covetous, each seeking his own advancement by the meanest tricks of a truculent trade-unionism, or by blind and ignorant efforts to carry on a stupid *protection* of class interests at the expense of those not yet admitted to privileges and immunities. There is a noble and a generous side, when the poor are cared for by the self-sacrifices of the well-to-do, and the claims of the needy and unfortunate upon the rich and thriving are responded to by large alms-giving and splendid hospitality; there is a tender and pathetic side, when we are confronted by the religious activity which exhibits itself in all the public and private life of these mediæval townsmen. Their beliefs were not quite identical with ours; their worship was, so we are pleased to assure ourselves, tainted with superstition, but their practical Christianity (make all the deductions you please) puts us to the blush when we reflect how they were living nearer to their creed than, I fear, we are; and how much more profoundly the religious sentiment influenced the thoughts and habits of the townsmen of the fourteenth and fifteenth centuries than it does ours.

Be it, however, as it may, while we read these pictures of a past which has gone, no wise man will wish to bring back that past—

> " Dead and gone is the old world's ideal,
>   The old arts and old religion fled;
> But we gladly live amid the real,
> And we seek a worthier ideal.
>   Courage, brothers! God is overhead."

CONTENTS

CHAPTER I
INTRODUCTORY

Old English towns—Foreign towns—Decayed towns—Contrast between English and foreign towns—" Belford Regis "—Growing interest in old municipal life—The birthplace of freedom 31

CHAPTER II
BRITISH AND ROMAN TOWNS

Mythical origins of British towns—Earthworks—Pit-dwellings—King Lud and London—King Coel—Bath and Prince Bladud—King Lear and Leicester—York—Edinburgh—Carlisle—Gloucester—Birmingham nail-makers—Chun Castle—Roman towns—Itineraries 44

CHAPTER III
A ROMAN CITY

Silchester—Results of recent excavations—Description of the old city—" Calleva Attrebatum "—Roads—Villas—Hypocausts—Pavements—Villa at Brading—Forum at Silchester and the Basilica—Discovery of Christian church — Baths — Amphitheatre — Decay of Roman cities—Roman London 57

CHAPTER IV
SAXON TOWNS

Saxon ravages—Saxon settlements—A thane's household—Their daily life—Merchants and craftsmen—Danish wars and their effects—Saxon civilisation—Their churches—St. Andrew's, Hexham—Brixham Church—"Domesday Book"—York—Northern England—Lincoln — Chester — Colchester — Death of Saxon freedom 73

CHAPTER V
CHURCH TOWNS

Monastic towns—Peterborough—Orders of monks—The Benedictine order—Reading Abbey in olden days—Piers Ploughman's description of a monastery—Dissolution of monasteries—Bishop's towns — Wells—Bishop's castles—Selby and its hermitage—Influence of the Church—Chaucer's "Poor Parson of a Town" . 93

CHAPTER VI
CASTLE TOWNS

Castles, the mothers of cities—Norman tyranny—Effects of the Conquest on the towns—English merchants—A Norman keep and fortress—Dungeons and their story—The burghers of castle towns—Their services to the lord—Corfe Castle—Social life in the twelfth century—

Fitz-Stephen's, London—Horse-racing at Smithfield—Tilting and tournaments 109

CHAPTER VII
THE GUILDS

Numerous kinds of guilds and their objects—Their origin—Ordinance of guild at Abbotsbury—Guilds and their plays—London—Cambridge—Exeter—The guild-merchant—Royal Winchester and its guilds—Guild-halls 126

CHAPTER VIII
THE TYRANNY OF GUILDS: MODERN SURVIVALS

Some disadvantages of guild-life—Irksome restrictions—Heavy fines—" Foreigners " and " Evil May-day "—Aristocratic tendencies—Basingstoke Guild—Guilds of the Kalendars and other forms of guild-life—Henry VIII. and the City Companies—Destruction of guilds—Preston Guild—Newcastle—Trinity House—Benefits conferred by the guilds 148

CHAPTER IX
MEDIÆVAL TOWNS

Towns built by special decree of the king—Hull—Merchants and their houses—Cannynge of Bristol—Richard Whittington and his cat—Sir John Crosby—John Taverner of Hull and his " Grace Dieu "—Ecclesiastical traders—An old town in mediæval times—Town houses—St. Mary's Hall, Coventry—Craftsmen's hovels—State of the streets—Plagues—" Black Death "—Fires—Foreign traders—Expansion of commerce . 169

CHAPTER X

IN THE STREETS

Street scenes—The London Livery Companies—The Mercers and their pageant—Triumphal return of Henry V. from Agincourt: a City welcome—Pageant for Henry VI. —River pageants—Chester's "setting of the watch" —Coventry plays and pageants—Kenilworth—Corpus Christi Day—Chester plays—Reading—Pillories and punishments—Master Lickpenny's adventures . . 182

CHAPTER XI

IN FAIR AND MARKET

Fairs and their origin—The royal right—Toll and tribute— Description of a fair—Strafford custom—Stourbridge Fair—Fairs in churches and churchyards—Boston Fair and the robber knights—Markets and market- places—Canterbury monks and citizens—The fight for freedom—A burgher's difficulties—Causes of his prosperity—The growth of manufacture—The coming of the Flemings—Henry VIII. and the destruction of municipal freedom 200

CHAPTER XII

THE GREAT METROPOLIS

Royal Winchester—Mercantile supremacy of London— Mediæval London—A tour of the walls of the city— A city of palaces—The Strand and the houses of nobles—Bishops' palaces—Riots—The "Intelligencer" of 1648—The "Newes" of 1665—The Plague— The Great Fire—Memorable buildings . . . 218

CHAPTER XIII

IN THE DAYS OF GOOD QUEEN BESS

"*Merrie England*"—*Ruins and desolation—Scene in Reading Abbey—Destruction of monasteries and disfigurement of churches—The Church and the people—Church-ales—Morrice-dancers and minstrels—Elizabethan houses—A merchant's household—Costumes of women—May-day—Pageants at Norwich—Rogues and vagabonds—Cruel laws* 231

CHAPTER XIV

MEMORABLE SIEGES OF GREAT TOWNS

In time of war—Exeter sieges—Alfred and the Danes—Exeter and the Conqueror—A siege in mediæval times—Perkin Warbeck—" Semper fidelis "—The siege of Gloucester—Colchester—The death of heroes . . 247

CHAPTER XV

UNIVERSITY TOWNS

Oxford and Cambridge—Mythical founders—The history of Oxford—Massacre of the Danes—Saxon Palace—Norman Castle—The flight of the Empress Maud—Old college life—First colleges at Oxford and Cambridge—The battles of scholars—Effect of the dissolution of monasteries—Begging scholars—Destruction of college libraries—Oxford in the Civil War—The homes of learning 256

CHAPTER XVI

CINQUE PORTS AND HARBOURS

Special privileges of the Cinque Ports—The fickleness of the sea—The navy in olden times—Old Sandwich—The troubles of Hythe—Rye and Winchelsea—The Armada —Drake and the "Golden Hind"—Feuds and piracies—Smuggling days 270

CHAPTER XVII

PALATINATE TOWNS AND CATHEDRAL CITIES

Mighty Durham—Its days of splendour—Lancaster and its Duke—Old county towns—Ely and its Palatinate— Chester and its memories—Cathedral towns and their associations—Wells and Salisbury—The bishop and canons 279

CHAPTER XVIII

MODERN CHANGES AND SURVIVALS

Contrasts—Changes in the appearance of manufacturing towns—Changed industries—The old town-halls—The market-cross — Scenes in the market-place — Burning witches—Norwich riots—Birmingham riots—Nottingham and the framework knitters—The parish church— Old windows—Desecrations—Preservation of ancient features of the church—Old Inns—The "Bull" Inn at Coventry—Ancient hostels—Curious signs—Conclusion 290

Our English Towns

CHAPTER I

INTRODUCTORY

Old English towns—Foreign towns—Decayed towns—Contrast between English and foreign towns—" Belford Regis "—Growing interest in old municipal life—The birthplace of freedom.

To those who love antiquity there can be no greater pleasure than to wander through the streets of some of our English towns, and to picture to our mind the strange events which have happened on the very ground upon which we are standing, and the manners and customs of the good townsfolk of ancient days. Every town thus becomes to us a "city of memories," and at every turn and corner we meet with something that reminds us of the past, and recalls the pleasing associations of old town life.

In most of our large towns the old features

are fast disappearing; historical houses, the old quaint, half-timbered and gabled shops, have been pulled down to make room for buildings more adapted to present needs; a new Town Hall occupies the site of the ancient Guild Hall wherein the Merchant Guild of mediæval times transacted their business; and everything is being hopelessly modernised. This process is, of course, inevitable; and these new abodes are doubtless more comfortable and serviceable; but perhaps we may be allowed to sigh over the disappearance of the picturesqueness of our old towns, and the destruction of many features of historical interest and association.

One of the great pleasures in visiting the old cities and towns on the Continent, which have preserved traces of their mediæval grandeur, is to recall the story which their walls, towers, and belfries have to tell of the busy life of past times. Standing beneath the belfry tower at Ghent, we hear the great bell send forth its sonorous note, and think of the time when, at the summons of the bell called "Roland," thousands of sturdy citizens would muster in the market-place, and bid defiance to kings and emperors, who had dared to trifle with the rights and liberties of the brave but turbulent burghers. So mighty was the tongue of "Roland," which seemed a living thing, endowed with a human voice, that the conqueror of Ghent, Charles V., thought fit to silence it for ever, lest it should again rouse the citizens to arms. Steaming down the Rhine in a few hours from Bingen to Cologne, passing by the ruins of many a lordly castle, we think of the time when our journey would not have been quite so speedy, when bands of armed warriors would have sallied forth from every castle wall, and demanded toll and tribute;—and if we refused to pay, there was always a convenient dungeon for us to occupy until we agreed to satisfy the lord's demands. And we might have seen the monks cultivating their vines on the steep, rocky banks, and, perhaps, heard the weird song of the Lorelei, who, seated upon a high rock, by the sweetness of her music, lured gallant sailors and fishermen to their destruction in the swift-flowing river. Or go to Rome itself, the city of cities, where, heaped together, we have the records of all the ages, and where every stone, palace, church, and cathedral have their story to tell of the strange events of the past.

But it is not necessary to journey to Rome, or Belgium, or the Rhine, in order to surround ourselves with the treasures of past ages. Have our own towns no story to tell us? Let us endeavour to discover how rich the towns and cities of England are in historical association, to depict their ancient appearance, and to describe their various origins. Let us live again in the past, and see the knights clad in their coats of mail riding along the streets with their men-at-arms, and the merchants in their sober suits of cloth meeting together at the Guild Hall to discuss the king's wars, or the "hard times," or the troublesome nature of apprentices and craftsmen. A lordly abbot mounted on a mule rides past us, and receives with the utmost complaisance the humble homage of the citizens. A friar too walks along, but he does not meet with the same amount of favour. Smock-frocked peasants and lazy apprentices move along the streets, and ladies with wondrous gowns and curious head-gear complete the picture.

We will endeavour to realise the conditions of municipal life in still earlier ages, long before the palmy days of ancient chivalry, and to discover who first built and inhabited our towns, and what were the causes of their development and growth. There is a wonderful variety in their origin and character. Some were called into being by the establishment of a great monastery; others by a royal decree. Others again owe their origin to the legionaries of Rome, or to the erection of a Norman fortress. There are Bishop's towns, Castle towns, King's towns, and many others, which we shall meet with in our wanderings, and try to mark their various characteristics and varied history.

Some too have sent their names across the seas, and many of their inhabitants also, and established themselves in new lands, in America and Australia, and there attained a pre-eminence unknown in the Old Country. New York, Boston, Melbourne, and many others have long ago eclipsed in size their mother towns and cities here at home.

We hope to visit also some of the decayed old market-towns of England, which now seem so still and peaceful, where, except on market-day, everybody appears to be asleep and no excitement ever comes. And yet through what stormy and tumultuous times these still country towns have passed! Many of them were very active busy places ere the railroads left them high and dry to wither and decay in the grave and sober respectability of old age. It is difficult to imagine that the grey-haired, wrinkled, quiet old man, who walks sedately down the street with bowed head and bent back, was ever the dashing young soldier who fought so bravely in the Mutiny, and stormed the rebel stronghold at Lucknow. Just as difficult is it to imagine that the nation's pulse ever beat quickly in the sleepy streets of Slowchester, or that any more exciting questions were discussed in the market-place than the price of pigs or the rate of wages.

The railroads destroyed the prosperity of many of these old coaching towns through which forty or fifty coaches used to rattle daily, where the inns were ever filled with streams of guests, and their huge stables with post-horses; but they did not destroy their picturesqueness. Indeed with regard to their appearance and beauty our English towns compare very favourably with those on the Continent. We have had wars in this country, but these have never been so incessant as they were in other lands. Hence there are few towns in England which were strongly fortified; whereas abroad almost every town was a stronghold, and no buildings or trees outside the walls were allowed to spring up, lest they should be used as a cover by an enemy. The poor live huddled together in large high houses, with narrow streets between them, and the filth and refuse which accumulate in the ill-drained thoroughfares generally give forth most disagreeable odours. There is always a peculiar smell about a German or Belgian town which is not particularly agreeable to English visitors. Our towns, unenclosed by fortified walls, have naturally extended themselves, and the lines of old English cottages, with their well-tilled gardens, their flowers and creepers, which form the approach to most of our country towns, add a charm and a delight to them.

Miss Mitford in her delightful book, "Belford Regis," thus describes the appearance of the town from which her novel takes its name, and which is none other than the good old town of Reading, our Berkshire metropolis, as it appeared at the beginning of the century:—

"No sooner do we get within a mile of the town, than our approach is indicated by successive market-gardens on either side, crowned, as we ascend the long hill on which the turnpike-gate stands, by an extensive nursery-ground, gay with long beds of flowers, with trellised walks covered with creepers, with whole acres of flowering shrubs, and ranges of greenhouses, the glass glittering in the southern sun. Then the turnpike-gate, with its civil keeper, then another public-house, then the clear bright pond on the top of the hill, and then rows of small tenements, with here and there a more ambitious single cottage standing in its own pretty garden, which forms the usual gradation from the country to the town.

"About this point, where our road, skirting the great pond and edged by small houses, diverges from the great southern entrance, and where two streets, meeting or parting, lead by separate ways down the steep hill to the centre of the town, stands a handsome mansion, surrounded by orchards and pleasure-grounds, across which is perhaps to be seen the very best view of Belford, with its long ranges of modern buildings in the outskirts, mingled with picturesque old streets, the venerable towers of St. Stephen's and St. Nicholas', the light and tapering spire of St. John's, the huge monastic ruins of the abbey, the massive walls of the county gaol, the great river winding along like a thread of silver, trees and gardens mingling amongst all, and the whole landscape environed and lightened by the drooping elms of the foreground, adding an illusive beauty to the picture by breaking the too formal outline, and veiling just exactly those parts which most require concealment.

"Nobody can look on Belford from this point without feeling that it is a very English and very charming scene, and the impression does not diminish on further acquaintance. We see at once the history of the place, that it is at once an antique borough town, which has recently been extended to nearly double its former size; so that it unites in no common degree the old romantic irregular structures in which our ancestors delighted, with the handsome and uniform buildings which are the fashion nowadays. I suppose that people are right in their taste, and that the modern houses are pleasantest to live in, but, beyond all question, those antique streets are the prettiest to look at. The occasional blending too is good. Witness the striking piece of street scenery which was once accidentally forced upon my attention, as I took shelter from a shower of rain in a shop about ten doors up the right hand side of Friar Street—the old vicarage-house of St. Nicholas embowered in greens, the lofty town-hall, and the handsome modern house of my friend Mr. Beauchamp, the fine church tower of St. Nicholas, the picturesque piazza underneath, the jutting corner of Friar Street, the old irregular shops in the market-place, and the trees of the Forbury just peeping between with all their varieties of light and shadow. I went to the door to see if the shower was over, was caught by its beauty, and stood looking at it in the sunshine long after the rain had ceased."

Thus does the charming authoress of "Our Village" describe an old-fashioned English town as it appeared at the beginning of the century. If she could visit it now, she would probably be grieved at the destruction of many beauties which her graphic pen so lovingly described. Prosperity has its drawbacks, as well as its advantages. But in spite of modern changes it is still possible to call to mind the stories of the past that cluster round its ancient abbey, its churches, streets, and those historic houses which the hand of the moderniser has as yet spared.

In many places huge manufactories, smoky mill-chimneys, iron-works belching forth their clouds of black smoke, chemical works which kill all the trees for miles round, collieries which blacken and disfigure the country, and such things, have obliterated all beauty and picturesqueness; but even then they have not quite destroyed all the interesting associations which cluster round the history of an English borough. And it is our endeavour to revive the recollections of the past, rather than to dwell on the outward beauty of our towns.

During recent years considerable attention has been paid to municipal history. Several large volumes of the corporation records and documents of some of our large towns have been published. Abbey charters and churchwardens' account-books have been ably transcribed and printed; many writers have thrown light upon the early history of English Guilds. Hence we have a mass of material to aid us in our investigations, and to enable us to realise the social manners and customs of our forefathers, and the growth of their constitutions and laws. In such matters all Englishmen must take a profound interest; and there is much truth in the saying that "they who care nothing for their ancestors, care little for their posterity—indeed, little for anything but themselves."

To the towns of England we, English people, owe a vast debt of gratitude; we owe to them our progress and our freedom. "In the silent growth and elevation of the English people," says Green, their historian, "the boroughs led the way: unnoticed and despised by prelate and noble, they had all along preserved or won back again the full tradition of Teutonic liberty. The rights of self-government, of free speech in free meeting, of equal justice by one's equals, were brought safely across the ages of tyranny by the burghers and shopkeepers of the towns. In the quiet, quaintly-named streets, in town-mead and market-place, in the lord's mill beside the stream, in the bell that swung out its summons to the crowded borough-mote, in merchant-gild, and church-gild, and craft-gild, lay the life of Englishmen who were doing more than knight and baron to make England what she is, the life of their home and their trade, of their steady battle with oppression, their sturdy, ceaseless struggle for right and freedom."

The progress of this achievement was peaceful, gradual, but sure. "The bell which swung out from the town tower gathered the burgesses to a common meeting, where they could exercise rights of free speech and free deliberation on their own affairs. Their merchant-gild, over its ale-feast, regulated trade, distributed the sums due from the town among the different burgesses, looked to the due repair of gate and wall, and acted in fact pretty much the same part as a Town Council of to-day. Not only were all their rights secured by custom from the first, but they were constantly widening as time went on. Whenever we get a glimpse of the inner history of an English town, we find the same peaceful revolution in progress, services disappearing through disuse or omission, while privileges and immunities were being purchased in hard cash. The lord of the town, whether he were king, baron, or abbot, was commonly thriftless or poor, and the capture of a noble, or the campaign of a sovereign, or the building of some new minster by a prior, brought about an appeal to the thrifty burghers, who were ready to fill again their master's treasury, at the price of a strip of parchment, which gave them freedom of trade, of justice and of government." Thus by sheer hard bargaining were the liberties of our towns acquired; and the freedom-loving burghers have taught the people of England in what true freedom really consists, and inspired them to win for themselves those privileges of liberty and justice which all Englishmen have learnt to prize.

CHAPTER II

BRITISH AND ROMAN TOWNS

Mythical origins of British towns—Earthworks—Pit-dwellings—King Lud and London—King Coel—Bath and Prince Bladud—King Lear and Leicester—York—Edinburgh—Carlisle—Gloucester—Birmingham nail-makers—Chun Castle—Roman towns—Itineraries.

WONDERFUL legends and stories are told by the early chroniclers of the number and strength and mythical origin of the towns of ancient Britain. Our ancestors must have had very lively imaginations. Even the venerable Bede in his Ecclesiastical History tells us that "the island was formerly embellished with twenty-eight noble cities, besides innumerable castles, which were all strongly secured with walls, towers, gates, and locks." Cæsar states that there were towns in Britain when he came to subdue our brave wode-dyed ancestors. "The numbers of their towns was great," he says; but in describing them he adds that the Britons call that a town where they have been used to assemble for the sake of avoiding an incursion of enemies when they had fortified the entangled woods with a rampart and a ditch.

Traces of these rude British towns may be found in every county, and probably many of my readers will have observed on the crest of some hill huge earthen ramparts, encircled by a deep ditch, which once constituted the fortifications of an old British town. Some have several ramparts, and were evidently important strongholds. But inside this enclosure the buildings were simply a few huts composed of wood and thatch, and sometimes the only habitations were holes dug in the ground, covered by a thatched roof. Buckland in his "Curiosities of Natural History" thus describes some pit-dwellings discovered at Brighthampton, near Oxford: "The ancient Britons were in the habit of digging holes for shelter. Not many weeks ago some labourers, when digging gravel at Brighthampton, near Oxford, came across several such excavations. They were simply pits dug in the earth large enough to hold one or two persons." At Worlebury, near Weston-super-Mare, there is a British "town," and the pit-dwellings may still be seen. Very suitable for purposes of defence were these ancient strongholds; the earthen ramparts were sometimes as much as twenty feet in height, and above them was fastened felled timber, which made them more impregnable.

These rude British towns were very different from the wonderful descriptions of them which we find in the early chronicles. We read of the great King Lud, who, according to Geoffrey of Monmouth, "became famous for the building of cities, and for rebuilding the walls of Trinovantum (London), which he also surrounded with innumerable towers. He likewise commanded the citizens to build houses, and all other kinds of structures in it, so that no city in all foreign countries to a great distance round could show more beautiful palaces. He was withal a warlike man, and very magnificent in his feasts and public entertainments. And though he had many other cities, yet he loved this above them all, and resided in it the greater part of the year; for which reason it was called Kaerlud; and by the corruption of the word Caerlondon; and again by change of languages, in process of time, London; as also by foreigners who arrived here and reduced this country under their subjection, it was called Londres. At last, when he was dead, his body was buried by the gate which to this time is called in the British tongue,

Parthlud (in Latin *Porta-Lud*), and in the Saxon, Ludesgata."

There is a story, too, of a son of Lud, who married Blanche, a cousin of Julius Cæsar, to whom a legend ascribes the origin of Norwich Castle. How the Roman Cæsar came to have a cousin named "Blanche" is not explained. And who has not heard of the fame of the mythical founder of Colchester, King Coel, or Cole, whose memory is recorded in the well-known rhyme of "Old King Cole"? But Cole, his fiddlers, and his pipe, exist only in legends, and Colchester derives its name from the river Colne, on which it stands, or perhaps, as some writers maintain, from Colonia, a Roman colony.

Familiar also is the mythical story of the origin of the city of Bath and of the discovery of the hot springs which cure rheumatism and many other ills of life. The legend tells us of a certain Prince Bladud who lived in the year 1853 B.C., or according to Geoffrey of Monmouth 910 B.C. This prince was educated in the learned city of Athens, but being afflicted with leprosy, he was exiled from his country, and became a swineherd. His pigs too became leprous, but by rolling in the black, steaming mud, where the hot springs now boil up, they became healed. The prince followed their example, and was thus cured of his malady. In gratitude for his deliverance he founded the city of Bath, then called Kaerbadus, "and made hot baths in it for the benefit of the public, which he dedicated to the goddess Minerva; in whose temple he kept fires that never went out, nor consumed to ashes, but as soon as they began to decay were turned into balls of stone. About this time the prophet Elias prayed that it might not rain upon earth, and it did not rain for three years and six months. This prince was a very ingenious man, and taught necromancy in his kingdom, nor did he leave off pursuing his magical operations, till he attempted to fly to the upper region of the air with wings which he had prepared, and fell down upon the temple of Apollo in the city of Trinovantum (London), where he was dashed to pieces."

We might narrate many other of these stories; of King Lear, immortalised by Shakespeare, whose real name was Leir, and who built Leircestre, or Leicester; of Hudibras, the father of Bladud, who built Kaerlem or Canterbury, Kaerguen or Winchester, and the town of Mount Paladur, now Shaftesbury. "At this place an eagle spoke," says the chronicler, "while the wall of the town was being built; and indeed I should have transmitted the speech to posterity, had I thought it true, as the rest of the history." About the time that David reigned in Judæa, our British king Ebrancus, after invading Gaul and enriching himself with an infinite quantity of gold and silver, built Kaerebranc, the city of Ebrancus, or York, and also Mount Agned (Edinburgh), "called in this time the castle of Maidens, or the Mountain of Sorrow." When King Solomon was building the temple at Jerusalem, our Leil, a peaceful and just prince, founded Kaerleil, or Carlisle. Gloucester owes its foundation to Claudius Cæsar, who gave his beautiful daughter, Genuissa, to the British prince Arviragus for a wife. The beautiful damsel gained so great an ascendency over his affections, that he valued nothing but her alone; insomuch that he was desirous to have the place honoured where the nuptials were solemnised, and moved Claudius to build a city there for a monument to posterity of so great and happy a marriage. Claudius acceded to his request, and commanded a city to be built, which after his name is called Kaerglon, that is, Gloucester. Although this account of the beautiful Genuissa and Arviragus is purely imaginative, it is quite possible that Gloucester was founded by Claudius and called

Claudii castrum, or Caer Glau. Tradition tells of strong-limbed hardy natives, who lived in the woods where Birmingham now stands, and made nails with their fingers from the iron which they found, and could drive them into a plank with their knuckles. These nails were probably as fabulous as the spear-staves, javelins, and heavy blades which these mythical workmen supplied to the native kings of Britain before the advent of Julius Cæsar and his victorious legions.

The Britons were a very patriotic race, and it delighted them to describe the past glories of their country, even though those glories existed only in their own vivid imaginations. Geoffrey of Monmouth, who wrote in the twelfth century, founded his early "British History" upon the traditions of the Welsh people. It is supposed that he had some early Welsh manuscripts to guide him, and the stories which these contained he probably improved. There still exist some Welsh manuscripts which contain these legends; but whether they were copied from earlier ones, or translated from Geoffrey's chronicle, it has not been satisfactorily determined. At any rate they show that the Celtic race were not unskilled in the invention of romantic myths.

We may dismiss then all ideas of the magnificence of ancient British towns. Strabo states that "the forests of the Britons are their cities; for when they have enclosed a very large circuit with felled trees, they build within it houses for themselves and hovels for their cattle. These buildings are very slight, and not designed for long duration." Diodorus Siculus calls them wretched cottages, constructed of wood and covered with straw. Most of them, like the pit-dwellings, were, according to Strabo, of circular form. Cæsar tells us that they resembled the houses of the Gauls; of these we have some representations on the Antonine column, the roofs of which are in the form of a dome. In the west of England there still remain some stone foundations and walls of these circular houses.

Chun Castle, in Cornwall, is a fine specimen of a British town. It has two circular walls, divided by a terrace thirty feet wide, and composed of rough masses of granite, piled up without cement. A wide ditch surrounds the outer wall. This wall is about twelve feet thick, and must have been about fifteen feet high. There is only one entrance, which is arranged and guarded with wonderful military skill. Within the enclosure adjoining the wall there are the remains of circular stone dwellings. The Herefordshire Beacon is a fine specimen of a British town or fortress protected by a triple rampart, and the famous Tynwald Mound, in the Isle of Man, on which the Manx laws are proclaimed every year, is an interesting relic of ancient British earthworks.

We may therefore conclude that the only towns in this country prior to the Roman conquests were these strongly fortified camps, containing rude collections of huts and pit-dwellings surrounded by ramparts constructed of earth or stone or felled trees.

It was not until the Romans established themselves in this island that real towns sprang into existence. Sometimes the conquerors built their walled towns on the site of these early British encampments, and their fortifications were constructed on the line of the old bulwarks. As each powerful tribe was subdued, the victorious Romans fortified the old British stronghold, or built a fortress near it, and connected all these towns and camps by military ways. The new towns were all regular in shape, bounded by lines as straight as the nature of the ground would permit, usually square or oblong; whereas the old strongholds which they occupied and adapted to their uses retained their original irregular form. We have a record of these Roman towns in the celebrated Itinerary of Antoninus, a Roman officer, who travelled along the old roads, probably in the suite of the Emperor Adrian, and recorded the places which he visited. We have also the valuable Itinerary of Richard of Cirencester, a monk of Westminster in the fourteenth century, which he collected from certain fragments left by a Roman general, and which differs somewhat from the Itinerary of Antoninus.

Very magnificent were many of these towns which the conquerors built in imitation of mighty Rome itself, and adorned with temples, courts of justice, theatres, statues, and other public buildings and monuments. Sir Francis Palgrave says: "The country was replete with the monuments of Roman magnificence. Malmesbury appeals to these stately ruins as testimonies of the favour which Britain had enjoyed; the towers, the temples, the theatres, and the baths, which yet remained undestroyed, excited the wonder and the admiration of the chronicler and the traveller; and even in the fourteenth century, the edifices raised by the Romans were so numerous and costly, as almost to excel any others on this side the Alps. Nor were these structures among the least influential means of establishing the Roman power. Architecture, as cultivated by the ancients, was not merely presented to the eye; the art also spoke to the mind. The walls, covered with the decrees of the legislature, engraved on bronze or sculptured in the marble; the triumphal arches, crowned with the statues of the princes who governed the province from the distant Quirinal; the tessellated floor, pictured with the mythology of the state, whose sovereign was its pontiff—all contributed to act upon the feelings of the people, and to impress them with respect and submission. The conquered shared in the fame, and were exalted by the splendour of the victors."

These Roman towns were of various degrees of rank and importance. Some were called colonies, which claimed the first rank. Roman soldiers were rewarded for their services by receiving a grant of land from the territory of the nations they helped to conquer. This was called a colony, which was a Rome in miniature, enjoying the same privileges, governed by the same laws as the great city of the empire. When St. Paul claimed the privileges of Roman citizenship, which prevented him from being imprisoned and beaten uncondemned, he signified that he was born a citizen of Tarsus, which was a Roman colony, just as some of our English towns were.

The names of these towns were Richborough, London, Colchester, Bath, Gloucester, Caerleon, Chester, Lincoln, and Chesterfield. At these places the remains of Roman buildings are constantly being found, and inscriptions to the memory of worthy citizens of the period. Here is an interesting one, which was discovered recently at Chester:—"To the memory of . . ." (the name is wanting) "a centurion's adjutant who was expecting to become a centurion, attached to the century of Lucilius Ingenuus, when he was shipwrecked and drowned." This stone memorial tells a mournful story of disappointed hopes, and a beautiful romance might be woven around this tragic end of a brave Roman soldier of Chester City.

Another class of Roman cities consisted of those possessing municipal rank and privileges, which were only conferred as a reward for especial services to the empire. The citizens could choose their own magistrates, make their own laws, and enjoyed the same privileges as the inhabitants of a colony. There were only two of this class in Britain, York, and Verulam, now called St. Albans. Ten other towns had the Latian right conferred upon them, viz., Inverness, Perth, Dunbarton, Carlisle, Catterwick, Blackrod,

Cirencester, Salisbury, Caister, in Lincolnshire, and Slack, in Longwood. The remaining towns were stipendiary; that is to say, they were compelled to pay tribute, and were governed by Roman officers. It is well known that all places whose names are compounded of castor, cester, or chester (Latin *castra*, a camp) usually were Roman military stations, *e.g.*, Worcester, Manchester, Doncaster, although this rule is not universally true. An old chronicler mentions twenty-eight of these ancient Roman cities, and to those already mentioned we may add Canterbury, Carnarvon, Norwich, Caermarthen, Grantchester (now Cambridge), Bristol, London, and Leicester.

We see now the country of Britain studded with camps and towns held by sturdy Romans, and connected by great roads. Outside their walls wild bands of Britons roamed; some became civilised and adopted Roman manners, others were enslaved; but the life of towns had begun, and we will try to realise what kind of places these Roman towns were.

CHAPTER III

A ROMAN CITY

Silchester—Results of recent excavations—Description of the old city—" Calleva Attrebatum "—Roads—Villas—Hypocausts —Pavements—Villa at Brading—Forum at Silchester and the Basilica—Discovery of Christian church —Baths—Amphitheatre—Decay of Roman cities—Roman London.

IF we desire to know the fashion of an old Roman town in Britain, it would be advisable for us to discover one that had not been much disturbed by subsequent building operations. Upon the sites of most of these old-world places new towns have been constructed; so that it is difficult to find out many relics of Roman times. But happily we have at least one very important city which has been left undisturbed since the Roman legions sailed away, and abandoned the poor Britons an easy prey to their enemies. It is true that the Saxons overran the place, and time has long since levelled the walls of the houses; but the city walls are still proudly standing, and the earth has kept safely for us during many centuries the treasures and memories of a bygone age.

Silchester was once a large, important, and flourishing place. It contained a forum, or market-place, having on one side a large structure called a basilica, which was a kind of municipal building or town-hall, in which prisoners were tried, business transactions executed, and the general affairs of the city carried on. On the other side of the square were the shops, where the butchers, shoemakers, or fishmongers plied their trade. You can find plenty of oyster shells, the contents of which furnished many a feast to the Romans who lived there 1700 years ago.[1] The objects which have been found tell us how the dwellers in the old city used to employ themselves, and how skilful the Romans were in craftsmanship. Amongst other things have been discovered axes, chisels, files for setting saws, hammers, a large plane, and other carpenters' tools; an anvil, a pair of tongs, and blacksmiths' implements; shoemakers' anvils, very similar to

---

[1] The vast quantities of oyster shells at Silchester and the position of the beds have led antiquaries to believe that the shells were brought there for making lime, and that they are not entirely the remains of Roman feastings.

those used in our own day, a large gridiron, a standing lamp, safety-pins, such as ladies use now, and many other things.

In order to protect the city it was surrounded by high walls, which seem to defy all the attacks of time. These massive walls are nine feet in thickness, and are still in many places twenty feet high. Outside the wall a wide ditch added to the strength of the fortifications. Watch-towers were placed at intervals along the walls, in which the Roman soldiers stood to mark the approach of an enemy who might dare to attack their stronghold. On the north, south, east, and west sides of the city there were strongly fortified gates, with guard chambers on each side, and arched entrances through which the Roman chariots were driven.

These walls enclosed a space of irregular shape, and were built on the site of old British fortifications. Silchester was originally a British stronghold, and was called by them Calleva. The Celtic tribe which inhabited the northern part of Hampshire was the Attrebates, who after a great many hard fights were subdued by the Romans, about A.D. 78. The conqueror, Agricola, tried to civilise the half-savage tribes of Britain, and taught them to have a taste for the arts and for refined pleasures. He encouraged them to build temples and forums and houses, and the Britons soon began to imitate Roman manners and to adopt the Roman dress. And so within the rude fortifications of ancient Calleva arose the city of Silchester with its fine houses, temples, and baths, its strong walls, and gates, and streets, the great centre of civilisation and the chief city of that part of the country.

When Rome was considered the very centre of the world it was said that "all roads led to Rome," but in this part of England it might be said with truth that all roads led to Silchester. There was the great street which led from the east gate to Staines and London. From the south gate issued the street which led to Winchester, straight as a dart, as all the Roman roads were made. From the western gate issued the main road to Salisbury and the West of England, and a branch road to Speen, near Newbury. This is marked by an old Roman milestone, commonly called the Imp stone, probably from the first three letters of the Latin word Imperator, or Emperor, carved upon it. Curious legends often cluster round these relics of ancient times. Just as the superstitious Saxons, when they saw the great Roman roads, made by a people who had quite vanished from the land, often attributed these great works to evil spirits, and called parts of these well-made streets the Devil's Highway; so they invented a strange legend to account for the position of the Imp stone, and said that some giant had thrown it from the city and left on it the marks of his finger and thumb. It is also said to turn round when the clock strikes twelve, but nobody has ever seen it perform this feat. From the north gate a road went towards the Thames to Dorchester.

These streets ran through the city, which was divided into rectangles by the roads. These rectangular spaces were called *insulæ*. When the corn is growing, you may see where the roads ran, for on the surface of the old roads where the ground is thin the corn is scanty. This was noticed by Leland in the year 1586, who says: "The inhabitants told me that it had been proved by long observation that, although this is a fertile and fruitful enough spot, yet in certain places, like little lines which intersect one another, the corn does not grow so equally abundantly, but much thinner than elsewhere, and along these lines they think the streets of the city formerly led." This, of course, was more observable three hundred years ago than it is now, as the soil has become thicker; but even now when the corn is young the course of the streets is perceptible. One is inclined to wonder where all the earth comes from which buries old buildings and hides them away so carefully, but any one who has read Darwin's book on "Worms" will cease to be astonished. It is chiefly through the action of these useful insects that soil accumulates so greatly on the sites of old buildings.

Within the walls of Silchester were gardens and villas replete with all the contrivances of Roman luxury, and filled with rich and costly things. The pit-dwelling Britons must have been very much surprised to see the kind of houses which the Romans built for themselves. These houses were built on three sides of a square court. A cloister ran round the court supported by pillars. The open space was used as a garden. At the back of the house were the kitchens and apartments for the slaves and domestics of the owner. The Romans adapted their dwellings to the climate in which they lived. In the sunny south at Pompeii the houses were more open, and would be little suited for our more rigorous climate. They knew how to make themselves comfortable, so they built rooms well protected from the weather, and heated them with what are called hypocausts. These were furnaces made beneath the house, which generated hot air; and this was admitted into the rooms by earthenware flue-tiles. The dwellers had both summer and winter apartments; the former on one side of the house, the latter on the other; and when the weather became cold the hypocaust furnaces were lighted and the family adjourned to their winter quarters. The floors were made of *tesseræ*, or small cubes of different materials and various colours, which were arranged in beautiful patterns. Some of these pavements were of most elegant and elaborate designs, having figures in them representing often the seasons, or some mythological characters.

The pavements at Silchester which have been discovered are of simple design, but the explorers hope to find some more elaborate ones later on. The Roman builders used mortar, which is very hard and tenacious: they also used small and thin bricks, varying from eight inches square to eighteen inches by twelve, and about two inches thick. Large quantities of these bricks are found at Silchester, and flue-tiles which were made for the hypocausts. Sometimes we find the impress of an animal's foot on these bricks and tiles, formed when they were in a soft state before they were baked, and one tile recently found bore the impression of a Roman baby's foot, which has thus been preserved for so many centuries. Another brick had the word *puellam* (a girl) scratched upon it, evidently by some youth attached to some Roman or perhaps fair British maiden.

The Roman villa at Brading is perhaps the most perfect type of a Roman gentleman's residence. There we find magnificent suites of rooms, colonnades, halls, and splendid mosaic pavements. The subjects represented on these pavements are very interesting and remarkable. We see two gladiators fighting, one armed with a trident, and the other with a net. A fox under a tree is probably contemplating the sourness of the grapes. What a man with the head and legs of a cock is doing, standing in front of a small house, with a ladder leading up to it guarded by two griffins, can only be guessed. In the centre of this group is a Bacchante with a staff. In another room we see Orpheus wearing a Phrygian cap and playing a lyre, by which he is attracting a monkey, a fox, a peacock, and other animals. Again we see "Winter," a female figure closely wrapped, holding a leafless bough and a dead bird, and the other seasons; Perseus and Andromeda;

an early astronomer; the head of Medusa, and many others which need not now be mentioned. There is here also a splendid example of a hypocaust. The floor of the room, called a *suspensura*, or suspended floor, is supported by fifty-four pillars. Flue-tiles admitted the hot air into the chamber, and on the outer side of the wall is the *præfurnium*, or furnace. A remarkable example of a *suspensura* was discovered at Cirencester.

Returning to Silchester, we enter the ancient forum, the great centre of the city, the common resort and lounging place of the citizens who met together to discuss the latest news from Rome, to transact their business or to talk about the weather, as Englishmen do to-day. On the west side of the forum, or market-place, stood the noble basilica, or hall of justice, a splendid building, its entrance being adorned with fine Corinthian columns, and slabs of polished Purbeck marble, and even green and white marble from the Pyrenees, covered the walls. It was a long rectangular hall, 233 feet in length by 58 in width, and at each end was a semi-circular apse, which was called the Tribune. Here the magistrate sat to administer justice, or an orator stood to address the citizens of ancient Silchester.

In the centre of the western wall was another apse where the *curia* met for the government of the city. Two rows of columns ran down the hall, dividing it into a nave with two aisles, like many of our churches. Indeed the form of construction of our churches was taken from these old Roman basilica. On the west of the hall were several chambers, one of which was another fine hall, used probably as a corn exchange or market. In another the records of the city were kept, indicated by the discovery of a Roman seal. At the south corner stood the treasury, among the ruins of which was found a bronze eagle, the proud standard of the Romans borne in front of the legions. Possibly it was hidden away when the city was captured, lest it should fall into the hands of the enemy. How the Romans came to leave their eagle behind, or whether it was of British manufacture in imitation of the Roman ensign, has never been clearly ascertained. Another interesting discovery has been made, a small stone statue of a female wearing a mural crown. This was probably the figure of the Genius of the city over whose destinies it was expected to guard.

By far the most important of the discoveries in this country is the interesting little church, which stood just outside the forum at Silchester. It is very similar in form to the early church in Italy, and resembles the basilica in construction. At the west end, where the altar stood on a mosaic square, is an apse. There is a nave and two narrow aisles, on the east side a porch, or *narthex*, into which the catechumens were allowed to enter. In the open space in front stood the laver, or *labrum*, in which the faithful used to wash their hands and faces before entering the church. This interesting memorial of early Christianity was probably erected soon after the Emperor Constantine's Edict of Toleration, A.D. 313. The size of the church is very small, only forty-two feet long by twenty feet wide, and could scarcely accommodate all the Christians in Silchester; so possibly we may unearth another Christian church before the completion of the excavations.

The Romans were very fond of baths, and no country house of any size was without its bath, constructed in a very complete manner. But in a large city like Silchester there were large public baths whither the Romans resorted daily. The excavations show these arrangements with various chambers connected with a quadrangle of buildings near the south gate, but possibly the great public baths of the city remain still to be discovered. The Romans used to spend a great part of the day in the bath-house, which was a favourite meeting-place for gossip and discussion. Amongst other things found at Silchester was a bronze implement which was used for scraping off the drops from the skin after bathing, thus answering the purpose of a rough towel. It is interesting also to notice the ingenious manner in which the waste water from the different chambers was utilised to flush the drains and sewers.

Theatrical displays were also a great delight to the Romans. No theatre has yet been found within the city walls, but outside there is an amphitheatre where the contests between gladiators, or between men and wild beasts, took place. The existence of a church shows that Christianity was preached at an early date at Silchester, long before the church was built. The Christians would often be persecuted here as in other places, and one of the common ways of treating Christians was to cause them to be killed in an amphitheatre by wild beasts, while the Roman ladies and men thronged to see them die. Most probably at Silchester Christians were—

"Butchered to make a Roman holiday,"

as in other parts of the great Empire. The amphitheatre consisted of a large open space called the arena, called so from the sand with which it was strewn, surrounded by mounds gradually sloping upwards, with five tiers of seats capable of holding several thousand persons. It is difficult to imagine this grass-covered slope occupied by a gay crowd of Romans and wondering Britons, all eagerly witnessing some fierce fight of men with men, or beast with beast, and taking pleasure in the sanguinary sport.

Of course, there was a temple dedicated to some heathen god whom the Romans worshipped, and a second has recently been discovered.

The Britons soon acquired the manners of the Romans, and loved their ways, their baths, and more luxurious manner of living. But the time came when Rome was threatened with invasion, when the Empire had grown so vast, and the race so weakened by luxury, that the legions were unable to guard such wide possessions. Then the soldiers were withdrawn from Britain, and most of their countrymen followed in the wake of the army. The Britons were left to defend themselves, and a poor business they made of it. The old fierce, war-loving heart had ceased to beat; Roman luxury and corruption had undermined the manhood of the race, and the sons of those who had more than once turned the arms of Cæsar were an easy prey to any enemy who might invade our shores. The prosperity of Silchester rapidly declined. In order to make the place more secure they walled up one of the arches of the west gate, and the buildings of the city had evidently fallen into ruins, for they used one of the beautiful capitals of the pillars to make their wall. The temples were deserted, the forum empty, the houses beginning to fall into decay, and a few listless, enervated Britons were left to mourn the ruined greatness of their once prosperous city.

At last the evil day arrived. Ella, the South Saxon chief, with a band of strong, brave Saxons, broke up their camp at Basingstoke, and marched on Silchester. This was in the year A.D. 490. It is said that the stout Roman walls for some time prevented his entrance into the city, and that he accomplished its destruction by attaching burning tow to the tails of swallows, which flew to their nests in the thatched roofs of the Silchester houses and set fire to the place. If there is any truth in the story, the conqueror probably fixed his burning tow to reeds or spears, and the legend of the swallows arose from the confusion between the two Latin words, *arundo* (a reed) and *hirundo* (a swallow). The Saxon conquerors sacked the place, and reduced the buildings to ruins, the city walls alone remaining as a memorial of its former greatness. The soil soon began to accumulate over the foundations of the houses, which alone were left. For centuries this has been increasing, and the memory of Silchester was almost buried with its buildings. It has been left to the men of this generation to uncover the waste places, and to restore in imagination the forgotten glories of this old Roman city in Hampshire.

The story of Silchester is similar to that of many other towns. York, Lincoln, Colchester, and other once great, flourishing centres of Roman life, tell the same tale of mournful decline when the power that once held them was withdrawn.

Roman London, the proud *Augusta*, was the great port of the country. Near the British stronghold of Llyndin (hence we derive the modern name of our famous metropolis) they built a strong citadel, and surrounded the city with a wall. This wall has marked the course of the city boundaries ever since; it has been renewed, strengthened, and repaired, but its course has never changed. Numerous were the ships which came up the Thames and landed their cargoes at the quays of Roman London. Silks and spices, wines and pottery, weapons and trinkets, were brought by the merchants, whose ships returned to foreign ports laden with slaves and iron and hides, which Britain supplied in plenty. Its population has been estimated at not less than 70,000. Nothing remains of Roman London but the famous London stone, near Cannon Street Station, a few fragments of the wall, a few mosaic pavements, a bath, and the amphoræ, fibulæ, cists, altars, and a few bronze statues, which the earth has preserved

The prosperity of the Roman towns in Britain declined after the departure of the legions. Trade and commerce practically vanished. Despair reigned in the ruined forums; black clouds boding troubles were gathering in all directions, and at length the storm burst, and Roman civilisation was swept away by the fierce Saxon sword.

CHAPTER IV

SAXON TOWNS

Saxon ravages—Saxon settlements—A thane's household—Their daily life—Merchants and craftsmen—Danish wars and their effects—Saxon civilisation—Their churches—St. Andrew's, Hexham — Brixham Church — " Domesday Book"—York—Northern England—Lincoln—Chester—Colchester—Death of Saxon freedom.

"MAN made the towns, but God made the country." So evidently thought the Saxons, although they did not know about God when they sailed in their ships to the shores of Britain. At any rate, they preferred to live in the country, to establish their village settlements in the forest clearings, to tend their flocks, and till the land, rather than to shut themselves up in walled strongholds. However, from the Saxons we derive the word "town." They called a lonely farmstead surrounded by a hedge or palisade a 'tun"; the lonely farmstead developed into a village, and these villages afterwards grew into towns with their teeming populations, and of far-reaching extent. All places whose names end in "ton," such as Bolton, were once Saxon settlements, very primitive in character, consisting of a few rude cottages, and very different from the towns or "tons" of to-day.

From the same people we derive our *stokes*, or stockaded places, such as Basingstoke; our *worths*, and *hams*, and *ings*, all denoting Saxon foundations. *Borough* and *burgh* owe their names to the same source, and signify places of shelter, being derived from Anglo-Saxon *beorgan*, and the German *bergen*, to shelter.

Terrible was the destruction which these fierce warriors wrought in the old towns and centres of civilisation. When they captured a city they burned it to the ground and massacred the inhabitants. The fierce Pagan Saxon, when he first came to our shores, knew no pity, and the land was strewn with the wrecks of cities, deserted walls, pillaged churches, and desecrated shrines. According to the British historians these "wolves," these miserable "dogs and whelps from the kennel of barbarism," were the emissaries of Satan and hateful both to God and man. But however savage and relentless they were in time of war, they possessed the makings of a great and powerful nation. Indeed the Saxon character is impressed upon all our institutions, laws, and customs. We Englishmen are a mixed race, as the late Poet Laureate sang—

"Saxon and Norman and Dane are we;"

but we are chiefly of Saxon origin; and most of the sturdy characteristics of the English people are derived from our Saxon forefathers.

The Saxons usually shunned the old walled cities, and considered them " as graves of freedom surrounded by nets." They imagined them as peopled with goblins and evil spirits, and loved to establish their colonies and farmsteads in the open country and forest clearings. Hence when an English town at length grew up, it partook entirely of the nature and constitution of the village communities around it. The original settlement consisted of a number of families holding a district, and the land was regularly divided into three portions. There was the village itself, in which the people lived in houses built of wood or rude stone-work; around the village were a few small inclosures, or grass-yards, for rearing calves and baiting farm-stock; this was the common farmstead. Then came the second division, the cultivated portion, or arable land, and around this the common meadows, or pasture land. Beyond this lay the uncultivated forest, which was left in its wild state, for timber, fuel, and rough pasturage for pigs. The names of places sometimes record these old divisions of land; for example, there are three villages in the suburbs of Reading, Earley, Grazely, and Woodley. *Ear*ley marks the ground where the Saxon farmers cultivated their corn, *Graze*ley the grazing land, and *Wood*ley the wild uncultivated land where their swine pastured. The pasture land was held by the whole community in common, so that each family could turn their cattle into it; but there was always a special officer elected by the people, whose duty it was to see that no man trespassed on the rights of his neighbour, or turned too many cattle into the common pasture.

The cultivated land was divided into three large fields, in which the rotation of crops was strictly enforced, each field lying fallow once in three years. To each householder was assigned his own lot, which was cultivated by the members of his family and his servants.

This was the kind of village which existed in early Saxon times, and the laws which governed its inhabitants were based on the grand principle of common sense, which still remains as a strong characteristic of the English people. How long these Saxon communities remained independent we cannot tell. In times of war it was necessary to have a leader. Chieftains were chosen to lead the forces of the hundred or the shire; they were the ealdermen, thanes, or lords: they became gradually powerful, and began to exercise rights over the communities, undertaking to defend them from hostile attacks, and in return demanding certain services. The classes who composed the community were the *socmen*, or yeomen, the *geburs* or *villans*, the *cottiers* or *bordarii*, and the serfs. All except the serfs enjoyed a certain measure of freedom, although according to their rank they were obliged to render certain services to the lord of the land, or to their lawful master. After discharging their dues they were entirely free. They managed the affairs of their own community in their meetings of freemen; they sent their representatives to the hundred court and to the shire-mote, where criminals were tried, disputes settled, and bargains of sale concluded.

The towns or burghs of Saxon times resembled these village communities in all respects. They were sometimes formed around the fortified houses of the nobles and chieftains, and were rather more strongly defended than the fenced homesteads of the villagers. The inhabitants were freemen; they tilled their own lands which girt the walls, and they had a popular assembly called the "tun-mote," over which an elected grieve, or reeve, presided. Attached to an old oak-tree in some accessible spot, was a bell; and when its harsh notes were heard each freeman left his plough or his axe, and seizing his sword hurried to the place of meeting. A clerk from the neighbouring monastery would record the proceedings; the reeve would settle all disputes, and arrangements be made for the ploughing and cultivation of the common fields belonging to the freemen of the town.

We will try to picture to ourselves the house of a Saxon gentleman of the period. The style of these buildings was very poor and unpretending, very unlike the stately Norman castles which were erected in later times. They consisted of an irregular group of low buildings, almost all of one story, constructed of stone or mud foundations, the upper part of the walls being made of wood. In the centre of the group was the hall, with doors opening into the court. On one side stood the chapel; on the other side a kitchen, and numerous other rooms with lean-to roofs;

a tower for purposes of defence in case of an attack; stables and barns were scattered about outside the house, and with the cattle and horses lived the grooms and herdsmen, while villans and cottiers dwelt in the humble, low, shed-like buildings which clustered round the Saxon noble's dwelling-place. An illustration of such a house appears in an ancient illumination preserved in the Harleian MS., No. 603. The lord and lady of the house are represented as engaged in alms-giving; the lady is thus earning her true title, that of "loaf-giver," from which her name "lady" is derived. The interior of the hall was the common living-room for both men and women, who slept on the reed-strewn floor. There, too, the women talked and worked at their embroidery; and when the hours for a meal approached, rude tables were laid on trestles, and the banquetters sat on benches. A peat or log fire burned in the centre of the hall, and the smoke hid the ceiling and finally found its way out through a hole in the roof. Subsequently the builders devised a solar or withdrawing room for the women of the household, where they could sit and spin and weave; then separate sleeping apartments were made for them, while the men still slept on the hall floor. Thither the bards and gleemen used to come and delight the company with their songs and stories of the gallant deeds of their ancestors, the weird legends of their gods Woden and Thor, and acrobats and dancers astonished them with their strange postures.

These gleemen did not confine themselves to singing or harping or reciting poetry; they were tumblers, and mimics, and dancers, and conjurers. Throwing up three balls and three knives alternately into the air and catching them in their fall was a very favourite trick. Sometimes two men dressed as warriors would perform a mock combat, while the musicians piped, and a female danced around the fighters. We have seen a curious wall painting in a village church representing the daughter of Herodias dancing before Herod, in which she is depicted as tumbling or trying to touch her heels with her head. This was one of their favourite styles of dancing. And if there were no gleemen in the hall there were always games to be played, such as dice-throwing, and even chess and backgammon were not unknown.

In course of time the Saxons furnished their houses with some degree of luxury. The walls were hung with beautiful tapestry woven by the deft fingers of their ladies. We find pictures of their bedsteads, very elaborate structures, with roofs like those of a house, and hung with curtains. Sacks of straw and bolsters laid on the hall floor were considered quite good enough for the retainers. The ladies too were not regardless of finery. They used curling-irons for their beautifully twisted locks; they adorned themselves with rich jewels, earrings, and bracelets, and even in some cases rouged their dainty cheeks.

The Saxons also enjoyed many outdoor sports, principally hunting wild boars, deer, and hares, and even goats. There were no cruel game laws to prevent them, as in later times; and hawking was also a favourite pastime.

Such was the inner life of a Saxon thane's household. The prosperous merchant in the town had a similar abode, and lived very much after the same fashion. The craftsmen lived in narrow streets, in small tenements built of wood. They were a hardy, happy, contented race; they enjoyed great freedom, and had food and work in plenty.

The Danish wars had a disastrous effect on the condition of our towns. Many of them were burnt to the ground by these fierce invaders, who plundered and ravaged the country just as the Saxons themselves had done a few centuries before. In addition these wars struck a heavy blow at the freedom of the citizens. The insecurity of property caused by them, the levying of the Danegelt and other enactments, made it legally binding that every man, whether town-bred or country-born, should have a lord over him. Hence many of the towns passed into the hands of the great thanes or under the dominion of the king. Mr. Green says: "A new officer, the lord's or the king's reeve, was a sign of this revolution. It was the reeve who now summoned the borough-moot and administered justice in it; it was he who collected the lord's dues or annual rent of the town, and who exacted the services it owed to its lord. When Leicester, for instance, passed from the hands of the conqueror into those of the earls, its townsmen were bound to reap their lord's corn-crops, to grind at his mill, to redeem their strayed cattle from his pound. The great forest round was the earl's, and it was only out of his grace that the little borough could drive its swine into the woods or pasture its cattle in the glades. The justice and the government of the town lay wholly in its master's hands; he appointed its bailiffs, received the fines and forfeitures of his tenants, and the fees and tolls of their markets and fairs. But when once their dues were paid and their services rendered, the English townsman was practically free. His rights were as rigidly defined by custom as those of his lord. Property and person were alike secured against arbitrary seizure. He could demand a fair trial on any charge, and even if justice was administered by his master's reeve, it was administered in the presence and with the assent of his fellow-townsmen."

We see therefore that the Saxons had made great progress since they landed on our shores. They had become civilised; many of them lived in towns, and were skilled craftsmen; above all they had become Christians. After their conversion they began to build churches in the towns and villages of England. Beside the thane's palace and adjoining the city market-place these little wooden structures arose, wherein the prayers of the faithful were uttered, and the sacred rites of the church solemnised. Very few of the old Roman churches remained, but Bede tells us that there were two at Canterbury, one of which was repaired by King Ethelbert and assigned to St. Augustine, who made it the seat of a bishopric. In 627 King Edwin of Northumberland built a chapel at York of timber, and the first cathedral of Lindisfarne was made in 652 of sawn oak, and covered with thatch. One of these old wooden churches still remains at Greenstead, in Essex, the nave of which is composed of the half-trunks of chestnut trees fastened by wooden pegs.

But the genius of Wilfrid, Benedict, Biscop, and others, introduced more permanent and beautiful structures than these rude timber churches, and they summoned to their aid builders from Normandy. Here is a description of the church of St. Andrew, at Hexham, taken from the writings of Richard, Prior of the monastery at Hexham, who bears witness to the skill of its saintly architect:—

"The foundations of this church St. Wilfrid laid deep in the earth for the crypts and oratories, and the passages leading to them, which were then with great exactness contrived and built underground. The walls, which were of great length, and raised to an immense height, and divided into three several stories or tiers, he supported by square and other kinds of well-polished columns. Also, the walls, the capitals of the columns which supported them, and the arch of the sanctuary, he decorated with historical representations, imagery, and various figures in relief, carved in stone, and painted with a most agreeable variety of colour. The body of the church he compassed about with pentices and porticoes, which, both above and below, he divided with great and inexpressible art, by partition walls and winding stairs. Within the staircases, and above them, he caused flights of steps and galleries of stone, and several passages leading from them both ascending and descending, to be so artfully disposed, that multitudes of people might be there, and go quite round the church, without being seen by any one below in the nave. Moreover, in the several divisions of the porticoes or aisles, he erected many most beautiful and private oratories of exquisite workmanship, and in them he caused to be placed altars in honour of the Blessed Virgin Mary, St. Michael, St. John the Baptist, and the holy Apostles, martyrs, confessors, and virgins, with all decent and proper furniture to each of them; some of which, remaining at this day, appear like so many turrets and fortified places."

From this description we gather that some of the edifices of Saxon construction were noble and magnificent, but little of Saxon work remains. There is a good specimen of a Saxon parish church at Brixham, near Northampton, also at Bradford-on-Avon, in Wilts. We have noticed that the Saxon towns enjoyed great freedom; they managed their own concerns, and, beyond paying to the king an annual sum for the Danegelt, and a few fines for criminals, they were not interfered with by any external authority. But the time came when William of Normandy conquered England, and he soon began to rivet fetters about the limbs of the Saxons. He claimed to be the lord of all common lands, and the lord of every man who had no other lord. The towns soon began to feel the weight of his arm. From his famous survey of England called "Domesday Book" we may gather some details concerning the old Saxon towns. Many of them were little better than villages. Norwich contained 738 houses, Exeter 315, Ipswich 538, Northampton 60, Hertford 146, Canterbury 262, Bath 64, Southampton 84, Warwick 225.

Let us try to picture to ourselves the condition of some of these chief towns of England before the Conqueror came with his hungry followers to seize the lands of our English forefathers and destroy their freedom. Amongst the most important ranked the ancient city of York, the dwelling-place of the Cæsars, a city renowned not only in Britain, but throughout the whole Roman Empire. London soon became a great centre of commerce; but York was the seat of empire, where Severus, Constantine, and Constantius, Roman Emperors, ruled. It was truly a great and mighty city, stretching far and wide, rich in the costly treasures, the culture, and the splendour which characterised the old Romans. And when they left our shores, and the Saxons came with fire and sword, doubtless York did not fall an easy prey to the conquerors. How or when it became English we know not; but in the course of a few years we find that it was the centre of the Northern Saxon kingdom of Deira.

To the lover of history, to the true Englishman who loves his country, who cares not to trace his ancestry to any of William's band of low-bred robbers—to those "who came over with the Conqueror"—but rather to those true Englishmen "who were here when the Conqueror came"—to him the northern part of England is especially full of interest. A great historian declares it to be "the brightest part of the whole island, the home of learning and holiness, the cradle of the history of our people." Whitby, on the Yorkshire coast, which, as its termination *by* proclaims, was a Danish settlement, was the home of Cædmon, the first of England's sacred poets, who sang of "Abraham returning from the slaughter of the kings;" and Jarrow was the home of Bede, the first of English historians, whose chronicles are so priceless to the student. The men of the north have ever been foremost in brave deeds. The barons of Northumbria were the leaders of those who extracted from the reluctant John the famous Charter of English liberties; and history tells us that the men of the north were ever ready to support a failing cause, and remained faithful to a dynasty abandoned by more fickle subjects.

We will now journey to Lincoln, a Roman colony. There we may see the massive arch of the gate which the Romans made, and which has stood for so many centuries. Briton, Roman, Englishman, Dane, Norman, have all inhabited this famous city and made it their own. In Roman times, if we entered the city, we should have seen a forum, or market-place; a basilica, or court of justice, possibly converted into a Christian church; several temples built in honour of Roman gods, as Jupiter or Mercury, but all deserted, or consecrated to the worship of the one true God. Then there were the shops and the houses of the inhabitants, built on three sides of a quadrangle, very well-planned structures, rich with the art of bygone times. Such was Lincoln in the days of the Romans. Then the Saxons came, and here the good Paulinus preached to them, and converted the chieftains to Christianity. Then the Danes came, as they did in goodly numbers and in many ships, and built their towns in all parts of Lincoln and Norfolk. All places ending in *by* were Danish towns; they left behind also the names of their chiefs and warriors, and the places, Grimsby, Ormsby, Osbernby, Asgarby, tell of the valiant deeds of Grim, Orm, Osbern, and Asgar. When the Danes settled in Lincoln they formed a league or confederation of towns. Five boroughs, Leicester, Lincoln, Nottingham, Stamford, Derby, united together for purposes of defence. In the Anglo-Saxon Chronicle we read:—

> "Five towns
>   Leicester
>   and Lincoln
>   and Nottingham
>   so Stamford eke
>   and Derby
> to Danes were erewhile,
> under North-men,
> by need constrained,
> of heathen men
> in captive chains,
> a long time;
> until again redeemed them
> for his worthiness

Lincoln was almost a complete commonwealth; it governed itself and made its own laws, independent of any external power. When the Normans came it held out for a long time, preserving its own laws and customs, but at length it had to bow before the stern Conqueror. William, however, did not unduly oppress the brave citizens; but he built a castle, as was his wont, to prevent any subsequent rebellion against his authority. Lincoln became the centre of a vast diocese, which stretched from the Thames to the Humber, Remigius, Bishop of Dorchester, in Oxfordshire, having decided to fix his episcopal seat in the famous city of the fenlands.

Two other Roman cities which, after many changes, passed under Norman sway were Chester and Colchester. The city, on the banks of the Dee, the great "city of legions," has preserved its walls. It was the last to yield to the Normans' might. The capital of Essex has also a complete circuit of walls, which are, in fact, Roman work, repaired where time and war have made breaches in them. The city suffered from many attacks and owned several masters. The Romans captured the British stronghold, and built the city, which was again taken by the Britons under the brave heroine Boadicea, who captured London,

Verulam, and this Roman station. But the poorly armed Britons, though led by such a noble leader, could not long resist the well-drilled legions. Colchester again became Roman. The Danes held it for a time, but were dispossessed by the Saxons. The city fared well at the hands of the Conqueror, many of the townsfolk being allowed to retain their houses. We have noticed the process which went on in several cities and towns of England which converted them from Roman to English places, and marked the footsteps of the Norman William as he trod upon the rights of his Saxon subjects, and reduced many of their towns to ruined heaps. There is a clear description of a Saxon stronghold in a curious poetical fragment, entitled "The Ruin," taken from the *Codex Exoniensis* :—

> "Wondrous is this wall-stone,
> The fates have broken it,
> have burst the burgh-place.
> Perishes the work of giants.
> The roofs have fallen in
> the towers tottering
> the hoar gateways despoiled
> Rime on the lime
> Shattered the battlements."

The old order changes, giving place to new.

Norman cooks and adventurers seize the lands and houses of the old English gentry. Strong castles overawe the citizens, and Saxon freedom perishes beneath the stern tread of the conquerors.

CHAPTER V

CHURCH TOWNS

Monastic towns—Peterborough—Orders of monks—The Benedictine order—Reading Abbey in olden days—Piers Ploughman's description of a monastery—Dissolution of monasteries—Bishops' towns—Wells—Bishops' castles—Selby and its hermitage—Influence of the Church—Chaucer's "Poor Parson of a Town."

SOME of our towns owe their origin to the Church. There are several monastic cities which were formed by the settlement of various people in the neighbourhood of some monastery. Thus Peterborough was founded; the settlement which grew up round the great fen-land monastery of St. Peter, then called Medeshampstead, gradually grew into a borough, and then into a city. The monastery was founded in a wilderness; but a number of artisans were constantly employed about it, constructing new buildings and repairing the old. These monastic houses, too, were the chief resting-places for travellers, who were entertained in a separate building, called the *hospitium*, and waited upon by the monks. Many of them were places of pilgrimage, whither the pilgrims flocked in order to fulfil their vows. This, too, would constantly bring an influx of visitors. The monastic house had large estates attached to it; and the Lord Abbot was a very important person, having a large retinue of servants, and a large amount of business to transact; consequently, many persons would constantly be brought thither, and by degrees a town would spring up, as at St. Albans, Reading, St. Edmundsbury, or Bury St. Edmunds, the name meaning the *town* of St. Edmund's—*i.e.*, attached to the Abbey of St. Edmund's.

There were various orders of monks, who had different rules of life, different dress, manners, and customs. The Cistercian monks, who arose in the twelfth century, shunned the haunts of men. They built their houses amid woods and wastes, by the banks of rivers, and covered the vales of England with their beautiful dwelling-places. Fountains Abbey, in Yorkshire, is a grand specimen of their architectural skill; but with the Cistercians we have little to do, as they shunned all cities and towns, and loved the sweet solitude of hills and streams. But another order of monks, the Benedictines, loved to build their monastic houses in towns, or towns soon arose around their majestic abbeys. Many people have strange and hazy notions about abbeys. They have seen the ruins of these once mighty dwelling-places, and have come to believe that all abbeys must be ruins. What they were before they were ruins, these people do not stop to inquire. It is important for us to consider what they really were, and what kind of life was lived by the inhabitants of these old English abbeys.

The Benedictine order was founded by St. Benedict, an Italian, in the year 529, and his rule was adopted by most of the monasteries in the Western Church. The monks took the vows of obedience, poverty, and chastity, and also of seven hours' manual labour a day. Labour was regarded as a sacred duty, not only as a means of support. They wore a black gown and hood over a white woollen cassock. By degrees, the rule of seven hours' manual labour was relaxed, and learned studies, the writing and illuminating of books, were substituted for the humbler form of toil. The monasteries became very wealthy, having large estates and rich possessions, and all the literature, art, and science of the period were to be found within their walls. The monks paid great attention to architecture, as their buildings testify, to sculpture, and painting; they taught the children of the townsfolk and neighbouring gentry in the monastic schools; they built hospitals, and nursed the sick, entertained strangers, and at regular hours each day they attended service in their abbey church.

The abbot exercised great power over the townsfolk who lived in the town which grew up beneath the shadow of the monastery over which he ruled.

The monks of the Abbey of Reading exercised complete control over the good townsfolk. They enjoyed freedom from all customs, tolls, and contributions throughout England and the seaports, and the privilege of trying thieves and other criminals within the territory of the abbey. The abbot was allowed to coin money, and even to confer the honour of knighthood. All judicial authority was in his hands; the mayor and corporation were merely dependents on the abbey. Even the right of selecting the mayor and burgesses of the town rested with the abbot, and it was not until the reign of Henry VII., after years of bitter fighting, that the burgesses were allowed to elect three persons, one of whom the abbot appointed to the office of mayor. No person could be admitted to the freedom of the borough without the abbot's consent, who duly received some share of the fine paid by the new freeman. His officers collected the fees from the stall-holders at the markets and fairs, were very careful to uphold the dignity and authority of their master, and continually came in conflict with the officials of the town. So supreme was the authority of a lordly abbot in ancient times. Very magnificent were the entertainments which sometimes took place here. When John of Gaunt married the rich heiress Blanche of Lancaster in the grand abbey church, the festivities lasted a whole fortnight, and feastings and tournaments with grand displays of pomp and chivalry were held daily. The parliaments of England often assembled here, and all the great barons of the kingdom flocked to meet their sovereign in the abbey precincts. Such were some of the scenes which constantly were witnessed in an ancient abbey.

An old writer, the author of "Piers Ploughman," gives a description of the appearance of a monastery in the fourteenth century. As he approached the monastic buildings, he was so bewildered by their greatness and beauty, that for a long time he could distinguish nothing certainly but stately buildings of stone, pillars carved and painted, and great windows well wrought. In the central quadrangle he notices the stone cross in the middle of the grass sward; he enters the minster, or church of the monastery, and describes the arches, carved and gilded, the wide windows, full of shields of arms and merchants' marks on stained glass, the high tombs under canopies, with armed effigies in alabaster, and lovely ladies lying by their sides in many gay garments. He passes into the cloister, where the monks used to read and study, and sees it pillared and painted, and covered with lead, and conduits of white metal pouring their water into bronze lavatories, beautifully wrought. The chapter-house, in which the monks assembled for monastic business, was, he says, like a great church, carved and painted like a parliament-house. Then he went into the refectory, where the monks had their meals, and found it a hall fit for a knight and his household, with broad tables and clean benches, and windows wrought as in a church. The head of the monastery was the abbot, who had a grand house adjoining the monastic buildings, besides two or three country houses, whither he used occasionally to retire. Under him were several officers—the prior; the precentor, who attended to the singing in the minster; the cellarer; the sacrist or sacristan (whence we derive our word "sexton"), who looked after the fabric and furniture of the church; and the hospitaller, who attended to the comforts of the travellers who came to the *hospitium* of the abbey. Besides these, there was the infirmarer, who presided over the infirmary attached to every abbey; the almoner, who distributed the alms to poor people; the master of the novices, who taught in the schools of the abbey; the porter, kitchener, seneschal, &c. In addition, there were the workmen and the servants of the monastery, a host of millers, bakers, tailors, smiths, grooms, gardeners, and others, who were all obliged to conform to the rules of the institution which furnished them with bread and employment. This large number of persons attached to a mediæval monastery will give some idea of its vastness and importance.

Within the monastic walls all was quietude and peace; without, the townsfolk plied their respective callings, while a goodly company were entertained in the *hospitium*, whither flocked a mixed and noisy crowd of knights and dames, monks and clerks, palmers, friars, traders with their wares, minstrels with their songs, and beggars, enjoying to the full the hospitality of the monks, who recognised it as one of their duties "to entertain strangers."

The arrangement of the buildings of a Norman abbey may be better understood by referring to the published plan of the remains of the Abbey of Kirkstall, in Yorkshire. The principal features are the same in all abbeys, although the details of the arrangements of the chambers differ. On the north of the abbey always stands the abbey church, a magnificent edifice with its grand massive pillars, immense central tower, semicircular arches, its monuments and tombs of departed abbots and great men. On the east side of the quadrangle always stood the chapter-house, wherein the monks used to assemble daily to hear a lecture on some portion of the Bilbe, or to transact the affairs of the abbey. The stone seats on which the monks sat may still be seen, ranged in two tiers; on the higher sat the monks, and at their feet the novices. The abbot sat in a raised chair at the east end of the chamber, and when he raised his hand, the monks would fall on their knees in token of their obedience. The refectory usually stood on the south side of the cloister court, and the dormitories on the east. A grand and noble place was an ancient abbey in the days of its glory. How we should like to see one now in its former beauty and grandeur! But even musing amidst its crumbling ruins in imagination we may picture its past magnificence, and restore the beauties of the ancient pile.

Sometimes we find traces of the monks and nuns in the old monastic gardens. Under the wall of a nunnery may be seen a curious plant with heart-shaped leaves and a yellow trumpet flower. It is not a native plant. It is called *Aristolochia*, or birthwort, and was grown by the nuns, who used to nurse the sick for miles around, and found this plant useful as a medicine in certain cases.

The ancient abbeys have passed away. They had done their work and conferred great benefits on the country. They preserved the love of learning, literature, art, and science during the dark ages of ignorance and lawlessness. The monks were the architects, the artists, and scientists of their age; they nursed the sick and fed the poor; and their homes were sanctuaries of peace in the midst of a turbulent and war-loving age. Some few had become corrupt; but nothing can excuse the covetousness and rapacity of King Henry VIII. and his ministers, who destroyed these beautiful houses, murdered the abbots, and seizing upon the property of the Church, converted it to secular and private uses. It was then that large estates and tithes which belonged to the monasteries were granted to the king's favourites, and the lay tithe-owner began to exist.

When the monasteries were dissolved, the buildings soon began to crumble; they were used as quarries for stone. Many a church, bridge, town-hall, and private house in the neighbourhood of an old abbey has been built with its stones. Some of the churches of the monastic houses have been converted into cathedrals or parish churches, but many of them have completely disappeared, save only a few massive foundations, which mark the site and tell the glories of the magnificent pile that once stood there.

When the abbey was destroyed, the town, which owed its existence to the monastic foundation, was quite strong enough to stand alone, and the mayor and burgesses were doubtless pleased to be freed from the dominion of a powerful master who was very careful to maintain his authority over them. But many classes suffered much by the dissolution of abbeys; and especially the poor missed their good friends, the monks, who gave them food and drink, the surplus of the meals in the refectory. The widows, orphans, and poor clerks had no one to provide cloth and shoes for them at Christmas, and when they were ill they missed their constant visitors and comforters. But good often comes out of evil; and it was for the ultimate advantage of this country that the monasteries ceased to exist.

Some other towns also owe their origin to the Church besides those which grew up under the shadow of some great abbey. As we have an abbot's town, like Peterborough, so we have a bishop's town, like Wells, which grew up at the gate of the bishop's palace and cathedral. In other countries, we find that the bishop often selected some city as his episcopal residence on account of the greatness, the importance, or the security of that city; but in England he fixed his seat in some church, as at Wells, within his lordship of Wells, and the little city arose around the bishop's house, and received its privileges and municipal rights from the grant of the bishop himself. Thus we have a bishop's town, or city. A city differs from a town in that it is, or has been, the seat of a bishop.

Bishops, too, built castles for themselves on

their estates. The Conqueror William appointed Norman prelates to the English Sees, who were strangers to the people, and were by no means loved by them. In order to protect themselves these bishops built their castles, and lived like barons, ever ready to make war upon a neighbouring baron, or to subdue with armed hand any revolt amongst their Saxon subjects. These strongholds were often necessary in those troublous times, as Bishop Walcher found, when he was appointed by the Conqueror Bishop of Durham, as the temporal and spiritual ruler of a fierce and unconquered people, who had slain two former earls, and wished to kill the bishop himself. At Durham, Llandaff, and Wolvesey, the bishop's palace was itself fortified on account of the opposition of the people; but generally the palace was without any fortification, and the bishop's castle was on his rural estate away from the city. For example, Bishop Roger of Salisbury, who built the cathedral, raised the castle of Devizes, where he could live as a lord, fly hawks, and make war like his neighbours; and around his castle the town began to grow, although there were probably some houses there before the Norman bishop began to build his stone walls.

Selby town began life as the cell of a hermit,

such as Lydgate describes in his Life of St. Edmund—

> "A litel hermitage
> Be side a ryver with al his besy peyne,
> He and his fellawis that were in nombre tweyne,"

or such as Spenser tells us of—

> "A little lowly hermitage it was,
> Down in a dale, hard by a forest's side,
> Far from the view of people that did pass
> In travel to and fro ; a little wide
> There was an holy chapel edified
> Wherein the hermit duly wont to say
> His holy things each morn and eventide ;
> Hereby a crystal stream did gently play,
> Which from a sacred fountain welled forth alway."

Selby's hermitage became afterwards a monastery, and then a town quickly sprang up around the hallowed walls.

It would not be too much to say that in late Norman and Plantagenet times every town was a church town, so great was the authority and wealth of the Church, so numerous were her buildings. It has been estimated by a recent writer, that at this period one fourth of the area of the City of London was occupied by ecclesiastical buildings, their courts and gardens. In other towns the case was similar. Wallingford in Berks, which now is well served by three parish churches, had then fourteen; Norwich had sixty; York had forty-five; London, one hundred and twenty. In addition to these there were the monastic houses belonging to the various orders, the nunneries, and friars' houses. Outside the walls of the town these churches and monasteries held vast estates and manors, and were as rich as a devoted and Church-loving people could make them. The power and authority of the Church was very real and very visible. English Churchmen used often to begrudge the wealth which alien potentates, who sat on the papal throne, drew from this country, complained angrily, and refused supplies; but they never dreamed of refusing to give largely to the Church at home.

We remark also how closely the ministrations of the Church were associated with the daily lives of the people. The craftsmen and merchants all belonged to guilds (of these we shall have much to say presently) which were religious fraternities, dedicated to some saint, and possessing a chantry or chapel in the parish church. The holy days of the Church were the holidays of the people. Each day they attended an early service in their church. All day long the bells of the churches and monasteries were ringing for some service. The parish priests were beloved and revered by their people, and certainly they were worthy of all honour and respect if Chaucer's description of the poor parson of a town, who was one of the Canterbury Pilgrims, be a true one.

> "A good man there was of religioun,
> That was a poure parsone of a toun ;
> But riche he was of holy thought and werk,
> He was also a lerned man, a clerk,
> That Criste's gospel trewely wolde preche,
> His parishens devoutly wolde he teche.
> . . . . . .
> A better priest I trow that nowhere none is,
> He waited after no pomp in reverence,
> He maked him no spiced conscience,
> But Christe's love, and his apostles twelve
> He taught, but first he followed it himselve."

Such men as these gained the confidence and love of their people. In all departments of their social life the presence and influence of the Church was seen and felt. Abbots' officers collected their market dues. Monks and nuns nursed them in their hospitals when they were sick. Monks housed them when they travelled abroad on a pilgrimage or to some distant fair. Monks taught their children; the clergy acted plays for them in the churches; the Church supplied thousands with work, and was a liberal mistress. From the dawn of life to its closing day the Church was the very centre and soul of the social life of the people of England; and in spite of many errors and shortcomings she continued for centuries to carry on her beneficent work in moulding and developing the national character, and in making the English race a noble and God-fearing people.

CHAPTER VI

CASTLE TOWNS

Castles, the mothers of cities—Norman tyranny—Effects of the Conquest on the towns—English merchants—A Norman keep and fortress—Dungeons and their story—The burghers of castle towns—Their services to the lord—Corfe Castle—Social life in the twelfth century—Fitz-Stephen's London—Horse-racing at Smithfield—Tilting and tournaments.

In wild and turbulent times, when every man's hand was against every man, places of security were naturally eagerly sought after. Hence when the Norman conquerors built their castles and strongholds, groups of houses quickly arose nigh the strong walls of the keep, silently soliciting the protection of its high towering battlements. Therefore castles became the mothers of cities, just as we have noticed the monasteries begat children; and very cruel stepmothers some proved themselves to be, at least as far as the English portion of the inhabitants were concerned.

Saxon writers lament over the sadness of the times when English lands were bestowed upon the followers and favourites of the Conqueror, who reared their mighty strongholds everywhere "filled with devils and evil men," who plundered the English, confined them in dungeons, and were guilty of every kind of act of cruelty and crime. The English were forced to work in building these castles, which must have seemed so strange to them, accustomed chiefly to wooden walls and humbler dwelling-places.

A glance at the famous Domesday Book reveals the disastrous effect which the Conquest had on the condition of our towns. Many of the inhabitants fled to the woods or were killed in the wars, and their houses were destroyed in the sieges, or fell into decay. Thus at York there were 1607 houses before the Conquest; afterwards only 967, of which 400 were much decayed; and one of the six scyræ, or wards, was entirely laid waste for the building of a castle to overawe the city. In Lincoln, where there were 1150 houses, 166 were destroyed for castle-building and 74 were in ruins. In Dorchester, which formerly contained 188 houses, 100 were totally destroyed. Oxford had 721 houses before the Conquest, 478 of these were afterwards in ruins. The records of

Shrewsbury, Ipswich, Northampton, Cambridge, all tell the same sad tale of devastation and ruin. Moreover many of the houses were occupied now by Normans, who were free from the burdens of taxation; some were given to the abbeys and were also free; and yet the few remaining English burgesses were required to contribute to the king's exchequer as much as the town had contributed before in the time of King Edward the Confessor, when there were double the number of householders, and all paid tribute.

The merchants of England before the Conquest had become rich and prosperous. William of Poictiers, the Conqueror's chaplain, tells us : " The English merchants to the opulence of their country, rich in its own fertility, added still greater riches and more valuable treasures. The articles imported by them, notable both for their quantity and their quality, were to have been hoarded up for the gratification of their avarice, or to have been dissipated in the indulgence of their luxurious inclinations. But William seized them, and bestowed part on his victorious army, and part on the churches and monasteries, while to the Pope and the Church of Rome he sent an incredible mass of money in gold and silver, and many ornaments that would have been admired even in Constantinople." *Væ victis!* Englishmen might well groan as they struggled in vain beneath the mailed foot of the Conqueror.

The gaunt rectangular or circular Norman keep, or donjons, stern in their passive strength, and mightily convincing of the power of the conquerors, were very similar in their construction. They were built for strength and not for beauty, and possessed little of the palatial character of the castles of later periods, such as Kenilworth. Sometimes a solitary keep frowned down upon the town, and reminded it of its chains; but a full-fledged Norman castle covered a considerable area of ground.

When we approach one of these old fortresses we see massive high walls with an embattled parapet surrounding the lower court, or ballium. A moat encircles the castle. We enter the fortress by a gate defended by strong towers. There is a barbican which protects the bridge. A portcullis has to be raised and the heavy door thrown back before we can enter, while above in the stone roof of the archway there are holes through which melted lead and pitch could be poured upon our heads, if we had attempted to enter the castle as assailants. On one side of the court we notice the stables; in the centre is a mound where the lord dispenses justice, and where traitors and criminals are executed. Another strong gateway flanked with towers protects the entrance to the inner court, or bailey, and straight before us frowns the donjon, or keep, of the castle, "four-square to every wind that blew," a mighty place, 150 feet in height. It contains several rooms, one above the other. The basement is used chiefly for stores. Here is a deep well to supply the garrison with water, in case they are surrounded by their foes. We ascend the spiral stone steps laid in the thickness of the wall, and reach the first floor, where the soldiers of the garrison reside. Above this as we ascend we arrive at the state apartments; there is a hall, as large as the walls will allow, with a chimney, where the lord of the castle and his guests had their meals, and in the thickness of the walls there are numerous chambers used as sleeping rooms, garderobes, &c., and the piscina outside one of the doors shows that the apartment is a small chapel or oratory. The upper story is divided by wooden partitions into small sleeping apartments. Unlike our modern houses, the kitchen is at the top of the keep, and opens on to the roof. In the hall or in the ladies' bower, or boudoir, the wife of the baron and her handmaidens live, and weave beautiful tapestry and hangings whilst her lord is away from home, crusading in the Holy Land, or fighting for his king in France. And sometimes a neighbouring baron bethinks him that this would be a favourable opportunity of possessing himself of his absent friend's property. Summoning his vassals and men-at-arms, he marches suddenly at nightfall, and tries to surprise the castle; but often he meets with a warm reception, and many a noble and brave lady, during her husband's absence, has refused to surrender, and courageously held the fortress until succour arrived.

Before the end of the reign of Stephen it is said that 1115 of these castles were built; and some of them were held by tyrannical and evil men, who placed their sentinels on the watchtowers, and when some convoy of merchandise was seen passing along the road, or some rich-looking travellers, a company of reckless soldiers would issue from the gates, seize the strangers, and drag them to their dungeons, and keep them there until a sufficient ransom had been paid.

Dreadful places were these dungeons. Let us descend the staircase in the north tower of our castle, which seems to go down into the bowels of the earth, down the cold grey stone steps, and enter a long corridor, dark and gloomy, where the silence is broken by many a groan from despairing captives in the cells on either side. In the cell of one were toads and adders; another had to repose on a bed of sharp flints, while the torture-chamber echoed with the groans of the victims of mediæval cruelty, who were hanged by their feet and smoked with foul smoke, or hung up by their thumbs, while burning rings were put on their feet. Knotted strings were drawn about a man's head and writhed till they went into the brain. Then there was the horrible rack, whereon a man was stretched, and drawn out until every bone in his body seemed on the point of breaking; the heated pincers, for tearing the flesh . . . but we will draw a veil over the horrors of those loathsome haunts. But why were men so tortured? It was almost always for money— to extract a heavy ransom, to obtain lands and estates, to know the secrets of buried treasure, and the like; it was this that made men such horrible wretches and devils in human form; and when men have stooped from their high estate as children of the Almighty, and given themselves over to sin and lust, their nature seems to become changed, and they learn to take a savage pleasure in terrible acts of shameless cruelty.

But there were certain persons for whom the baron had some regard, and those were the burghers of the town which had grown up around his castle walls. They were well able to protect themselves, having obtained charters and privileges from their sovereign, which were ratified by the lord, who feared to use any acts of violence against them. Commerce soon began to gain its peaceful victories, and to have interfered with the trade of the burghers would have been as foolish as the conduct of the old woman who killed the goose that laid the golden eggs. When their lord was in financial difficulties, as was not infrequent, the thrifty burghers were quite willing to advance money to him on condition that he would grant them privileges and immunities, and enable them to ply their trade and live at peace under the protection of his castle walls and armed hosts. The strength which comes from uniting together for common purposes, the establishment of merchant-guilds of which we shall have more to say presently, enabled our townsfolk of former times to hold their own even against the rapacity and injustice of a hard and cruel lord; and this united action of the burghers laid the foundations of English freedom.

The tenants of the lord had to render certain

services for the land which they held of him. At Nottingham, in the time of Henry IV., all who held a bovate of land were obliged to plough and harrow one day in the year for their lord, receiving as their recompense three pennyworth of wheaten bread and pease, *i.e.*, about 3s. of our money. At other times they had to sow and weed, make hay and reap corn, for which they received, with other things, 4d. to drink, and a pair of white pigeons. On one estate in the same county, a right royal feast was spread each night for the tenants who mowed their lord's hay, consisting of beef, pork, lamb, pigs, ducks, and veal, and various flagons of beer. It is probable that the tenants prolonged their labours for as many days as possible.

What strange sad tales of war and cruelty the stones of these proud castles could tell, if only they could speak! Every one has heard of Corfe Castle, where Edward, commonly called the Martyr, was stabbed by his step-mother Elfreda at the castle gate, when he was quenching his thirst after a long ride. Here King John starved to death twenty-two foreign supporters of his rival Arthur. Here Peter of Pontefract was drawn and hanged, his head being placed on a spike at the entrance gate as a warning to others. If all the terrible

I do not think there is a city with more commendable customs of church attendance, honour to God's ordinances, keeping sacred festivals, almsgiving, hospitality, confirming betrothals, contracting marriages, celebration of nuptials, preparing feasts, cheering the guests, and also in care for funerals and the interment of the dead. The only pests of London are the immoderate drinking of fools and the frequency of fires. To this may be added that nearly all the Bishops, Abbots, and magnates of England are, as it were, citizens and freemen of London, having their own splendid houses to which they resort, where they spend largely when summoned to great Councils by the King or by their Metropolitan, or drawn thither by their own private affairs."

Such is the picture which Fitz-Stephen draws of ancient London. He tells us also of the tradesmen and craftsmen plying their respective callings in their own particular localities, of the famous Chepe (hence our Cheapside), a large open space surrounded by sheds or stalls where all manner of fine things could be bought. The mercers, the grocers, the armourers, the leather sellers, and many others, have all their own quarters in the city, which we will examine more carefully at a later period of their existence. He tells us too of the weekly market at Smithfield, held every Friday, where horses and cows and hogs were sold, and how the young men raced their horses when the fair was over. The worthy monk becomes quite enthusiastic in describing the sport. He says: "When a race is to be run by this sort of horses (hackneys and war-steeds), and perhaps by others which also, in their kind, are strong and fleet, a shout is immediately raised, and the common horses are ordered to withdraw immediately out of the way. Three jockeys, sometimes only two, according as the match is made (for such as being used to ride, know how to manage the horses with judgement): the grand point is to prevent a competitor from getting before them." This surely is obvious, Master William, even to a monk! "The horses on their part are not without emulation—they tremble, are impatient, and continually in motion; and at last, the signal once given, they strike, devour the course, hurrying along with unremitting velocity. The jockeys, inspired with the thoughts of applause and the hopes of victory, clap spurs to the willing horses, and brandish their whips, and cheer them with their cries."

The sturdy young citizens had many other sports; they shot their arrows at the butts; they wrestled; they played hockey, baited bulls and bears, and even horses; they skated in winter on the shallow water in Moorfields. The Norman knights introduced tournaments with all the pomp and gallant display of ancient chivalry, although for many years they were prohibited on account of the supposed danger to public safety which a large concourse of armed men and excited spectators might entail. But the young townsfolk went mad over tournaments. They tilted at each other on the ice, their feet being shod with bones in lieu of skates. They tilted at each other in boats on the river, which sport Stow describes as follows:—"I have seen also in the summer season upon the river Thames, some rowed in wherries, with staves in their hands, flat at the fore-end, running one against the other; and for the most part, one or both of them were overthrown and well ducked." They tilted at shields stuck on posts at Easter—as an old writer says:—"They fight battles on the water. A shield is hanged upon a pole fixed in the midst of the stream. A boat is prepared without oars, to be carried by the violence of the water, and in the forepart thereof standeth a young man ready to give charge upon the shield with his lance. If so be he break his lance upon the shield, and do not fall, he is thought to have performed a worthy deed. If so be that, without breaking his lance, he runneth strongly against the shield, down he falleth into the water, for the boat is violently tossed with the tide; but on each side of the shield ride two boats furnished with young men, which recover him that falleth as soon as they may. Upon the bridge, wharves, and houses, by the river side, stand great numbers to see and laugh thereat." This was called the water quintain. They tilted on land, and riding on horseback charged a shield, or wooden figure, attached to a beam of wood which easily turned round upon the top of a post. At the other end of the beam was a heavy bag of sand, which, when the rider struck the shield with his lance, swung round and struck him with great force on the back if he did not ride fast and so escape his ponderous foe. Queen Elizabeth was much amused at Kenilworth Castle by the hard knocks which the inexpert riders received from the rotating sand-bag, when they charged "a comely quintane" in her royal presence in 1575. And well might the tournament itself inspire our young English townsfolk to imitate the knights and barons in their martial sports, in which commoners were not allowed to take part. Sometimes they would see a tournament, the lists superbly decorated and surrounded by the pavilions belonging to the champions, ornamented with their arms, banners, and bannerols; the scaffolds for the spectators hung with tapestry and embroideries of gold and silver; the splendid appearance of the knights, their horses gorgeously arrayed, and their esquires and pages, together with minstrels and heralds all clothed in costly and glittering apparel; the gay throng of sumptuously dressed women and brave men who watched the fight; a show of pomp and splendour which never could be forgotten; while the cries of the heralds, the clangour of the trumpets, the clashing of arms, the rushing together of the combatants, and the shouts of the beholders, impressed the mind, and kindled an enthusiastic love for knightly deeds and martial ardour.

It is unnecessary here to describe the details of a tournament, and we have many other games and amusements of the people to record, which added brightness to the lives of our forefathers, and relieved the burdens of their daily toil. When our towns have grown a little, we shall see these sports and pastimes more fully developed. But even at this early period of their existence, English youths appear ready for anything from fighting and footballing, wrestling and bowling, to bob-apple and bird-catching; while their sisters and sweethearts scorned not the dance, and herein resembled the young women of to-day.

CHAPTER VII

THE GUILDS

Numerous kinds of guilds and their objects—Their origin—Ordinance of guild at Abbotsbury—Guilds and their plays—London—Cambridge—Exeter—The guild-merchant—Royal Winchester and its guilds—Guildhalls.

FEW institutions have contributed more to the "making of England," to the improvement of the condition of the craftsmen and merchants, and to the development of our commercial industries, than the ancient guilds. If we would understand the social conditions of the townsfolk of this country, and the origins of our municipal government, we must study the history of our guilds.

There was a time when almost every inhabitant of the country belonged to some guild. In towns, membership of a guild was necessary to the carrying on of any trade, business, or handicraft, and woe betide the luckless man who dared to try to sell cloth or make boots, and who did not belong to the honourable company of clothiers or shoemakers! Instances will be quoted to show the severe punishment and ruin which would overtake so adventurous a tradesman. But in country villages, also, every one belonged to some guild which was of a religious nature, and had part of the church assigned to it. Men, women, and children, each had their own guild. Just as our churches are dedicated to some patron saint—St. James, St. Paul, &c.—so each guild had a patron saint, with a separate altar, over which stood an image of the saint, and before it a light was kept continually burning. The object of this light was to drive away evil spirits. The candles which shed the light were made of wax provided by the members of the guild, and fines for a breach of the rules were very often levied in wax; for example, in the Guild of St. John the Baptist at York, every member bound himself, that if he was wrath with another member without reasonable cause, he would pay the first time a pound of wax, the second time two pounds of wax, and the third time he would do whatever the warden of the guild should direct. Sometimes members left money in their wills to support the lights, as Robert Mylwarde did, A.D. 1530, who bequeathed "to the lads' light 2d., and to the maidens' light 2d." The festivities of Plough Monday, when Old Bess rattled her money-box whilst the ploughmen drew their plough along from village to village, owe their origin to the same source. The money collected on this occasion was devoted in pre-Reformation times to the support of the ploughmen's light, which burned before the altar of the ploughmen's guild. The Reformation put out the light, but could not extinguish the custom.

We will now enumerate at greater length the object for which these institutions were founded, and the various kinds of guilds which have existed in England. The word is derived from an Anglo-Saxon word which means "to pay," and signified that each member subscribed something towards the common fund of the association, which in return conferred certain advantages on each member. In the early times of our country's history they took the place of friendly or benefit societies; only they paid much more attention to the claims of religion and morality than our modern societies do. Each member was a "brother" or a "sister," and was treated as one of a large family. If he became ill, or poor, or infirm, he was supported by the guild. If his cattle were stolen, or his house blown down, or in case of any loss by fire, flood, shipwreck, or violence, his brethren of the guild would come to his rescue, and supply his needs and replace the loss. When "any good girl of the guild" wanted to be married, the guild provided a dowry for her; and when any brother or sister died, the guild paid the funeral expenses. In the times before the Reformation, special merit was attached to pilgrimages to Rome or to the shrine of some saint, such as St. Joseph at Glastonbury Abbey, or St. Thomas-à-Becket at Canterbury: if any member wished to go on a pilgrimage, his brethren helped him on the way, and some guilds provided lodgings for pilgrims when they passed through the town.

From all this it will be seen how many benefits these old guilds conferred upon their members, and how much good they accomplished. But the list is not yet exhausted. They took in hand the repair of the parish churches and the expense of public worship. The Guild of Swaffham, in Norfolk, undertook "the repair of the church, and the renovation of vestments, books, and other ornaments in the said church." Each guild had a chaplain, who was paid for taking the services and for praying for the souls of the members.

The warden of the guild received the offerings from the members, paid the expenses of the special services, and handed over the remainder to the churchwardens for the general expenses and repairs of the church. In those days every parishioner contributed something to the cost of the maintenance of Divine worship; no one was left out, and if any one omitted to send his yearly offering his name was recorded on the black list in the churchwardens' account-books. Thus the people looked upon their church as their own, and gladly contributed their Easter offerings; hence there was always money to keep the fabric in good order, and in this matter the guilds were the chief supporters and helpers.

Again, the repair of bridges and roads, of walls and gates of fortified towns, was often undertaken by the guilds; and they exercised their benevolence in many works of charity, feeding poor people, providing lodgings for poor strangers, and almshouses for their poor townsfolk.

Thus we see the extreme usefulness of these grand institutions, and how great is the debt which England owes to them. They were based on the principle of co-operation, and the mutual respect, honour, and faith which each brother felt for another. It was not simply a matter of money with fixed contributions and fixed rates of disbursements, like our modern friendly societies; but each brother gave what he could afford, and in case of distress received what he required.

Not the least advantage which the guilds procured for their members was that of protection. By uniting together the townsfolk became strong, and could resist the tyranny of unjust kings or powerful earls and barons, securing their property and goods from robbery and confiscation. In the days when the law of right was the law of might, and when the barons in their strongly fortified castles ruled as little kings, recognising no laws which were not agreeable to their wishes, it was a great thing for the liberties and rights of the people of England that a power should spring up which by the force of unity could cope with the lawless robbers, and protect and preserve the freedom of the English race. This and many other advantages and privileges did the old guilds gain for our country.

The guilds of England are of such ancient origin that it is impossible to state when they were first formed. Even in the old Roman towns and cities there were institutions of a nature somewhat similar to the guilds of Saxon and Norman times. They were called *collegia opificum*, or colleges of workmen; they had their own property, their meeting-house, their president and governing body; the richer members helped their poorer brethren; and on certain days the whole company visited the common sepulchre in which the brethren were buried, and decked with violets or roses the tombs of their departed friends. It is impossible to say whether the Saxons, when they came to England, founded their guilds on the model of these Roman colleges, as some writers have supposed; there is a resemblance between the Roman and early Saxon institutions, but in all probability the origin of guilds is not to be sought in pagan institutions. They were doubtless first formed by Christians, for mutual support in things temporal and spiritual, and for the mutual promotion of well-being in this world and the next.[1] It has been already stated that the religious guilds were the earliest in England, and we are fortunate in possessing a copy of the rules by which the members were governed. Orcy, a friend of King Canute, founded a famous guild

---

[1] Gross, *Gildæ Mercatoria*, vol. i. p. 170.

at Abbotsbury, in Dorsetshire, of which the following is the Guild Ordinance:—

"This writing witnesseth that Orcy hath granted the Guildhall at Abbotsbury, and the site thereof, to the honour of God and St. Peter, and for a property to the Guild, both during his life and after his life, for a lasting commemoration of himself and his consort. Let him that would set it aside answer it to God in the Great Day of Judgment! Now these are the covenants which Orcy and the Guildsmen of Abbotsbury have ordained to the honour of God, the worship of St. Peter, and the hele of their own souls. Firstly, three days before St. Peter's mass, from each Guild-brother one penny or one pennyworth of wax—look which the minister most needeth; and on the mass eve, from every two Guild-brothers one bread-loaf, well sifted and well raisid, towards our common alms; and five weeks before Peter's mass, let each Guild-brother contribute one Guild-sester full of clean wheat, and let this be paid within three days, or forfeit of the entrance, which is three sesters of wheat. If one brother misgreet another within the Guild in hostile temper, let him atone for it to all the fellowship with the amount of his entrance, and after that to him whom he misgreeted as they two may arrange; and if he will not bend to compensation, let him lose our fellowship and every other advantage of the Guild."

If a brother died contributions were levied for the soul's hele, and if any one was sick and felt that he was about to die, he was conducted to the place where he desired to go while he lived. The steward was directed to collect as many of the brethren as possible to attend the funeral, to bear the corpse to the minister, and to pray for the soul. "It is rightly ordained a Guildship if we do thus, and well fitting it is both towards God and man; for we know not which of us shall first depart."

"Now, we have faith through God's assistance that the aforesaid ordinance, if we rightly maintain it, shall be to the benefit of us all. Let us earnestly from the bottom of our hearts beseech Almighty God to have mercy upon us, and also His holy Apostle to make intercession for us, and take our way unto eternal rest, because for His sake we gathered this Guild together; He hath the power in Heaven to admit into Heaven whomso he will, and to exclude whomso he will not, even as Christ Himself spake unto him in the Gospel, 'Peter, I give unto thee the keys of Heaven, and whatsoever thou wilt have bound on earth, the same shall be bound in Heaven.' Let us hope and trust in Him that He will guide us here in this world, and after death be a help to our souls. May He bring us to eternal rest? Amen!"

This ordinance clearly sets forth that religion and charity were the chief objects for which the guild was founded, and the rule for preventing quarrelling, or "misgreeting," was admirably conceived. In later times the religious guilds used to act a miracle play, *i.e.*, a play based on some Scriptural subject, such as "The Creation of the World," "Noah and the Deluge." These were performed on the annual festival, which was celebrated on the feast of the patron saint of the guild.

In later times the trades guilds, composed of persons engaged in particular industries, performed various plays, and one of the objects of building a new guildhall at York in the fifteenth century was to provide a convenient place for the plays to be performed in. The Chester plays were very famous, composed by a monk and acted by the trade guilds. Here is part of their programme, which was arranged for a whole week:—

"1. The Bakers and Tanners bring forth the 'Falling of Lucifer.'
2. Drapers and Hosiers—'The Creation of the World.'
3. Drawers of Dee and Waterleaders—'Noah and his Ship.'

4. Barbers, Waxchandlers, and Leeches —'Abraham and Isaac.'

5. Coppers, Wiredrawers, and Pinners—'King Balak, Balaam, and Moses.'

6. Wrights, Slaters, Tylers, Daubers, and Thatchers—'The Nativity of our Lord.'

7. Painters, Brotherers, and Glaziers —'The Shepherds' Offering.'

8. Vintners and Merchants—'King Herod and the Mount Victorial.'

9. Mercers and Spicers—'The Three Kings of Colin.'"[1]

Many of these pieces were childish representations of the sacred narratives, mingled with much that to our eyes would seem irreverent and profane, but doubtless they did not seem so to our forefathers. At Hull the miracle plays were usually performed on Plough Monday by the members of the trade guilds. The representatives of each guild had their peculiar dresses, badges, and banners, and as they marched through the streets to the sound of music and the pealing of church bells, they must have presented an imposing and brilliant sight.

But these miracle plays have carried us away from the history of the early guilds. One of the earliest in the country was one in London, which

[1] "The Three Kings of Colin" represented the wise men from the East, who came to worship the Infant Saviour. "Colin" was in reality Cologne, on the Rhine, whence they supposed the wise men came.

was a kind of insurance association against theft and for the maintenance of peace. If a member lost any of his stock or slaves (for slavery was in existence in those times, *i.e.*, A.D. 900) the guild endeavoured to recover the same, or to recompense the loser from the common fund. If a horse was stolen and could not be found the owner received half a pound, for a cow he received twenty pence, for a hog tenpence, for a sheep one shilling. A slave was valued at the same rate as a horse, but if the slave have "stolen himself," *i.e.*, run away from his master, he shall be stoned, and his master receive compensation from the brethren of the guild.

A very ancient guild existed at Cambridge, in which it was ordained that all the members should swear to be faithful to each other as well in religious as in worldly matters; and that in all disputes they should always take part with him that had justice on his side. There were also sundry regulations for the funeral of brethren of the guild, for their relief in times of distress, and for preventing quarrels.

In the city of Exeter we find a very ancient guild of the religious type, which was held "for the sake of God and our souls, that we may make such ordinances as tend to our welfare and security, as well in this life as in that future state which we wish to enjoy in the presence of God, our judge." At the meetings the priest was ordered to sing two masses, one for the living and one for the dead. If any member went abroad, his brethren contributed fivepence towards the expenses of his journey, and one penny if any man's house was burnt. Here we have the earliest notion of a fire insurance association, which must have been most useful in the days when wooden houses with thatched roofs were the usual habitations. From the study of these rules and regulations, it is evident that our Saxon forefathers were very civilised, shrewd, and provident people.

Most of our towns have a mayor and corporation, who look after the welfare of the town, manage its concerns, make its by-laws, &c. This body is a descendant of the old guilds which existed in early Norman, or Saxon, times. The inhabitants of a town, who formed the *communitas*, were all members of the Frith or Peace Guild, and were bound to each other for the maintenance of the public peace. Thus a corporation was formed. In those days all the men who were engaged in any particular industry, such as weaving or shoemaking, united themselves into a company or guild for the purpose of protecting their industry and obtaining a monopoly for themselves. They would not allow any one who was not a freeman of their guild to practise their trade; they were most severe "protectionists." Thus in most towns there would be several companies, each watching over the interests of special industries. In course of time these companies united in one body, "*convivium conjuratum*," which called itself the Guild-merchant of the town, and discharged all the duties which we now expect our town councils and corporations to perform for us, the old guild-law becoming the law of the borough. In London, this union took place as early as the time of Athelstan; in the town of Berwick-on-Tweed, in 1283. This body often became a very powerful one, which could possess property, enjoy privileges, make laws, and was as mighty in the town as the lordly baron in his castle. They won from the kings of England charters of privileges which were the great bonds of society, conferring liberty and security, and which were the means of raising the arts and sciences in this country to a degree of perfection almost unequalled on the face of the earth.

Generally the good burghers had to pay for

their privileges. The king often needed money for foreign wars, to support his army, and to furnish his ships; he would apply to the "loyal merchants" of Winchester or Bristol for a large sum of money, which the thriving citizens were delighted to pay to the royal exchequer on condition that they might have some long-coveted privilege granted, and be allowed to ply their trade unfettered by adverse restrictions. In most cases the charter and privileges were granted to the guild-merchant of the town, which thus became so powerful a body that it could at length defy the threats of any lordly abbot or turbulent baron who attempted to levy toll on the merchants' goods or to deprive them of their hardly-won privileges.

As an example, the free charter granted by Henry I. to the royal city of Winchester, where his son Henry was born, may be quoted. The king was so thankful to have a son that, in 1112 A.D., he granted this charter to the city which gave his child birth. Here are the words:—

"Henry, king of England, duke of Normandy and Aquitaine, earl of Andalusia, to all archbishops, bishops, abbots, earls, viscounts, and all our faithful subjects, both French and English, greeting; know ye that we have granted unto our citizens of Winchester, *incorporated by the name of Guild-merchants*, full license and liberty to buy and sell all wares and merchandise in fairs or markets, and to export or import the same free from payment of any gift, tax, or custom usually levied on these occasions; and that they may have free passage of all such wares and merchandise throughout these my dominions from custom of carriage and passage over bridges toll free, and that they be not molested hereafter on this account."

In 1207 the privilege of coining money was granted to the merchant guild of the same city, and the rent of certain mills was assigned to the same body for building and keeping in repair the city walls. In the days of compulsory service no citizen of Winchester was obliged to go to war, nor could he be sued or impleaded in any action outside the walls of his own city. He could buy or sell without paying any toll, nor could he be fined or punished except according to the laws and customs of his own city.

Very much the same privileges were gradually obtained by favour or purchase by the merchant guilds of other cities and towns of England; so these places gradually became like little independent states in the heart of the realm, each managing its own concerns and looking after the interests of its people.

It seems to have been the policy of the Plantagenet kings to build up the powers of the towns, and great privileges were granted to them by Henry I. and his successors. Wallingford was especially favoured by Henry II. on account of the important services rendered by the towns-folk during the late war. It may be noticed that the charters refer to the towns as Free Burghs. *Sit Liberum Burgum, Liber Burgus*, are frequent expressions. In what did this freedom consist? It was a freedom to buy and sell without disturbance, a liberty from paying toll, pontage, passage-money, lastage, stallage, &c. Personal freedom could also be obtained by residence in a free burgh; for it was enacted that if a bondman remained in a burgh a year and a day as a burgess or member of it, he gained his freedom.

The chief officer in the town was the reeve or bailiff, who collected the tolls for the over-lord. London had its port-reeve, whose duty was to look after the customs and tolls of the port of London for the king. Tradesmen and merchants were said to be *in dominio*, and carried on their business under the protection of the over-lord. In course of time these tolls and customs were let out in fee-farm to the com-munities of cities or burghs, and the lord's reeve became the chief officer of the burgh as well as the representative of the lord, who received an annual compensation, always less than the true value, in lieu of the tolls and customs. The reeve was the ancestor of the mayor of more recent times, and was sometimes designated the alderman; while at Ripon he was known as the wakeman, who was elected annually from among the twenty-four aldermen of the city. His duty was to walk throughout the whole city, and give a supper, and cause a horn to be blown by night during the year of office, at nine o'clock, at the four corners of the cross in the market-place. One of the unpleasant duties of the Ripon wakeman was to make good any property stolen during his year of office, a duty which would make him very careful lest his city should harbour any thieves or vagabonds.

If we lived at Winchester when William the Conqueror came to England, we should have found that besides the merchant guild, which was becoming gradually a powerful body, there existed also two other guilds. There was the knights' guild, which was composed of youths of good family, pages, nobles, or young freemen, who were allowed to wear swords. To this body was committed the charge of the city defences, the ordering of the watch, &c. There was also the palmers' or pilgrims' guild, which possessed a house where pilgrims were entertained when they passed through the town on their way to some holy shrine. The room in which they slept still remains, and their rude carvings may yet be seen upon the beams that support the roof.

When any business of importance had to be transacted, and the rights and liberties of the people were in danger, the great bell swung in the town tower and summoned the burgesses together to a common meeting, where they discussed the various questions that arose freely and openly. Sometimes loud and angry were their deliberations when the neighbouring lord or powerful abbot had presumed to trespass upon the rights of the good townsfolk.

If we went to old Winchester at the time of a fair we should have found that the Bishop of Winchester's authority was greater than many of the citizens cared for. During the sixteen days of the fair the officers of the guild were entirely displaced by the officers of the bishop. All civic authority came to an end; all the shops were closed; and no one might trade within the city or the neighbourhood while the fair lasted. To the fair flocked merchants from all parts of England, and the proceeds of the fair went to the bishop's exchequer.

How useful the guilds were in opposing the wills of unscrupulous monarchs and preserving the lives of its members may be seen from another incident in the history of the same royal city of Winchester. Queen Isabella, the wife of Edward II., being enraged against the king's favourite, Hugh le Despencer, pursued him and hanged him. She then proceeded to take vengeance on all who had espoused his cause, and several rich citizens of Winchester, known friends of the Earl, were apprehended, and some were cruelly put to death for harbouring and entertaining him; but the mayor pleaded the privilege of a statute passed in the reign of Henry II., whereby it was enacted that no inhabitant of Winchester free of the guild of merchants (*i.e.*, a member of the same) should be sentenced for any capital offence whatever except for treason, nor then, unless convicted by lawful trial before his peers. The mayor, therefore, insisted upon the lives of his brethren being spared, and at length prevailed upon the queen to cease her cruel vengeance, and to set the captive citizens at liberty. This is only one instance out of many where the privileges of guild membership saved the lives of citizens and restrained the fury of despotic authority.

Where we now have town-halls our ancestors used to have guildhalls, which were used for a variety of purposes. There the members met to transact their common business. It was the centre of the trade of the town, and, in addition to its other uses, it was a kind of a club-house where the members used to meet and "drink their guild," and, perhaps, gossip and talk scandal like the members of more modern clubs. In Reading the guildhall was close to a brook in which the women washed their clothes, and made so much noise by "beating their battledores" (which was the usual style of washing clothes in those days) that the worthy brethren were often disturbed in their deliberations; so they petitioned the king to grant them the use of an old church, which was placed at their disposal. In some towns the old guildhall still stands, quaint-looking buildings, often supported on pillars and open beneath. In many places the time-honoured building has been swept away to make room for a more convenient but less interesting edifice. The guildhall of London still stands, although much altered externally; the actual hall is the same in which Buckingham pleaded so earnestly with the reluctant citizens of London to espouse the cause of the wretched Richard III., where

Garnet the Jesuit was condemned for his connection with the Gunpowder Plot, where Anne Askew was doomed to be burned at the stake for her religious belief, and many other exciting scenes took place. Although the Great Fire wrought much damage to the guildhall and destroyed the roof, the old walls still form part of the present building.

CHAPTER VIII

THE TYRANNY OF GUILDS—MODERN SURVIVALS

Some disadvantages of guild-life—Irksome restrictions—Heavy fines—" Foreigners" and " Evil May-day"—Aristocratic tendencies—Basingstoke Guild—Guilds of the Kalendars and other forms of guild-life—Henry VIII. and the City Companies—Destruction of guilds—Preston Guild—Newcastle—Trinity House—Benefits conferred by the guilds.

A SPEAKER at a recent Labour Congress attributed the poverty of the working people of England to the suppression of the trades guilds. Of course, there were other reasons assigned also, but this was one of the causes given for the increase of the number of poor people in the last and present century. But I question very much whether our tradesfolk and craftsmen would care to live under the severe restrictions which the old trades guilds imposed. They were like the old-fashioned stage coaches, which were very nice for those who rode upon them, but they cast a great deal of mud upon those who had to trudge behind them, and if one of these unfortunate people tried to get on the coach he received little mercy from the occupants, who used all their force to cast him back again into the mud. The case was similar with the old guilds. The members were obliged by their rules to be kind and brotherly to their fellow-members, but no one outside the select brotherhood was entitled to any consideration. Any one who came to ply his trade in a town was a "foreigner," who must be banished at once, so as not to interfere with the privileges of the guild. Here is an example taken from the annals of an ancient town:—"In July, 1545, one, Robert Hooper, a barber, being a foreigner, was this day ordered to be gone out of the town at his peril, with his wife and children," and the town sergeants were ordered to shut up his shop and see poor Robert Hooper and his wife beyond the borough boundaries.

It seems strange to us to think of the time when a man could not sell what he liked, or live where he liked, or work at any trade he pleased; but such freedom was impossible under the old guilds. No one was allowed to go and work where he pleased, but he must do his work only in that part of the town which was assigned to the members of his craft. The shoemakers must make shoes in Shoemakers' Row, and in no other part of the town. The shoemakers must not mend shoes, for that was the special work of the cobblers, and their privileges must not be interfered with.

A clothier was not allowed to make as much cloth as he wished, but might only have two looms, or, perhaps, if he were a favoured person, who had done good service to the town, he might have four. The old guild-rules would not have countenanced our modern co-operative stores, where everything is sold from a shoe-lace to a ship-load of furniture, for under their despotic government a tailor might not sell cloth, for that would be against the interests of the clothmakers; nor might he sell woven hose, for that would trespass upon the privileges of the haberdashers. A stranger at Southampton might not even bargain for or buy any goods brought into the town if a guildsman were present and wished to purchase the goods. If the stranger persisted, the goods were forfeited to the king. The "middleman" could not exist under the old guild-rules of Southampton, for it was provided by common consent of the guild that "no one shall sell any fresh fish, either in the market or street, but the person who had caught it in the water. And those who bring fresh fish in or about shall bring it all into the market at once. If the fisherman deliver any part of the fish for sale by another than himself he shall lose all, and if any huxter woman buy fish to sell it again she shall lose all." The old guildsmen did not approve of "sweating" the labourer, and allowing a middleman to make all the profit, nor did they see why they should pay for their goods a price higher than was fair and just.

Heavy fines were inflicted on those who dared to disobey the rules of the guild. At Reading no barber was allowed to shave any one after nine o'clock in winter, or ten o'clock in summer. This curious law was passed in 1443, at the commencement of the dispute between the rival houses of York and Lancaster, and was probably intended to prevent unlawful meetings being held in places so frequented as a barber's shop. The fine exacted for a breach of this rule was 300 tiles to the guildhall of Reading. The peculiar form of this fine may be accounted for by the fact that thatch was beginning to be superseded by tile roofs, and the barbers had to supply the materials. One John Bristol was fined 2100 tiles for shaving seven persons contrary to the order, but the number of tiles was reduced to 1200 on account of his poverty.

The price of commodities was fixed by the guild in many cases, and not left to the regulation of the law of supply and demand, as it is now. Beer, bread, &c., were sold at a regular charge, which was fixed by the guild.

In course of time, when the claims of feudal service were relaxed, the "foreigners," or "outsiders," who were not members of any guild, gave a great deal of trouble to the brethren. They settled outside the walls of a town, and, being unfettered by any restrictions, were able to undersell the tradesfolk in the town, and interfered greatly with their business. In the reign of Henry VIII. we find that an instance of this occurred in the City of London. "Foreigners" had injured the trade of the citizens, who were enraged, and thirsted for revenge. They took advantage of the May-day games and festivities in the year 1517, and turned the usual joyous pastimes into a violent insurrection against "foreigners." They secured the help of a preacher named Dr. Bell, who preached a Spital sermon in Easter week, and inflamed the minds of the people by his representation of the evils wrought by the "strangers," who ate their bread and devoured their commerce. The result of this was continued rioting and tumults, which terminated in a ferocious attack on the shops of the "foreigners" on May-day. Crowds had assembled to take part in the usual games, but the apprentices, watermen, and servants of the merchants began to insult the obnoxious "strangers" who did not belong to the guild, and plundered and destroyed their houses and warehouses. About 300 of the rioters were seized and sent to prison, but it does not appear that the poor foreigners received any compensation for their losses.

The old merchant guilds gradually became rather aristocratic in their tendency, and looked down upon the humbler working men, who formed amongst themselves craft guilds. In earlier times the craftsmen often belonged to the merchant guilds, for there was little difference between the two classes, the craftsmen being merchants and large traders as well as workers. But in course of time the full citizens became rich, and began to look down upon the poorer handicraft men, who were excluded from guild membership on the ground that they had not sufficient property. An ordinance appears in many a guild statute which states that no one with dirty hands, or with blue nails, or who hawked his wares in the streets, should become a member of the guild. The haughty burghers tried also to rule over the craftsmen, to tyrannise and oppress them; and this conduct led to many a conflict and bitter strife. If the workers had not united, they must have been brought into complete subjection; but they formed craft guilds, and by combination, firmness, and perseverance, preserved their rights, and in the fifteenth century won the day against their haughty rivals. The victory of the crafts was perfected in England in the time of Henry VI., and subsequent charters were usually granted to the men of a town, not to the old guild-merchant.

The rules of these guilds are very similar, and show much forethought and wisdom. They were very careful to secure the good quality of the work, and paid attention to the temporal and spiritual welfare of the members. No one was allowed to work longer than from the beginning of the day until curfew, nor "at night by candle light." This was intended to prevent bad workmanship, and to give opportunities of leisure for other duties. The working-men of those days had regular holidays from Christmas to the Feast of the Purification (February 2nd), and no work was allowed to be done on Saturdays after noon, nor on the eve of great festivals. Working-men were able in those days to find time for their social and religious duties. There was no "sweating," no incessant, grinding toil which often turns men into slaves; and the artificers of the Middle Ages owed their liberty and their privileges to self-help and co-operation. Men combine now in trades unions, but these lack the old religious spirit which animated the ancient guilds of England, and often establish a tyranny, well-nigh unbearable, and ruinous to the best interests of both employers and employed.

Besides those which have been already enumerated, there were other guilds which were formed for special purposes. At Basingstoke, near the railway station, there is an old ruined chapel, which was formerly the chapel of the Guild of the Holy Ghost. This association was established for educational purposes; the accounts have been published, and from this book we find that the guild existed in the thirteenth century, and was confirmed by a charter from Henry VIII. It shared the fate of many other similar institutions in the time of Edward VI., and was suppressed; but the inhabitants loved their guild and asked Queen Mary to restore it again. When Cromwell and the royal forces were fighting around Basingstoke, the buildings were laid in ruins and the estates lost; but later this vigorous guild, which no one could quite kill, revived again, and now supports a flourishing grammar school, formerly called the "Holy Ghost School."

Some of the entries in the accounts, which were kept most carefully and accurately, are curious. Evidently the annual dinner was not forgotten, for we find sundry items such as the following:—

It'm payde for iij quarters of a pound of pepper	xxiij^d
It'm payde for vj lb^s of prunis (prunes) . .	ix^d
It'm payde for ii oz of cloves	x^d
It'm payde for iiii lb^s of currans (currants) . .	xx^d
It'm payde xij lb^s of great reasons (raisins) .	ii^s

There are other items for sugar, spoons, salts, four dozen trenchers, butter, eggs, and loins of mutton, also for tending of the fire and the dinner. Evidently the feast was a great occasion, and the brethren fared sumptuously on that day at least. In Queen Mary's time, we find items paid for making the image, for painting the rood, making the "Holy Water Pot," &c.; but these cease when with Elizabeth reformed principles revived.

The clergy had their guild, called the Guild

of the Kalendars, which arose out of the monthly meetings of the clergy who assembled to deliberate about Church matters. There was a famous guild of this nature at Bristol, which was not confined to the clergy, but laymen and their wives were also admitted. The ladies were only allowed to become members and be present at the feasts on one condition—that the wife of the lay brother whose turn it was should provide the meal and wait at table. The brethren were evidently very careful and prudent men! This guild recorded all the public events which occurred, and had the charge of a library to which the citizens were admitted. They kept their books "in the roodloft or chamber next unto the street on the north side of All Saints' Church," and in 1318 a disastrous fire occurred during which many of the charters, writings, and records were "lost and embezeled away." The library was afterwards enriched, but another fire occurred in 1466, "through the carelessness of a drunken point-maker," which again destroyed the valuable collection of books. These guilds, which were numerous, had their own guildhall, which was a kind of club-house where the members, both ecclesiastical and lay, used to meet daily and "drink their guild."

There was also a class called Social Guilds, which were devoted to good fellowship and the encouragement of benevolence, and did not concern themselves with trade or religion. Sometimes guilds were founded for some special purpose, such as the support of a church, the maintenance of an altar, the performance of a play. The order of the Knight Templars, which was a very famous society in the Middle Ages, and played a conspicuous part in the Crusades, was originally a guild. The order of the Freemasons was based upon the old guild form; at one time each branch was separate and distinct, and it is comparatively recently, within the present century, that the lodges in England were brought into subjection to one chief lodge, which holds its court in London.

Having glanced at the various forms of guild-life in old England, we will now consider the effect which time had upon these venerable institutions. The merchant guilds became very rich and powerful, the possessors of large property; the craft guilds had likewise won their way, and gained wealth, honour, and privileges. Then came the Reformation in the sixteenth century, which very considerably disturbed the peaceful existence of all the guilds in this country as well as on the Continent. The city guilds of London were especially wealthy, and therefore attracted the covetous eyes of Henry VIII. He was not content with plundering the Church of her property, and enriching his favourites with the spoils, bestowing upon his courtiers wealth, lands, and plate which had been left to the Church, but he must needs deprive the guilds, too, of wealth which he deemed superfluous. In 1544 the king "borrowed" from the city guilds of London the large sum of £21,263 6s. 8d. for his wars in Scotland. It was very unwise of the members to lend so large a sum, but probably they were compelled, and this was the beginning of a system of extortion which both the Tudor and Stuart kings very successfully practised upon the old companies and guilds of London and other large towns.

In 1545 a severe blow was aimed at all institutions which were likely to yield booty for the royal spoiler. This was an Act for the dissolution of colleges. It stated that diverse colleges, chauntries, free chapels, hospitals, fraternities, brotherhoods, guilds, and stipendiary priests, having perpetuity for ever, had misapplied the possessions thereof in various ways; and enjoined that all the same should be dissolved, and the proceeds applied for supporting the king's expenses in wars, for the maintenance of the crown, &c.

In the following reign the evil ministers of Edward VI. proceeded at once to take advantage of this Act, and to begin the work of spoliation. Special commissioners were appointed, who proceeded to send to each town very minute inquiries concerning the guilds, brotherhoods, fraternities, and especially concerning the property, goods, ornaments, chattels, &c., which they possessed.

Perhaps the good people loved their guilds too well to return a full account of all their possessions; but although a great number of these ancient institutions were swept away by the unjust and scandalous measures of the king's advisers, some managed to weather the storm and to maintain their existence.

In one town in England the old guild has lived on through so many centuries, and although the objects for which it was first founded have long passed away, it is still celebrated with much of its ancient glory and magnificence. I refer to the town of Preston, where every twenty years the guild is held with much festivity, and the whole town is *en fête* for a fortnight. This is the proclamation which is issued by the mayor when the year of the guild comes round :—" The Guild Merchant for the Borough of Preston will be opened with the usual solemnities in the Town Hall on the first Monday after the feast of the decollation of St. John the Baptist, when all persons claiming to have any right to freedom or other franchise of the same borough, whether by ancestry, prescription, or purchase, are to appear by themselves or their proxies to claim and make out their several rights thereto, otherwise they will according to ancient and immemorial usage forfeit the same."

A court is formed consisting of the mayor, the three senior aldermen, who are called seneschals or stewards, four other aldermen, called aldermen of the guild, and the clerk of the guild. Before this court all who desire to be enrolled as freemen of the guild have to appear and make good their claim. In olden days we have seen how important it was for a man to become a freeman of the guild mercatory; otherwise he would not be able to carry on his calling, and was liable to a heavy fine every time he sold a piece of cloth or made a pair of boots. But in these days to become a freeman of a borough is little more than an honourable distinction; we have long ago swept away the absurd restrictions which hampered and hindered trade in the Middle Ages; and although Trade Unionists would like to revive some of these obsolete ideas, and prevent men from doing an honest day's work who did not belong to their union, I do not think such notions commend themselves to the common sense of English people. But it was a great thing to be a freeman of the Guild of Preston in former times, and now it is an honourable distinction.

The first Preston Guild of which we have any record was celebrated in the reign of Edward III., although there was probably a guild existing there long before. It is supposed to be of Saxon origin, as many guild merchants were established in seaports in Saxon times for the purpose of carrying on commercial enterprises with Hanse privileges, and Preston was one of the early ports selected for this purpose. These are some of the laws of the Preston Guild (temp. Henry II.):—

"1. So that they shall have a guild merchant with Hanse, and other customs belonging to such guild; so that no one who is not of that guild shall make any merchandise in the said town, unless with the will of the burgesses.

2. If any bondman hold any land, and be of the guild, and pay scot and lot with the burgesses for one year and a day, then he shall not be reclaimed by his lord, but shall remain free in the town."

Every twenty years since the year 1329 the festival has been held, except on two occasions —during the Wars of the Roses, and during the troubles of the Reformation—and the commemoration is of a most gorgeous descripton. The companies of the trading fraternities assemble early in the morning, and, accompanied by the noblemen and gentry of the county, they wend their way, as in the good old days, to the parish church. After the service a grand procession is formed, and the companies, decorated with the insignia of their trades, parade the town. First march the tanners, skinners, curriers, and glovers; then follow the weavers and spinners, the cordwainers, carpenters, butchers, vintners, tailors, plasterers, smiths, gardeners, printers and bookbinders, freemasons, &c. The ladies, too, take a prominent part in the functions, and march in procession, headed by the mayoress, accompanied by the ladies of the best families in the county. Banquets, balls, plays, concerts, follow each other in rapid succession, and for a whole fortnight the town keeps high festival.

At the conclusion of the guild the masters and wardens of the companies attend upon the guild mayor in the guildhall. The companies have their guild orders sealed and regularly entered in the books. Proclamation is next made, and the name of each inhabitant burgess called over, when the grand seneschal, or town-clerk, affixes the corporation seal upon the guild-book, which afterwards holding up, he says, "Here is your law." The sergeants then make proclamation: "This grand guild merchants' court is adjourned for twenty years, until a new guild merchants' court be held and duly proclaimed."

Such is the relic of olden times which has come down to us. A few years ago the festival was held, and if we live until the year 1902 we shall probably witness another Preston Guild, if all good old institutions have not quite passed away before that distant date.

Pope Julian II. offered some strong inducements to the good people of Boston, in Lincolnshire, to join the Guild of the Blessed Mary in that town. He granted a pardon, which provided that any Christian person who should aid and support the chamberlain of the guild should have five hundred years of pardon! He allowed the brothers and sisters of the same guild to eat during Lent, or on fast days, eggs, milk, butter, and flesh, by the advice of their spiritual pastor, without any scruple of conscience, and accounted the "merit" of membership equal to a pilgrimage to Rome. Evidently the guild had subscribed liberally to Peter's Pence, and enjoyed the high favour of the Pontiff. The guildhall still remains.

The records of the guilds of Newcastle are full of interest. They show the hostile feelings which the northerners entertained to their neighbours over the Border, and no Scotchman was allowed to become an apprentice to any trade in the town. The members were very careful also to keep the guild-light burning before the altar of their patron saint, and to provide for the performance of the annual play. For instance, a tailor, when he set up his shop, paid £40, with a pound of wax and a pot of oil, 13d. for our Lady-light, and 8d. to the play, "The Descent into Hell." All the brethren of all the guilds were required to come in their guild liveries and join in the grand procession on Corpus Christi Day, and to set forth their plays and pageants, otherwise they were fined a pound of wax.

The observance of Sunday was also strictly enjoined by all the guild rules. On that day no one was allowed to ply his trade, nor on Saturday after eight o'clock in the evening; but should keep holy the Sunday vigils and festival days on pain of six pounds of wax for every default. The rule for abstaining from all work on Sunday is a notable feature in nearly every guild ordinance.

Not only landsmen were benefited by the action of our ancient guilds, but it is to one of these most useful institutions that the seamen of olden times owed the erection of lighthouses and beacons to direct their course when approaching our coasts. The Trinity House Guild of Deptford, on the Thames, founded in 1512 on some ancient mariners' fraternity, and composed of "the chiefest and most expert masters and governors incorporate within themselves," was empowered to erect sea-marks on the shores and forelands "to save and keep seafaring men and the ships in their charge from sundry dangers." This guild has risen into one of vast importance. The greater number of our lighthouses belong to, and are managed by, this corporation; all ships pay toll to the guild for the maintenance of the lighthouses; pilots are appointed and licensed by it; poor and aged seamen are supported; and England owes the protection of navigation and commerce to this most useful and venerable institution. At Newcastle there was a similar association, also dedicated to the Holy Trinity, which was empowered by Henry VIII. to build two towers at the entrance to the Tyne haven, in which a light was burned for the guidance of ships entering the port. Every foreign ship paid 4d., and every English ship 2d., to the guild for the support of the light. To this fraternity were assigned the appointment of pilots, the maintenance of beacons and buoys, &c., and the care of aged seamen and widows. At Hull there existed a similar institution.

From this brief description of the ancient guilds of England it is evident how important a part they played in "the making of England," in the foundation of so many of the institutions which we value so much at the present day. To them we owe our municipal system of government, our borough laws, our trade, commerce, our light-houses, &c. To them our forefathers were indebted for the protection of their rights and liberties in lawless times, for prosperity and peace and settled government in the days of oppression and tyranny. To them they owed many social pleasures and happy days of harmless mirth which diversified their lives and made our forefathers a light-hearted and contented people.

CHAPTER IX

MEDIÆVAL TOWNS

Towns built by special decree of the king—Hull—Merchants and their houses—Cannynge of Bristol—Richard Whittington and his cat—Sir John Crosby—John Taverner of Hull and his " Grace Dieu"—Ecclesiastical traders—An old town in mediæval times—Town houses—St. Mary's Hall, Coventry — Craftsmen's hovels — State of the streets— Plagues—" Black Death"—Fires—Foreign traders— Expansion of commerce.

WE have already spoken of the towns which arose around the abbeys, and castles, and bishop's seat, of those which date their origin to Roman times; but there are others which owe their foundation to the foresight and enterprise of wise monarchs, which were built for special purposes, and did not spring into existence by accident, or trace their descent from ancient times. In the twelfth, thirteenth, and fourteenth centuries, kings and feudal lords found it a wise policy to encourage trade, and grant protection and privileges to traders. They founded commercial towns and gave them charters, and did their utmost to increase the power of the burghers in order to check the power of the nobles. Such towns are not so numerous in England as in other countries, but we have a notable instance of the creation of a great commercial city in the history of the foundation of Hull.

When Edward I. was returning from Scotland, after the battle of Dunbar, he visited Barnard Castle, and when hunting one day he chanced to ride to the village of Wyke-upon-Hull, which belonged to the abbey of Meaux, and appeared suitable for the erection of a fortress and port. Having gained possession of the site, he offered freedom and great commercial privileges to all merchants who would build houses and inhabit them. The king erected a manor-house for himself, and in 1299 the borough was incorporated. The merchants quickly availed themselves of the king's offer and proceeded to build houses, and Hull soon became a flourishing town. It was fortified with walls and towers; a great church was built in 1312, and the powerful family of the De la Poles were foremost in carrying out the king's wishes, and rose rapidly in wealth and power. One, Michael de la Pole, "builded a goodly house of brick, against St.

Mary's Church, like a palace, with a goodly orchard and garden at large, enclosed in brick. He builded also three houses in the town besides, whereof every one had a tower of brick." These bricks were brought over from Holland.

Very fine and stately buildings were these town houses of mediæval merchants, and very important persons were their owners, often the younger sons of old county families, who were not of opinion that work and trade were derogatory to their dignity. Kings honoured them with their confidence, stayed with them in their houses, and often conferred upon them titles, honours, and estates. Such a great merchant was William Cannynge, of Bristol, who founded the noble church of St. Mary, Redcliffe, a grand memorial of his greatness and piety. His king, Henry VI., delighted to honour him, and styled him "his beloved and honourable merchant." Vast was his fleet—his shipping, amounting to 2470 tons, was seized by the victorious Yorkist monarch—and vast were his commercial enterprises, whereby he made Bristol a large and flourishing port. Another was the famous Richard Whittington, "thrice Lord Mayor of London." The story about his wonderful cat probably arose from the fact that he had a ship which bore that name, and which enriched its owner by its numerous and successful voyages. But it is quite possible that there was some truth in the old story; and does not his portrait hang on the walls of Mercers' Hall, to which honourable company he belonged, with the figure of a cat in the corner? At any rate the other part of the famous story is quite untrue; he was not a poor man's son who sought his fortune in London, but the son of the good knight Sir William Whittington, or Whytington, of Pauntley in Gloucestershire, a worthy gentleman, and he was apprenticed to his cousin Sir John Fitzwarren, a rich mercer, whose daughter he married. This famous Richard amassed great wealth as a trader, was Lord Mayor three times, and proved himself to be "a worthy and notable merchant, the which while he lived had right liberal and large hands to the needy and poor people." He built and endowed a college which was suppressed, and an almshouse which remains, and moreover entertained his sovereign Henry V. right royally, bestowing upon him as a parting gift as much as £60,000. It was during his tenure of office as Lord Mayor of London that the famous

Liber Albus, or "white book," of the City of London was drawn up, which contains a very full account of the laws and rules regulating commerce and social life in the City of London.

Near Liverpool Street Station, in Bishopsgate, still stands the house of Sir John Crosby, alderman of London in the reign of Edward IV., the last of the residences of the old London merchant princes. A notable house it was in ancient days. Here Richard III. lived, before he became king, and plotted his deep designs for the usurpation of the crown. Here he feasted and gathered round him his adherents. Here too lived several Lord Mayors of London, and at one time the French ambassador with four hundred knights and nobles feasted royally in Crosby Hall.

Hull too can boast of its merchant princes, and one John Taverner of that town is said to have "by the help of God and some of the king's subjects, built a ship as large as a great carrack (the largest ships of the Venetian traders), or even longer, which the king directed should be called the carrack *Grace Dieu*, moreover granting him to carry wool, tin, lambskins, and other hides to Italy, and to bring back bowstaves, wax, and other foreign produce necessary to the country, to the great benefit of the revenue and of the nation."

In the Middle Ages every one traded who could, ecclesiastics not excepted. The Cistercian monks were the greatest wool-merchants in the kingdom, until in 1344 Parliament docked them of the privilege. One worthy abbot of St. Albans traded in herrings, having agents and a storehouse at Yarmouth, "to the inestimable advantage as well as honour of his abbey."

These old merchants were very liberal with their wealth. They built and endowed numerous beautiful churches, and many of those in Lincolnshire and Norfolk, which are remarkable for their vastness and grandeur, owe their existence to the munificence of the merchants of olden days.

The houses of these mediæval traders were very unlike the homes of modern citizens. The numerous apprentices and workmen lived under their master's roof, and partook of their meals in the large hall together with the family. The merchant and his family sat at the high table, which stood on the daïs, or low platform, at one end of the hall, while his servants were seated at a long table, which was placed in the lower part of the building.

Outside the strong walls of a mediæval town was a tract of land, both pasture and arable, which was the common land of the townsfolk. Massive towers stand at intervals along the walls, which bear the names of old heroes, or preserve the memory of their founders. Each gate is guarded by a strong tower; a moat surrounds it, which is crossed by a drawbridge, and before we cross the bridge there is the barbican, or watch-tower, to protect it.

On entering the town, we see wide streets and beautiful houses with picturesque gables, a great many churches with graceful spires and towers, several guildhalls, where the members of the guilds meet, transact their business, and "drink their guild" each day; and as we go along the streets we hear the town bell calling the burghers to their "mote," or meeting, or summoning them to protect the walls against a foe; and an army of sturdy citizens is called into being, each bearing his pike and bow, ready for the fray, resolved to protect their hearths and homes, no matter who their foe might be.

And the houses of these great merchants, which could accommodate a number of apprentices and workmen, all living under their master's roof, were large, important, and well-constructed buildings. Domestic architecture was at its height about the year 1520, and some specimens of the art of that period still exist. There was a large quadrangular court, like that of an Oxford or Cambridge college; at the entrance there was a gatehouse, with a strong iron-bound door. The principal room was the grand hall, with windows filled with stained glass, the walls supported by buttresses, and at one end of the hall was a large oriel; at the other end there were screens, and over them a gallery in which the musicians played on state occasions. It was a very stately building, with its high timber roof and mullioned windows and tapestry-covered walls. The fireplace was either in the centre of the room, and the smoke arose from the burning logs and found its way out through a hole in the roof, or a fireplace was built into the wall, and a wide open chimney conveyed the smoke upwards. Then there were solars, and withdrawing-rooms (hence our word "drawing-room"), whither the ladies used to retire after dinner, and a chapel generally formed part of a merchant's house. Behind the kitchen there was a tower, which could be defended in case of assault. An example of this may be seen at St. Mary's Hall, Coventry.

But all the town houses in mediæval times

were not so great as those which I have just described, and we will picture to ourselves the home of an ordinary citizen. The house had a narrow front, its gable-end facing the street. On the ground floor was the shop, about three feet above the street, the basement being the cellar. The shop was open to the street, a board, or counter, being placed across the opening, behind which the tradesman sat and sold his wares. A stone outside staircase led into the house. Above the shop was the hall, in which the citizen, his family, and apprentices lived, the kitchen being at the back of the hall; but many houses had no kitchen. On the second floor was the dormitory, a long undivided sleeping-room, and the space in the roof above was utilised as a store-room. The lower part of the house was built of stone or brick, the upper of wood, the timber being arranged in patterns and sometimes painted; a whole street formed of such houses presented a very picturesque appearance.

Coventry still preserves a large number of such old houses, with the beautifully carved woodwork of their gable-ends, their upper floors projecting; and one or two of the narrow streets remain in which it would be possible to shake hands across the road. St. Mary's Hall, in the same town, is one of the most interesting buildings in England. Coventry was very rich in its number of religious and trading guilds, and St. Mary's Hall belonged to three of the most important ones. On entering the quadrangle, down some steps on the right, we see the crypt where the merchants deposited their goods. There are also holes in the wall where they could place their strong chests. Then there are the kitchens, with several fireplaces, and on an arch is carved an angel holding a shield charged with a merchant's mark, and dated 1440. These marks are very numerous and various, and some examples are given in the accompanying illustrations. The large hall is a very imposing building, with its minstrels' gallery, and a daïs, and several suits of armour, a very small portion of the great store of offensive and defensive weapons which once belonged to the burghers of Coventry.

The craftsmen lived together in narrow filthy streets and dark courts; their houses were humble dwellings built of wattle-and-daub, of one or two storeys. A fire burned in the centre of the room wherein the craftsmen worked and lived, and often slept. All kinds of refuse were thrown into the street, from which arose most pestilential odours. No wonder that plagues raged wildly in these wretched hovels, and fevers and sweating sickness carried off their victims. When the Black Death found a congenial soil in these filthy lanes of our towns, historians tell us that one-third of the whole population of England died. Great pits were dug outside the town walls, and the bodies of the victims of the plague were buried to the number of one or two hundred a day. Labourers and artisans, who were the chief sufferers, became so scarce that wages rose enormously. Fires also frequently arose in the poor men's hovels, and swept through the towns and destroyed their fair buildings, their merchants' palaces, guildhalls, and stately churches. Famine, too, often raised its hideous head, when during the civil wars the land lay desolate, and the poor folk were reduced to make their bread from fern roots. However, these three dread visitors, Fire, Famine, and Pestilence, only came at intervals, and in their absence there was much happiness and growing prosperity in our towns in mediæval times.

There was a strong foreign element in our trade and commerce. The armorial bearings of the Lombard merchants, the Medicis of Florence, consisting of three gilded pills (hence the three balls of the modern pawnbroker), might be seen over the doorways of their agents in some of our chief towns, and the great Hanse merchants had established themselves in London, Boston, and Lynn. Leland tells us that "merchants of the stiliard cumming by all partes by est were wont greatly to haunt St. Botolph's town, or Boston." The Stiliard, or Steelyard, was their London house, which was assigned to these German merchants by Edward IV., and stood upon the site of Cannon Street Station.

English traders objected to the privileges bestowed upon these foreign merchants; hence we find a quaintly worded "Act touching the merchants of Italy" which states that they were resident in great numbers both in London and in other cities of England, and were in the habit of taking warehouses and cellars in which to store the wares and merchandises they imported, and "them in their said warehouses and cellars deceitfully pack, meddle, and keep unto the time the prices thereof been greatly enhanced, for their most lucre, and did then sell to all manner of people within the ports as in other divers places as well by retail as otherwise." "Moreover, they will not take upon them any laborious occupation, as carting and ploughing, and other like business, but use making of cloth and other handicrafts and easy occupations, and bring and convey from the parts of beyond the sea great substance of wares and merchandises unto fairs and markets, and all other places of your realm, at their pleasure, and there sell the same, to the great hurt and impoverishing of your subjects, whereby your said subjects for lack of occupation fall to idleness, and been thieves, beggars, vagabonds, and people of vicious living to the great trouble of your highness and of all your said realm." Many restrictions were imposed upon the foreigners, but most of them were happily inoperative; and our trade, whether carried on by Englishmen or by these strangers from beyond seas, advanced by leaps and bounds, and laid the foundations of England's greatness among the nations of Europe.

CHAPTER X

IN THE STREETS

Street scenes—The London Livery Companies—The Mercers and their pageant—Triumphal return of Henry V. from Agincourt: a City welcome—Pageant for Henry VI. —River pageants—Chester's "setting of the watch"— Coventry plays and pageants—Kenilworth—Corpus Christi Day—Chester plays—Reading—Pillories and punishments —Master Lickpenny's adventures.

WE have entered a mediæval town and marked its walls and bulwarks. We have seen the citizens at work, the merchants in their palatial halls, the tradesmen in their shops, and the craftsfolk in their hovels. Now let us walk through the streets and notice the crowds that throng them. We will see the pageants and "ridings" as they pass, the excitement of the spectators, the gorgeous dresses of the ladies, and the no less splendid robes of the Livery Companies, the open-air plays, the sports and pastimes, and all the varied scenes of English out-door life in the Middle Ages.

The Lord Mayor's Show, shorn of much of

its former magnificence, the procession of trades guilds which occurs once in twenty years at Preston, the Coventry pageant of Lady Godiva, are the few worn-out relics of the ancient pageants which delighted our forefathers. The Livery Companies of the City of London were foremost in these displays, and very gorgeous the brethren looked, resplendent sometimes in "one livery of red and white with the connuzances of their mysteries embroidered on their sleeves," and sometimes in "scarlet and green," or "scarlet and black," or "murrey and plunket," "a darkly-red," or "a kind of blue." But these were only for ordinary occasions; at special festivals, on the coronation of a sovereign, or at some state function, the companies shone in splendour with "blew gowns and red hoods," or "brown-blew with broderyed sleevys," or "red, with hoods red and white." The effect of such vivid colours must have been very striking, and brilliant must have been the scene when the brethren, clad in their new liveries, marched in procession through the streets to attend the services of the Church, or when, in their festal halls, they entertained nobles and princes, and the mighty "baron" made the table groan, and "frumertie with venyson, brawn, fat swans, boar, conger, sea-hog," and other delicacies crowned the feast, while the merry music of the minstrels or the performance of the players delighted the gay throng. We might linger long in contemplating the ancient glories and civic state of the Livery Companies, their magnificent shows and gorgeous ceremonies.

See the Mercers pass along the streets, their livery robes faced with satin, the gentlemen ushers with velvet coats and chains of gold. Gowns and scarlet satin hoods distinguish the bachelors; others wear plush coats; while trumpeters, drummers, fifemen, and pensioners in red gowns complete the procession. Then is drawn along a huge pageant representing a rock of coral with seaweeds; at the summit sits Neptune mounted on a dolphin, accompanied by tritons, mermaids, and other marine attendants. Then follows another pageant, a triumphal chariot, adorned with a variety of paintings, enriched with gold and silver and rare jewels, and figures bearing the banners of kings and mayors and the companies, with the arms of their founder, Richard II. A virgin, representing the arms of the Mercers, sits upon a high throne, dressed in a robe of white satin, decked with gold and jewels; her long, dishevelled, flaxen hair is adorned with pearls and gems, and crowned with a rich coronet of gold and jewels. Her buskins are of gold, laced with scarlet ribbons, and she bears a sceptre and a shield, with the arms of the Mercers. She has a goodly company of attendants, Fame blowing her trumpet, Vigilance, Wisdom, and other personified virtues, and the Nine Muses, while eight pages of honour walk on foot, and Triumph acts as charioteer. Nine white Flanders horses draw the huge machine, each horse being mounted by some emblematical figure, such as Asia, America, Victory, and the like. Grooms and Roman lictors in crimson garb, and twenty savages, or "green men," throwing squibs and fireworks, complete the pageant.

Never did London show its loyalty with greater splendour than on the occasion of the triumph of Henry V. after his victory at Agincourt. Twenty thousand citizens marched with the Lord Mayor to Blackheath to welcome the conquering monarch, the brethren of the Livery Companies wearing red gowns, with hoods of red and white, "well mounted and gorgeously horsed, with rich colours and great chains, rejoicing at his victorious returne." A huge giant was stationed at the entrance of London Bridge, who recited an ode of welcome and congratulation. On the top of one of the temporary towers stood a lion and an antelope, on the other a choir of angels who sang "Blessed is he that cometh in the name of the Lord." Glad hurrahs greeted the king as he rode through the crowded streets which were canopied with rich cloths, and silks and tapestries adorned each window. On a tower at Cornhill were stationed the patriarchs, who chanted "Sing unto the Lord a new song," and threw down live birds that flew thick about the king. At Cheapside the conduits ran wine, instead of water, and the twelve apostles sang psalms, while twelve kings knelt before him. Angels on towers sang his praises and showered down gold pieces, or imitations of the same. Mitred bishops received him at St. Paul's Cathedral with all the pomp of mediæval ceremonial; the bells clanged joyously, while the choirmen poured forth a glad *Te Deum Laudamus*. Such scenes delighted well our forefathers.

When the young king Henry VI. was welcomed to London by the citizens, they devised many surprises for the boy monarch. Three ladies clad in gold and silk, representing Grace, Nature, and Fortune, endowed him with various gifts of wisdom, strength, beauty, and prosperity. Then came the Seven Gifts of the Holy Spirit, and Seven Gifts of Grace, all represented by richly attired ladies, who with sundry rhymes and divers chantings imparted their virtues to the king. Nor were Truth, Wisdom and her seven sciences, Mercy, and Cleanness backward in bestowing their royal gifts. The garden of Paradise bloomed afresh behind the conduits in Cheapside; Mercy, Grace, and Pity drew wine, not water, from the fountains for all who wished to drink; and Enoch and Elias greeted the monarch.

The river, too, was often a scene of surpassing splendour, as when Elizabeth, the wife of Henry VII., was crowned, and all the worthy citizens united to do her honour. "At her coming forth from Greenwich by water there was attending upon her there the maior, shrifes, and aldermen of the citie, and divers and many worshipfull comoners, chosen out of every crafte, in their liveries, in barges freshly furnished with banners and streamers of silke, richly blason with the arms and bagges of their craftes; and in especiall a barge, called the bachelor's barge, garnished and apparelud, passing all other, wherein was ordeyned a great redd dragon, spowting flames of fyer into the Thames; and many other gentlemanlie pagiants, well and curiously devised, to do Her Highness sport and pleasure with."

Nor was this love of pageants confined to the metropolis. In many other towns we see the people assembling in gay crowds to see the pageants pass and to revel in such innocent pastimes and diversions. At Chester, on the eve of the festival of St. John the Baptist, the citizens used to delight in a famous pageant called "the setting of the watch," in which the following company took an active part: four giants, one unicorn, one dragon, one dromedary, one luce, one camel, one ass, six hobby-horses, and sixteen naked boys representing cupids. The spectators lined the old Rows of Chester, to witness the spectacle; but a Puritan mayor arose who liked not these diversions, and slew the dragon with the skill of a St. George, broke the pasteboard giants, and whipped away the cupids. However, the Chester folk did not approve of these proceedings, and a few years later the giants were restored, and moreover two shillings' worth of arsenic was mixed with the paste for the making of the giants, to prevent them from being devoured by rats.

Coventry also was famous for its pageants and plays. On Hock Tuesday the people had a merry diversion representing the fight between the Saxons and Danes. The players divided themselves into two companies to represent the Saxons and Danes; a great battle ensued, and by the help of the Saxon women the former were victorious, and led their foes captive. This play was performed before Queen Elizabeth, who laughed much at the pageant, and bestowed upon the performers two bucks and five marks in money. Sir Walter Scott has made every one familiar with the splendid pageants which were performed in honour of the same queen at Kenilworth Castle—the mighty, gigantic porter at the gate who recited sonorous verses to greet her majesty, the gods and goddesses who offered gifts and compliments on bended knee, the Lady of the Lake surrounded by tritons and nereids, who approached the queen on a floating island, and the strange conduct of Orion and his dolphin—for an account of all these wonders we refer to "Kenilworth," and Gascoigne's "Princely Progress" will furnish the lover of pageants with much to interest him.

But see—a more serious procession approaches. It is the festival of Corpus Christi, instituted in honour of the Holy Sacrament, and observed on the Thursday following Trinity Sunday. The priests, clad in splendid vestments, bear the Host through the streets; censors swing and the monks chant, and the people prostrate themselves as the silver pix containing the hallowed bread is borne along—a very solemn spectacle, which is thus described very faithfully by Master Googe, a stern Reformer who did not regard it with favourable eyes:—

>Then doth ensue the solemne feast
>   of Corpus Christi Day,
>Who then can shewe their wicked use
>   and fond and foolish play.
>The hallowed bread with worship great
>   in Silver Pix they beare
>About the churche or in the citie
>   passing here and theare.
>His armes that beares the same, two of
>   the wealthiest men do holde:
>And over him a canopey
>   of silke and clothe of golde.
>Christe's passion here derived is
>   with sundrie maskes and playes.
>Fair Ursley with her maydens all
>   doth pass amid the wayes.
>And valiant George with speare thou killest
>   the dreadful dragon here,
>The devil's house is drawne about
>   wherein there doth appere
>A wondrous sort of damned spirites
>   with foule and fearfull look,
>Great Christopher doth wade and passe

IN THE STREETS

Sebastian full of feathered shaftes
   the dint of dart doth feele.
There walketh Kathren with her sworde
   in hand, and cruel wheele.
The Challis and the singing Cake
   with Barbara is led,
And sundrie other pageants playde
   in worship of this bred. . . .
The common ways with bowes are strawde
   and every streete beside,
And to the walles and windowes all
   are boughes and braunches tide.
The monkes in every place do roame,
   the nonnes abroad are sent,
The priestes and schoolmen lowd do rore,
   some use the instrument.
The stranger passing through the streete
   uppon his knees doth fall,
And earnestly upon this brede
   as to his God doth calle. . . .
A number grete of armed men
   here all this while do stand,
To look than no disorder be
   nor any filching hand.
For all the church goodes out are brought
   which certainly would be
A bootie good if every man
   might have his libertie.

Master Googe's fingers evidently itched to seize the goodly booty and to rob the Church of her rich chalices, while he scowled at the roaring priests and at the bowed worshippers.

The streets of our towns were the theatres of the people in mediæval times. The stage was constructed on wheels, in order that it might be "drawn to all the eminent parts of the city for the better advantage of spectators." It consisted of three platforms; the highest represented Heaven, where God and His angels dwelt; glorified saints played their parts on the second platform, and below them acted the living men and women. In one corner was "hell's mouth," a huge, dark cavern, resounding with yells and shrieks, sending forth fire and smoke. Strange to say, this was the centre of the comic element of the performance; troops of merry demons constantly issued forth from this cave of horrors, and made the spectators roar with laughter by their buffoonery and strange jests. In course of time the upper platforms were removed, and only living characters represented.

They played in every street, we are told with regard to the Chester Mysteries. They began first at the Abbey Gates, and then "the stage was wheeled to the High Cross before the mayor, and so to every street; and so every street had a pagiant playing before them till all the pagiants for the day appointed were played; and when one pagiant was near ended, word was brought from street to street, that so they might come in place thereof exceeding orderly, and all the streets had their pageants afore them all at one time playing together, to see which plays was great resort, and also scaffolds, and stages made in the streets in those places where they determined to play their pageants." York, Chester, Hull, Coventry, were all famous for such performances; but it must not be supposed that these *mysteries* were confined to them. When we examine the records of any old town, we find traces of the players. The churchwardens' books of St. Lawrence's Church, Reading, will furnish us with an example:—

1507. It. Paid to the Labourers in the Forbury for setting up of the polls for the scaffold . ix^d
It. Paid to the Beerman for beer for the play in the Forbury . . . . . . x^d
It. Paid for 1 ell quarter of crescloth for Adam to make 1 pair of hosen and 1 ell for a doublett . . . . x^d
It. Paid for coarse canvass to make xiii capps with the making, and with the hers (ears) thereto belonging . . . . . ii^s iiii^d
It. Paid for ii ells of crescloth for to make Eve a coat . . . . x^d

There are sundry other entries referring to "dyed flax for wigs, a quior of paper, a doublett of leather," and many other items, which tell us the story of the performance of Adam and Eve and the expulsion from Paradise.

We go all the way to Ober-Ammergau to witness the Passion Play, but here in England were passion plays performed in most of our town churches. These took place usually on Palm Sunday, and were enacted for the most part in the rood-loft. The Passion Play was followed by the Resurrection Play; we read of one Sybil Darling of Reading, who received "for nails and for the sepulchre and for resin to the resurrection play ii^d," the resin being used for the illumination at the moment of the Resurrection.

We have lingered long over this important feature of ancient town life. It has many attractions, and there is still much more to say about it. But as we walk through the streets there are many other sights to be witnessed, and the players must retire to enjoy their "bred, ale, and bere," which seems to flow freely after the play is over. Now we see a noisy crowd dragging a poor man upon a hurdle. He is evidently a fraudulent baker, as the faulty loaf, the cause of his punishment, is hanging from his neck.

Cheating bakers were always rather severely handled, and officers of the City of London were ordered by the *Liber Albus* to drag such an one "through the great streets where there may be most people assembled, and through the great streets *that are most dirty*, to the pillory in the Chepe, there to remain at least one hour in the day." This was the favourite punishment. In after days we read of the terrible burnings, the mutilations, brandings, and ruinous fines, but as yet these tender mercies of the wicked were unknown. The pillory was considered the best doctor for social sores, and cured "Lies, Slanders, Falsehoods, and Deceits." Sellers of putrid meat, the forestallers of poultry, and many other fraudulent tradesfolk, suffered from his treatment. For practising the "art magic," for soothsaying, for having false dice, for taking away a child to go begging, cheating vagabonds were condemned to the pillory. To be forced to stand for an hour or more in a bent and cramped position is the reverse of comfortable; but to be made also a target for a copious shower of rotten eggs and market refuse, rendered the punishment of the pillory no light penalty.

We will follow the fortunes of Master Lickpenny, as described by John Lydgate in a famous ballad, called the "London Lickpenny." This worthy man came to London town to consult some one learned in the law, and encountered many pleasing adventures. We first see the poor countryman at Westminster. He does not progress far on his way before some street thieves snatch his hood from his head, and run away laughing. The Flemish merchants stroll to and fro, like pedlars, offering us hats and spectacles, and shouting lustily, "What will ye buy? What will ye buy?" It is now noon, and at Westminster gate there is plenty of bread, ale, wine, ribs of beef, and tables fairly set for such as had wherewith to pay. Making our way along the Strand, a country road, we are astonished to see the palaces of the nobles on either side, and the groups of armed men who stand about the gates and laugh at poor Lickpenny's hoodless state and rustic appearance. After passing under Ludgate Arch we hear the cries of the hawkers shouting peascods, strawberries, cherries, pepper, saffron, and spices; and at the Chepe there is an immense crowd of busy folk, and shopkeepers standing at the doors of their booths, offering all kinds of beautiful things,—velvets, silks, lawn, and Paris thread; nor do they cease from pestering us to buy, and even seize Master

Lickpenny by the hand to drag him into their shops, although he did not seem to have a well-lined purse. At London-stone the linen-drapers are equally clamorous and urgent; while certain noisy sellers of food cry out "Hot sheep's feet!" "Mackerel!" and the like. In East Cheap we see companies of minstrels who harp, and pipe, and sing the old street carols of Julian and Jenkin; there too we find a good supply of ribs of beef, pies, and pewter pots. At Cornhill there are several noted tradesfolk, who buy stolen goods, and lo! while we are examining some of the articles, Lickpenny beholds his own hood which was snatched from his head that very morning at Westminster. He is so overcome by this discovery that he must needs drink a pint of wine, for which he pays one penny to the taverner. And then we hurry down to the river at Billingsgate, where the watermen cry out to us "Hoo! go we hence!" And nothing loath, our friend Lickpenny gladly hies him over into Kent, and protests that he will never come to London again, or have anything to do with lawyers.

In our peregrinations through the streets we have noticed much of the gay splendour of the times,—the pageants, the plays, the gorgeous dresses and liveries, the pomp and external magnificence of the metropolis, and the comparative grandeur of the ecclesiastical and civic displays in other great towns. It was all very fine, very imposing. There was misery enough now and then, when wars raged and there was little food, and the plague stalked with relentless foot through the land, and men died by thousands, and cattle rotted in the fields, and the air was filled with the dread infection. But that was only occasionally, and men were light-hearted and forgot their troubles in the enjoyment of the present.

And if to us who live in the serious and solemn nineteenth century their shows and pageantry seem somewhat childish and useless, let us remember that these out-door festivities added greatly to the pleasures of the people. Although the English race no longer revels in the pomps and pageants which delighted our forefathers, nevertheless we have little changed in our love of active forms of amusement. Sports and games, hunting, racing, rowing, are dear to the hearts of our English people, and foreigners who come to our shores, and go away without witnessing a football match in the North of England, Epsom Downs on a Derby Day, the University boat-race, or Kennington Oval on the day of a great cricket match, cannot pretend that they know the English people. Melancholy philosophers may assert that we have lost our light-heartedness and that Englishmen take their pleasures sadly, but actual observations of our mannners and customs would lead us to doubt the truth of the assertion. We probably prefer open-air amusements of a more or less violent kind to watching processions, although the crowds that assemble to witness the Lord Mayor's Show declare that the love of pageantry is not quite defunct amongst us. Forms of expression may change, but the old characteristics of the race remain; and to those who live in our crowded, overgrown, smoky towns, it is pleasant to recall in imagination the scenes which once took place in the streets we know so well, to watch the pageant pass, and to witness the amusements of a contented and happy people in the days when England's life was young.

CHAPTER XI

IN FAIR AND MARKET

Fairs and their origin—The royal right—Toll and tribute—Description of a fair—Stafford custom—Stourbridge Fair—Fairs in churches and churchyards—Boston Fair and the robber knights — Markets and market-places — Canterbury monks and citizens—The fight for freedom—A burgher's difficulties—Causes of his prosperity—The growth of manufacture—The coming of the Flemings—Henry VIII. and the destruction of municipal freedom.

TOILING along the narrow streets on a certain day in the year we see a vast company of wains and pack-horses, merchants and traders, monks and packmen, keen-eyed foreigners from Antwerp and Bruges, dark-eyed Italians and hook-nosed Jews, a very miscellaneous company, all struggling through the deep mire of the streets to the market-place. It is the day of the great fair. No man knoweth at what date this mighty concourse of traders was first inaugurated. From time out of mind the merchants had always flocked to the fair on this day, and men were too busy bargaining to stop and inquire about the origin of things, or whence their customs arose. The monks could have told them that the word "fair" was derived from the Latin word *feria*, meaning a festival; and the fact that it usually took place on the feast of the patron saint of the Church shows its ecclesiastical origin. In early times it was the custom for the inhabitants of the town to keep open house, and to entertain all their relations and friends who came to them from a distance. They used to make booths and tents with the boughs of trees near the church, and celebrated the festival with much thanksgiving and prayer. By degrees they began to forget the prayers, and remembered only the feasting; country people flocked from far and near; the pedlars and hawkers came to find a market for their wares. Their stalls began to multiply, and this germ of that vast concourse of traders, called a Fair, was formed.

In such primitive fairs the traders paid no toll or rent for their stalls, but by degrees the right of granting permission to hold a fair was vested in the king, who for various considerations bestowed this favour on nobles, merchant guilds, bishops, or monasteries. Great profits arose from such gatherings. The traders had to pay toll on all the goods which they brought to the fair, in addition to the payment of stallage, or rent for the ground on which they displayed their merchandise, and also a charge on all the goods they sold. Moreover the town tradesfolk were obliged to close their shops during the fortnight, or such time as the gathering lasted, and compelled to bring their goods to the fair, so that the toll-owner might gain good profit withal.

The roads and streets leading to the market-place were thronged with traders and chapmen, the sellers of ribbons and cakes, minstrels and morrice-dancers, smock-frocked peasants, and sombre-clad monks. How they all contrived to convey themselves and their merchandise to the general rendezvous, it is difficult to conjecture. The streets were often well-nigh impassable on account of the masses of refuse therein accumulated. The builders worked in the streets, and made there the framework of new houses; dealers in wood threw down planks and blocks of timber in the public highway; butchers cast the refuse of their shambles into this common receptacle for all the manure, waste, and dirty water of the town. The Nottingham records tell us that the bell-founders cast hot cinders into the streets, so that none could walk therein; and moreover before each house lay great heaps of corn which had been winnowed by being thrown out of an upper window, the wind blowing away the chaff. Such was the condition of the narrow roads through which the crowd wended their way to the fair. Then a horn or trumpet sounded, and the lord of the manor, or the bishop's bailiff, or the mayor of the town proclaimed the fair; and then the cries of the traders, the music of the minstrels, the jingling of the bells of the morrice-dancers, filled the air, and added animation to the spectacle.

Curious local customs were observed on these occasions. In Stafford there was a procession of twelve men, having stag's antlers on their heads, who danced along in a wild procession. Many of these fairs have lingered on, the ghosts of their former greatness; the trade of the country has drifted into other channels; but shorn of their former dignity the fairs remain, wherein shows and round-abouts have superseded the minstrels and morrice-dancers, and only the traders are absent. However, on the Berkshire Downs, at a little village of West Ilsley, the great sheep fair is still held; once a year herds of Welsh ponies congregate at Blackwater, in Hampshire, driven hither by inveterate custom. Every year, in an open field near Cambridge, the once great Stourbridge fair is held, first granted by King John to the Hospital of Lepers, and formerly proclaimed with great state by the Vice-Chancellor of the University and the Mayor of Cambridge. This was once one of the largest fairs in Europe. Merchants of all nations attended it. The booths were planted in a cornfield, and the circuit of the fair, which was like a well-governed city, was about three miles. All offences committed therein were tried before a special court of *pie-poudre*. The shops were built in rows, having each a name, as Garlick Row, Booksellers' Row, Cook Row, &c.; there were the cheese-fair, hop-fair, wool-fair; every trade was represented, and there were taverns, eating-houses, and in later years play-houses of various descriptions. As late as the last century it is said that one hundred thousand pounds' worth of woollen goods was sold in a week in one row alone. This enables us to form some conception of the vast extent of these old fairs, without which the trade of the country could scarcely have been carried on.

The churchyard of the parish church was often used as a fair-ground, and even into the church the throng of traders surged, and there bought and sold their merchandise and displayed their wares. It is true that Edward I. prohibited such dealings, and declared that "henceforth no fairs or markets be kept in churchyards," but several hundreds of years elapsed before such trading in consecrated places was deemed sacrilegious. As we have already stated, the church was considered the home of the people. Its bell summoned them to an assembly of citizens, or bid them arm for the defence of their liberties. Thither they brought their goods when danger threatened, a place "where thieves could not break through nor steal," unless they wished to undergo the terrors of excommunication; there too were the weapons of defence, stored in the steeple, a goodly supply of harness, bows, helmets, and shields, all ready for use. The guild lights burned before their respective altars. Not for worship only did the crowds of burghers assemble on Sundays, but to hear the news, to discuss intricate matters of public business, and to devise new schemes for the development of the greatness of their town. Intensely loyal and patriotic were these old burghers as regards the interests of their own town or city. They cared little for the rest of the country;

kings and nobles might fight in France or against each other; it mattered not to them, so long as they could sell their goods, and make their town great, beautiful, and prosperous. Some strange scenes took place occasionally at fairs, and Boston had good cause to remember one such gathering of merchants in the reign of Edward I. One Chamberlain, and a number of knights, rode to the mayor and informed him that they intended to hold a grand tournament during the fair-time, which would attract large companies to the town, and add greatly to the glories of the fair. They would show the foreign traders how well brave English knights could tilt, and ride, and fight, and how dangerous it would be for any foreign foes to invade these shores. Nothing loath, the mayor gladly permitted the holding of the tournament. Then followed a strange scene. The fair of staples was at its height, when a company of monks entered the market-place. Suddenly cloaks and cowls are cast aside; the worthy knights stand revealed; and without delay set fire to the merchants' booths and plunder their goods. Silver and gold pieces ran in streams down the market square, and much booty was seized by the knights. It is satisfactory to know that their leader was captured and executed.

In the fairs the great wholesale trade of the country was carried on; in the weekly markets the principal retail business was transacted, and these began to supersede the more magnificent fairs and monopolise the general trade of the merchants. The holding of markets was also a right which appertained only to the king, and this right for various considerations was gradually conferred on nobles, or ecclesiastics, or town corporations. On market-day all the neighbouring farmers flocked to the town, with their wives and daughters, bearing their butter, eggs, and poultry, which they deposited in stalls in the market-place, and paid toll for the privilege. There too were gathered the principal tradesfolk of the town, the goldsmiths, mercers, saddlers, and all the other numerous dealers. Every town was in the Middle Ages an independent community, providing all things needful for the life and comfort of its inhabitants; and therefore it was necessary to have tradesmen of all descriptions. The usual shops were closed on market-day, and all men flocked to the market to buy or sell their goods. Very wroth were the good citizens of Canterbury with the monks of Christ Church monastery, whose tenants had houses with windows looking on the market, who did not scruple to open these windows and sell goods without paying toll. The quarrel lasted many years. The monks refused to buy their fish in the market, and sent for a supply to the sea-coast. The mayor was very wroth at such conduct, and waylaid the messengers who brought the fish; so the monks were deprived of their dinner, and in revenge advised their tenants to keep open their shops and defy the mayor. At last the mayor removed the market to another part of the town, and there the ecclesiastics and their tenants refused to trade. So the miserable quarrel went on in spite of lawsuits, turmoils, and attempted arbitrations, and probably was never ended until the monastery was swept away in the wild torrent of the Reformation.

Very fierce and bitter were these disputes between the burghers and monasteries established within their town walls. The monks were exempt from all taxation; they contributed nothing to the wealth of the town; they enjoyed many rights and privileges; their precincts were exempt from all the regulations and laws ordained by the citizens for the welfare of the town, and were moreover the refuge for all the disorderly persons who merited punishment for their crimes. Hence there was continual bitterness, and many angry disputings between the two rival authorities, neither of whom would give way.

The constant tolls and fees required from traders were another source of trouble and heart-burnings, and long and continued was their fight to obtain free passage of their goods from fair to fair, and market to seaport. In towns wherein the king was the over-lord the road to freedom lay easy. The right of trying prisoners, holding free meetings, and enjoying immunity from irritating tolls, was soon obtained in return for money advanced or other consideration. When an earl was the lord of the town, liberty was not quite so easily obtained. But during the Wars of the Roses the power of the nobles was broken, their fortunes gone, their purses empty, and they were quite willing to grant to the thrifty burghers the rights craved by them, in return for the money which they so sorely needed. But when a bishop or abbot was lord of the town, the struggle was fierce and prolonged. We have seen something of the continued contest which the men of Reading waged with their abbot; the same took place in many other places—always the same stern, dogged, determined fight for freedom.

When we look back upon the struggles of

those times we can but admire and wonder at the amazing perseverance and grand determination of these brave burghers. Nothing seemed to daunt them in the pursuit of the objects they had in view. They forgot, doubtless, the important fact that they owed their prosperity to the over-lord, whether abbot or earl, and that, but for the existence of the abbey or castle, their town would never have become so great and prosperous. No feelings of gratitude checked their strivings for power. For hundreds of years the fight lasted, one generation taking up the quarrel where their fathers had relinquished it; on and on the tide of progress and freedom flowed, bearing all before it—now driven back for a moment, and then mounting higher and higher till it swept away the stone walls and bars of privilege, and all that withstood the prosperity and freedom of the burghers.

And besides the battle of privilege, the burgher had to fight other battles too. He had to provide a company of soldiers, fully armed and victualled, for the king's service. He had to be always on the alert at home, lest an enemy should attack the town, or a company of lawless soldiers, the retinue of some warlike lord, should take it into their heads to try to pillage the town and slay its citizens. With his own hands he and all his fellows laboured to repair the town walls and to dig the protecting moat. On the sea-coasts heaps of brushwood were always ready to be fired in case of an invasion of piratical French folk or other unwelcome visitors. So the burgher was always on the alert, always ready, and might have adopted as the motto on his escutcheon *Semper paratus*. But he cared little for mottoes; he loved better the goodly treasures of his own town, and all that concerned its welfare. These he guarded with ever watchful eye. He loved too to see the town plays, "Adam and Eve," or the "Three Kings of Colin," and the minstrels and players, and the passion plays, and the setting of the watch on St. John's Eve, and the pageants and the ales, and all the endless variety of social festivity and pomp which a mediæval town provided for its worthy citizens.

Moreover he took a great pride in his town. There was no place like it in the world. Although he liked not the monks who defrauded him of his rightful dues, and never paid taxes, he loved his church, and with his own hands helped to build and repair its walls, and strove to make it as fair and beautiful as any other church in the world. He had traded with other towns, or been on a pilgrimage to the shrine of St. Thomas, or to that of Our Lady at Walsingham, and had noticed some better buildings, wider and cleaner streets, a guildhall with an open space beneath for the stalls on market-days; he had seen a market-cross made of stone, towering high, sculptured with many devices, with a covered penthouse for the shelter of market-folks, such as at Chichester or Salisbury. He had seen all these changes, and resolved with his fellow-townsmen to improve the condition of his own beloved town. The streets were paved, every man being ordered to pave the street before his door as far as the middle of the road; the market-cross erected, the church beautified; and gradually the appearance of the old town changed, and shared in the fortunes and prosperity of the burghers.

Moreover they did not see why their town should not have arms, and as early as the end of the thirteenth century began to devise for themselves these marks of dignity. Chester and the Cinque Ports led the way. The latter fashioned some curious monsters for their escutcheon, half lion, half ship, while the fishing folk of Great Yarmouth cut in half the lions of England, and made up the other half with three herrings.[1] The arms of the lord were often adopted, with some alteration, as those of the burgh over which he ruled. Sometimes the townsfolk exercised their wit by making a canting allusion to the name of their town. Thus those of Kingston-on-Hull placed three crowns on their shield, showing that they knew that the name was derived from the King's-town. The citizens of Oxford chose for their bearings an ox passing through a river. The dagger in the arms of the City of London is popularly supposed to represent the weapon with which Sir William Walworth slew Wat Tyler, and some rhymes in the Hall of the Fishmongers support the notion. It is really the sword of St. Paul combined with the cross of St. George, and the arms had been in use before the rebellion of Tyler. Southampton was incorporated by Henry VI.; hence the red roses of the House of Lancaster appear on the arms of the town, while the white roses on the shield of Ludlow, incorporated by Edward IV., denote the adherence of the burghers to the House of York. The principal trade of the town is sometimes denoted, as at Gloucester, where the nail-makers abounded, and

[1] "English Municipal Heraldry," by W. H. St. John Hope (*Archæological Journal*).

where horse-shoes and nails appear on the arms; and at Leeds, where the shield bearing the golden fleece alludes to the famous wool trade which there found a home. Thus the burghers sought to enhance the importance of their town, and showed their patriotism.

Moreover the burgher might aspire to be a member of Parliament and to meet the king at Westminster; but this privilege he was never very eager to enjoy. The increasing wealth of the towns made them important in the eyes of the king as a means for increasing his revenues. The rich townsfolk could pay taxes as well as other royal subjects; hence in the Parliament of 1265, two burgesses for each town were summoned to attend. Only few obeyed, but in 1295 Edward I. gathered together two burgesses from each city, borough, and leading town to sit in the great council of the nation, and to take their places with the nobles, knights, and great men of his kingdom. The result was pleasing to the sovereign, inasmuch as he was able to increase largely his exchequer by the liberal grants of the borough representatives. However, the thrifty burghers were not eager to send a member to Parliament, as they had to pay his expenses, amounting to two shillings a day, and the member was loath to abandon his trading for so long a period as the sitting of Parliament, even for the sake of the honour of consorting with princes and nobles in the nation's council chamber. Hence many boroughs petitioned that they might be exempted from sending a representative, and writs and fines had to be issued to compel reluctant members to attend. The ambition of the burgher did not extend beyond the walls of his own guildhall.

The story of the growth of the prosperity of the burghers is a long and complicated one. How did we English folk learn to become manufacturers? We were a farming folk, and our rich fleeces were sent to the Netherlands, the centre of the industry of the world, there to be made into cloth. The citizens of Ghent, and Bruges, and Antwerp, in the Middle Ages, were the richest and most prosperous people in Europe. They were very turbulent also, and riots and wars did not improve their trade.

The wise king, Edward III., seeing how prosperous the Flemings were on account of their skill in manufacturing cloth from English wool, bethought him that perhaps it would be well to make the wool into cloth before sending it abroad. So he prohibited the export of all wool, and invited a number of cloth-weavers from Flanders to settle in England, and instruct his subjects in the art. Many of these weavers settled in Bristol, in Temple Street, and commenced a manufacture which made the town long famous. The looms were also set up in the pleasant vales of Gloucestershire, and English folk learned to work them.

Grievous troubles dawned upon the ill-fated Netherlands. The Inquisition, the Duke of Alva and his Spanish soldiers, brought ruin on the fair provinces, and the Dutch weavers, finding the flames of persecution too fierce, fled to England, and brought with them the secrets of their craft, and that skill and ingenuity which had made them so successful. Then Dutchmen, Flemings, and Walloons settled in several of our towns. Norwich was made prosperous by them, and East Anglian dames delighted in the silk dresses which their new visitors made for them. They fixed their looms also in the West Riding of Yorkshire, in Rochdale and Saddleworth, and laid the foundation of the thriving industries of Lancashire. There are some cottages attached to the walls of the refectory of the Abbey of Reading, which were built by Queen Elizabeth for some Dutch weavers driven from their country by the fiercest and most cruel persecution that ever man has seen. English manufacturers and merchants owe a great debt of gratitude to these industrious refugees.

We have witnessed the growth and development of our towns, their struggle for liberty and their conquests. We have noticed the rise of a powerful burgher, or middle class, in which the main government of the town was vested. Brave, rich, determined, the product of centuries of stern and unflinching struggling, the burgher was a mighty man who with his fellows in the guildhall ruled the town, its craftsmen and small traders, with a firm and severe discipline. But still a mightier man arose, one before whom even the haughty burgher had to bow his head and make obeisance, even the imperious Henry VIII., who by his statecraft and determined will overthrew the power of the towns as separate organisations, and made the sovereignty of the crown felt in every council chamber in the land. It was a mighty change, perhaps beneficial for the country as a whole—this welding together of the shreds of sovereignty—but it destroyed much for which the dwellers in our towns and cities had long contended, and liberty died to rise again in less troublous times.

CHAPTER XII

THE GREAT METROPOLIS

Royal Winchester — Mercantile supremacy of London — Medieval London — A tour of the walls of the city — A city of palaces — The Strand and the houses of nobles — Bishops' palaces — Riots — The "Intelligencer" of 1648 — The "Newes" of 1665 — The Plague — The Great Fire — Memorable buildings.

OF all great towns and cities in England, London, of course, reigns supreme. In fact, it is becoming so much the centre of all our commercial and social life, that all places seem destined to be mere suburbs of London, that mighty city which grows ever larger and larger, and absorbs everything within its pale. There was a time when London had a great struggle for the sovereignty amongst the other towns and cities of England. In Saxon and early Norman times Winchester was the home of English kings. Under Cnut, it was the capital of a kingdom stretching across the seas to Scandinavia; and under the Normans, a large part of France was in subjection to it. Here kings were born, and royal weddings were celebrated with great pomp in its grand cathedral, where at last their bones were laid. If royal patronage could have preserved the glories of ancient Winchester, it would have remained the capital of England; but another force arose, the power of commerce. London was the centre of the commercial activity of the country, and, in the end, Winchester was forced to yield supremacy to its more powerful rival. The two cities quarrelled as to which of them should have the honour of providing a cup-bearer to Henry III.; but, alas, Winchester was only grasping at the shadow, when the reality of her power had passed away.

London in the Middle Ages was of course very different from that great, over-crowded, noisy, and far-extending metropolis which we see to-day. It is difficult for us in these days to realise the small extent of ancient London, or, indeed, to go back in imagination even a century or two ago, when the good citizens could go a-nutting on Notting Hill, and when it was possible to see Temple Bar from Leicester Square—then called Leicester Fields—and, with a telescope, observe the heads of the Scotch rebels which adorned its spikes. When we fly along in a hansom from Paddington to the City, we can scarcely believe that it ever required three hours to traverse the distance, as in the early coaching days, on account of the impassable roads; but Kensington, Islington, Brompton, and Paddington were simply country villages, separated from London by fields and pastures; and the names of such districts as Spitalfields, Bethnal Green, Smithfield, Moorfields, and many others now crowded with houses, indicate the once rural character of the neighbourhood.

We will walk round the walls of old London, and begin with the Tower, which was built by the Conqueror, not, as may be imagined, to secure the capital against foreign foes, but simply to keep in order the citizens and check any revolts. The wall extended thence to Aldgate—the "old gate"—and thence to Bishopsgate—near the Bishop of London's palace, I suppose; at any rate, his lordship was accustomed to use this gate as he passed out of the city to hunt in his woods at Stepney. A wide ditch protected the wall at this point; hence the name Houndsditch, which took its title from this old moat. London Wall preserves the course of the rampart, until we arrive at the northern gate, called Aldersgate.

Along Carth Street remains of the wall may still be seen, and at Cripplegate, in the churchyard of St. Giles, there are also some remains of the old fortification. Thence we go to Newgate and the Old Bailey, and then southwards to Ludgate, where the wall was protected by the Fleet, a small river, whence the name Fleet Street is derived. On the south of the Ludgate, on the bank of the Thames, stood another strong castle erected by the Conqueror, called Baynard Castle, which has entirely disappeared; and then the wall was continued along the north bank of the river back to the Tower, Dowgate and Billingsgate being two entrances on that side of the old city. The walk along the top of the walls would not have been a very exhausting one, as the whole city did not cover a wider area than that of Hyde Park.

Westminster Abbey was founded by Edward the Confessor, and around it a number of houses sprang up; but Charing was a village in the time of Edward I., and lay between the two cities of London and Westminster. The Strand was a country lane when Edward III. reigned. St. Giles'-in-the-Fields was literally in the fields, and Long Acre was a meadow. The palace of the kings of England stood where the Houses of

Parliament now stand, and Henry VIII. built his "mews" at Charing Cross for his hawks.

The walls of old London for a long time embraced the whole of the city; no "foreigner," or stranger from another town, was allowed to trade within the city boundaries unless he became a freeman of some guild; and by degrees houses sprang up outside the walls, in which many of these foreigners lived, and plied their trade without complying with the rules and regulations of the guild merchants. Grievous heart-burnings and jealousies ensued, and so enraged were the citizens at this interference with their trade, that on May-day 1517, when Cardinal Wolsey was the king's minister, a formidable riot ensued, and an angry crowd of servants and apprentices of the citizens plundered and destroyed the houses and warehouses of these "foreigners," the tumult continuing until daybreak.

In our review of the towns and cities of England we have frequently referred to London, and described the past glories of its civic life and the habits and customs of the citizens. We have seen that they were a very religious people, and that one-fourth of the area of the city was occupied by monastic buildings and churches. The beautiful church of St. Bartholomew,

Smithfield, is a splendid relic of early Norman London, and we have still the Charterhouse to admire and to remind us of pre-Reformation days.

London was also a city of palaces. All the great nobles of England had their town houses or inns, as they were called. These noblemen had vast retinues of armed men. In 1457, at a meeting of the great estates of the realm, Richard Duke of York came with four hundred followers, who lodged in Baynard's Castle. The Earl of Salisbury lodged in the Herber at Dowgate with five hundred horsemen. The Earl of Warwick stayed at his inn in Warwick Lane, with six hundred men, "where," says Stow, "there were oftentimes six oxen eaten at a breakfast." The Dukes of Exeter and Somerset, the Earl of Northumberland, and many others had their town houses, every vestige of which has passed away, though their names are preserved by the streets and sites on which they stood. The Strand, for example, is full of the memories of these old mansions. Northumberland Avenue tells us of the house of the Earls of Northumberland, which stood there till 1875; Burleigh Street and Exeter Street recall the famous Sir William Cecil, Lord Burleigh, whose son was created Earl of Essex.

The Savoy Hotel and Theatre mark the spot where Peter de Savoy, a relation of the queen of Henry III., built the old Savoy Palace, which afterwards became a nunnery and then a hospital. Lord Craven's house stood near Craven Buildings in Drury Lane. Clare House, the mansion of the Earls of Clare, survives in Clare Market. Arundel Street, Howard Street, and Norfolk Street tell us of the Howards, Earls of Norfolk, and Essex Street of the ill-fated favourite of Queen Elizabeth. Leicester Square points us to the residence of another favourite of the Virgin Queen, and Villiers Street and Buckingham Street are the memorial of yet another court favourite, the infamous Duke of Buckingham. The bishops also had their town houses, and the sites are recorded by such names as Ely Place, Salisbury Square, Bangor Court, and Durham Street.

Many scenes of riot and bloodshed have the old City walls witnessed, and very turbulent and rebellious were the citizens of olden days, ever ready to rush to arms, and more eager to support the cause of the people than that of the sovereign. After the coronation of Richard I., they plundered, robbed, and murdered the poor Jews who lived in Old Jewry. Led by a base Mayor, Fitz-Richard, they rose in favour of the barons against Henry III., and the pleasure of committing havoc and destruction prompted them again to plunder the Jews, and to attack the houses of rich merchants, and fire and sword raged horribly throughout the city. They pelted the poor queen with rotten eggs and dirt as she tried to escape from the Tower to Windsor. They sided with the shameless Queen Isabella against her unfortunate husband, Edward II., and murdered the Chancellor, a priest, in the Newgate Prison; but the "Black Death" checked their turbulent spirits in the following reign, and, it is said, carried off 50,000 souls. Again, in the troubles of the sixteenth century, they espoused the cause of the parliament against the king; and who has not read with sorrow the description of that sad and solemn scene at Whitehall, when, after a mock trial, Charles I. was beheaded by his own subjects? I have before me a copy of the *Intelligencer* of 1648, the newspaper of the period, which describes the mournful spectacle — the king protesting his innocence of the charges brought against him, praying, in the words of St. Stephen, that his death might not be laid to their charge, showing consideration to all, and exclaiming with his last words, "I go from a corruptible to an incorruptible crown, where no disturbance can be." That scene will not be forgotten while history remains.

Another old newspaper, called the *Newes,* "published for the satisfaction and information of the people," July 6, 1665, tells of the alarm of the citizens when the plague broke out, and the infallible remedies which were suggested for its removal. The *Intelligencer* of August 28, 1665, announces, "an excellent electuary against the plague, to be drunk at the Green Dragon, Cheapside, at sixpence a pint," and various "Lozenges or Pectorals approved as sovoraign Antidote against the Plague," manufactured by one Theophilus Buckworth at his house on Mile-end Green, and sealed up with his coat of arms on the papers, are strongly recommended for the cure of the malady.

Sad were the scenes in London streets at that disastrous period, when 90,000 inhabitants died; when there was wailing in every street, and scarcely a house which did not bear the ominous red cross, with the words "**Lord have Mercy upon us**" written over it, to mark the presence of the plague. The streets became deserted and moss-grown, and the rumble of the death-cart was alone heard, bearing the bodies to the pits, where all the dead were buried together.

The story of the Great Plague is a thrice-told tale, and need not be here repeated. Those who desire to study the sad records of its ravages should read Daniel Defoe's narrative, and Pepys' diary, and also Harrison Ainsworth's powerful novel, which is based upon the diary of a worthy and pious citizen, who during five long months shut up his house, and though the plague raged all around him, he and his family were mercifully spared until the scourge had passed away. London did not suffer alone by the presence of plagues. All the chief towns in England were periodically visited by pestilence. The entire absence of all sanitation, the abundance of pigsties, manure heaps, and other nuisances, the shameful neglect of common decency, provided a fruitful soil for the seeds of disease to grow. Indeed the wonder is that the periodical plagues were not more frequent and virulent. Outside the city of Winchester, near the west gate, there is an obelisk which is a standing memorial of the plague and its ravages, which carried off so many of the good citizens in the years 1665 and 1666. In its foundations is preserved the "Broad Stone" on which, in a pan of vinegar or water, coins were placed in exchange for provisions which the country-folk brought to the gates of the city, and by this means escaped the contagion. There exists also a still vigorous Society of Natives, a charitable institution, the primary object of which was to aid those who lost their parents in the times of the plague.

Another thrice-told tale is that of the **Great Fire** which broke out in the following year, and consumed 13,000 houses and about 400 streets. The wooden houses of the artisans in the narrow streets furnished fuel for the flames, and many stately palaces, and almost all the original halls of the city companies were swept away by this mighty conflagration. Its course was only stayed by the destruction of some houses by gunpowder; thus a gap was formed which the flames could not leap, and the fire burnt itself out.

The fire was really a blessing in disguise, as it purified the city of London and destroyed the germs of the plague, which used to break out two or three times every century. It also made it possible to build wide streets and more substantial houses; it enabled Sir Christopher Wren to erect the grand pile, St. Paul's Cathedral, upon the site of the old, desecrated, and half-ruined house of God, which the flames of the Great Fire had removed.

But the history of London is the history of England, and it is beyond the scope of this work to describe the many scenes and spectacles its old walls have witnessed. That task has already been accomplished by several writers whose works are known to all who love the old records of famous London town. We visit again with ever renewed interest the numerous places about which old associations cling—the Tower with its traditions of Norman supremacy and the sad stories of its dungeons and its block; the Temple Church and its courts, which once echoed the tread of mailed warrior monks; Westminster Abbey, the burying-place of our national heroes; the Charterhouse; the Inns of Court, the haunts of the famous literary men of the last century. We turn aside from the busy City streets and find ourselves in the calm seclusion of an ancient Livery Company's Hall, and are at once transported from this noisy nineteenth century to a less hurried period of our nation's life, and meet again the worthy merchants of three or four centuries ago, who regard us from their gilded frames while we read their names on the silver cups which they presented to their beloved most worshipful company.

In spite of modern "improvements" and the

destruction of many of its ancient features, London still remains one of the most interesting cities in the world, the centre of its commerce, the metropolis of an empire upon which, as yet, the sun never sets.

CHAPTER XIII

IN THE DAYS OF GOOD QUEEN BESS

"Merrie England" — Ruins and desolation — Scene in Reading Abbey — Destruction of monasteries and disfigurement of churches — The Church and the people — Church-ales — Morrice-dancers and minstrels — Elizabethan houses — A merchant's household — Costumes of women — May-day — Pageants at Norwich — Rogues and vagabonds — Cruel laws.

WE are accustomed to associate "Merrie England" with the brilliant days of the Virgin Queen, and to picture to ourselves the bright sunny scenes of splendour which delighted the hearts of a joyous people during the glorious reign of that powerful and imperious sovereign. Then surely was England "merrie" when the heart of the nation was young, and laughter reigned in every street; when old fetters had been thrown off, and prosperity smiled, and her marts were laden with the spoils of distant climes, and her land was filled with song, while her children danced, and all was merry as a marriage-bell. Certainly many details of the picture are true, but the study of the social condition of the towns of England at this period reveals many dark corners; many dreary scenes of misery present themselves when the whole canvas is spread before our eyes. We love to revel in the sunshine, to watch the pageants as they pass, to see the ships enter the harbours bearing the "elephants' teeth" and the spoils of the Indies, to hear the wild talk of the sailors who had scoured the Spanish main and singed the beard of the Spanish monarch. But side by side with the great expansion of commerce, and the prosperity of the middle classes, there was great want, privation, and misery among the labouring population of England. To this fact the Acts of Parliament and the records of our towns bear abundant witness, and to these we shall presently refer.

The appearance of our towns, too, had greatly changed. Where were all the stately monasteries, with their magnificent minsters, once so gorgeous with painted walls and windows, and gilded canopies? Where were the abbots and monks, black friars and grey friars, veiled nuns and chantry priests? And what had become of all the stores of Church plate, silver-gilt chalices, and numberless patens, and all the gold ornaments and rich vestments which the piety of generations had collected for the worship of God in our parish churches? All were gone to swell that hideous heap of spoil which a rapacious monarch and his myrmidons had amassed. The monks and nuns had been turned out into the world to starve or beg; the abbots had ended their miseries on the scaffold; and their houses were all ruins. It was a sad spectacle.

When the abbot's head had fallen and the monks expelled from the cloister shade, a whisper was heard among the townsfolk of Reading that the body of Henry I. lay before the high altar in the minster in a coffin of gold. The rumour was wrong, as rumours often are; for did not Matthew of Paris, or some other chronicler, record at monotonous length a not very edifying account of the embalming of the king's body, specially stating that it was wrapped in bulls' hides and placed in a stone coffin? But perhaps no one in the crowd had read Matthew of Paris, or any other work—the days of free education and board schools as yet were not—at any rate they heeded not. "Gold, gold!" was their cry, as they rushed into the deserted aisles of the grand minster. Soon picks and spades were busy on the beautifully tiled pavement; but they only found a skeleton in stone cist, which they cast away in disgust. Imitating their betters in appropriating anything they could find, they then hurried away to the Greyfriars' monastery, where there was a goodly booty of precious metal for industrious pilferers. And then the masons and labourers came to quarry the ruins for stone and timber.

Thus we read in the churchwardens' accounts of St. Mary's, Reading:—

Payede for the taking downe of the Quyer in the Abbye
      and the carraige home of the same . xxj. Lodes x^s vi^d
Payed for the Rowfe in the Abbye . . . vj li x^s viij^d

Some of the minsters became cathedrals; some monastic buildings were pulled down and the materials sold; some were handed over to baser uses; and others remain to this day, melancholy memorials of a past age and of their ancient magnificence.

See also the sad condition of our town churches. They too have been despoiled by ruthless, avaricious hands. The beautiful chalices are all gone, the altars stripped of their ornaments, the ancient rood-screen pulled down (we notice in the account-books a scornful *item* relating to the charge for "carting away of the rubbish"), the carved front broken, and all the curious mural paintings have disappeared. In the account-books we read the following *items*, which explain the disappearance of the pictures:—

Paid for iiij boketts for the werkmen to whytelyme the churche . . . . xii^d
Paid to Alexander Lake a mason for xxiij dayes for hym and his assistant in white lymymg of the churche at ix^d the day . . . . . . xvij^s iij^d

As it was in one church, so in all; everywhere destruction, spoliation, desecration.

Happily the Church herself survived this rude treatment of her ancient fabrics. The same rectors and vicars lived on, many of them, through all the changes of that changeful time. The churchwardens continued their work. There was no violent disruption. The Church continued to be the centre of the social, as well as of the religious, life of the people. The vestry was the council chamber of the parish; the church was the home of the inhabitants, associated with all their joys and sorrows, their business and their festivals. One curious *item* in the old account-books shows the identity of post-Reformation and pre-Reformation arrangements, and that is "Smoke farthings." This was a hearth tax, and was formerly known as Peter's Pence, which was paid by each householder to the Pope. After the Reformation the money was still paid, but it did not go to the support of papal dignity, but to the bishop of the diocese, for the welfare of the Church at home. One curious Church custom we must not omit to describe, as it formed a notable feature in the social life of each town and country parish, and that was the "Church Ale." Easter and Whitsuntide were the two seasons at which church-ales were usually held, but they were not confined to those times, and if the church needed a new roof, or some poor people were in sad straits, the parishioners would decide to have a church-ale, and the funds required would soon be forthcoming. The churchwardens bought, and received as presents, a large quantity of provisions, which they employed in brewing and baking, and on the appointed day "the neighbours met at the Church House, and there fed merrily on their own victuals, contributing some petty portion to the stock, which by many smalls groweth to a meetly greatness: for there is entertained a kind of emulation between these wardens, who by his graciousness in gathering, and good husbandry in expending, can best advance the Church's profit. Besides, the neighbour parishes at those times lovingly visit one another, and this way frankly spend their money together. The afternoons are consumed in such exercises as old and young folk (having leisure) do accustomly wear out the time withal. When the feast is ended the wardens yield in their account to the parishioners, and such money as exceedeth the disbursements is laid up in store to defray any extraordinary charges arising in the parish or imposed on them for the good of the country, or the Prince's Service, neither of which commonly gripe so much, but that somewhat still remaineth to cover the purse's bottom."

Aubrey thus describes the Church House, the scene of these entertainments:—"In every parish was a church-house, to which belonged spits, crocks, and other utensils for dressing provisions. Here the housekeepers met. The young people were there, too, and had dancing, bowling, shooting at butts, &c., the ancients (*i.e.*, the old folk) sitting gravely by and looking on. All things were civil and without scandal. The Church Ale is, doubtless, derived from the Agapai, or Love Feasts, mentioned in the New Testament."

Here is an account of a goodly feast preserved in an old churchwardens' book:—

Imprimis for fleshe	xij^s
It'm for beare	iij^s
It'm for ale	xv^d
It'm for bread	ii^s
It'm for spices and frute	xx^d
It'm for Butter and Sewet	xij^d
It'm for flower	iiij^d
It'm for wood	iiij^d
It'm for Sawlte	iiij^d
It'm for Hayle	xij^d

The maidens too were busily engaged on these occasions; they erected an arbour of boughs in the churchyard, called Robin Hood's Bower, and collected money for the ales by "Hocking." The process was simple; they waylaid the men, and held them with a rope wound round them, until their prisoners redeemed themselves by the payment of money. Here is a record of the old custom:—

1505 A.D. *Item*, Received of the maidens' gathering at Whitsuntide by the tree at the church door . . . . ii^s vi^d

The morrice-dancers and minstrels, the ballad-singers and players, were in great force at these feasts, and were entertained at the cost of the parish, as the following *item* shows :—

Paid to morris-dancers and the minstrels, meat and
    drink at Whitsuntide . . . . . iij^s iiij^d

When we turn from the contemplation of these social gatherings, we see a great transformation in the appearance of our town-houses and of the princely mansions of the nobles. Increased prosperity and security produced an era of building. Palaces rose as if by the power of a magician's wand. There was the royal palace of Nonsuch, near Cheam, Surrey, extolled by all beholders as a marvel of architectural design. There was the splendid Wollaton, in Nottinghamshire; Somerset House, in the Strand; Buckhurst House, Surrey; Longleat, Burleigh, Hatfield, Audley, Hardwick, Bolsover, and a host of other lordly mansions, while the country gentry rebuilt their manor-houses and studded the land with fair edifices. The town-houses still retained their ancient form, but they were more beautifully ornamented. Rich carvings adorned the windows, and within rich hangings, a goodly store of plate, and many evidences of increased luxury meet the eye. The servants and apprentices still lived in their master's house, and were up betimes, at six o'clock in the morning. They dined at eleven and supped at six. After evening prayers companies of the apprentices might be seen practising with "bucklers and wasters" before their master's door. Very ready these London youths were with their weapons, and the cry, "'Prentices! 'Prentices! Clubs! Clubs!" was the signal for many a savage onslaught, which often ended fatally.

At the door, too, sat the ladies decked out in fine array, with monstrous ruffs and enormous fardingales, wilhe their faces were not ignorant of cosmetics. Very fine were these city dames; nor were their country cousins less gorgeous in their attire. The wife of the famous Jack of Newbury is described as being attired in a fair train gown stuck full of silver pins, having a white cap on her head with cuts of curious needlework under the same, and an apron before her as white as driven snow. Her maidens, too, were dressed in stamel red petticoats, with milk-white kerchers on their heads, and their smock-sleeves like the winter's snow, tied with silken bands at the waist.

Many were the sports and games in which the lads and lasses revelled during these "golden days of good Queen Bess," especially when

May-time crowned the year, and there were many shouts and horn-blowings and the twining of garlands, and all the delights of a May-Day Festival. Troops of young men and maidens are returning from the woods bearing branches of birch and spring flowers, and here comes the May-pole drawn by thirty yoke of oxen, their horns decorated with the trophies of spring. It is covered with flowers and gay ribbons, handkerchiefs and flags streaming in the wind. And then, with shouts of laughter and glad songs, the strong arms of the young men raise the mighty shaft, and then (as the Puritanical Stubbes observes) "they straw the ground round about it; they bind green boughs about it; they set up summer-halls, bowers, and arbours hard by it; and then they fall to banqueting and feasting, to leaping and dancing about it, as the heathen people did at the dedication of their idols."

A company of morris-dancers approach, and a circle is made round the May-pole in which they can perform their merry diversions. First comes a man dressed in a green tunic, with a bow, arrows, and bugle-horn. It is our old friend Robin Hood, and by his side, attended by her maidens, walks Maid Marian, the May Queen. Will Stukeley, Little John, and other companions of the famous outlaw follow; and then comes the hobby-horse, which careers about, prances, and curvets, now rushing among the crowd, and now kicking and rearing frantically at the sight of a formidable-looking dragon, which hisses and flaps his wings. And then the maidens dance again, and the archers set up their targets in the butts, where a close contest ensues, and the victor is crowned with a laurel wreath. Such were some of the sights and sounds of May-Day in olden times.

Volumes could be filled with descriptions of the amusements of this period; we have tried to draw the outlines of that bright picture of light-hearted gaiety which characterised the reign of good Queen Bess. The monarch contributed much to the happiness of her subjects by her ceaseless wanderings through the kingdom. Wherever she went there were pageants and processions and displays of courtly grandeur which must have entailed a vast amount of elaborate preparation and rehearsing, and afforded much amusement both to the performers and spectators. For example, at Norwich, which the Queen visited in 1578, there was displayed before her Majesty "a choice assemblage of rare and splendid scenery and personifications, among which Mercury paraded before her in a coach, the whole whereof was covered with birds, and naked spirits hanging by the heels in the air, and clouds cunningly painted out, as though by some thunder-crack they had been shaken and tormented." And besides the usual goodly company of gods and goddesses, knights and heroes, there was a pageant representing the trade of the country, little girls spinning and knitting, while a youth addressed the Queen in laudatory verse. This show pleased her Majesty greatly, we are told. Wherever the Queen went she was welcomed and entertained by these curious exhibitions, which afforded the townsfolk much innocent enjoyment. The nobles did not so much covet the honour of a royal visit, as the enormous expense of her entertainment crippled and well-nigh ruined many rich estates.

We have seen something of the outside splendour of Elizabeth's reign, the growing prosperity, increased luxury, merriment, and song, which echoed through the land and cheered the hearts of young and old; but there was plenty of misery too, terrible pictures of beggary and pauperism, while crowds of sturdy vagabonds scoured the country, living by theft and rapine, utterly regardless of all law or order. The dissolution of the monasteries was a fruitful source of mendicancy. Not only were the occupants of the monastic houses driven from their homes and forced to support themselves by the donations of the charitable, but the crowds of domestics and tradesfolk who had clustered around an ancient abbey and had derived their livelihood from it were suddenly deprived of their employment and had no means of subsistence. Then the monks and nuns had been the chief friends of the poor, who could always find food and lodgings in the abbey precincts: whither could they go now that the *hospitium* was in ruins and the monks expelled? In addition to these classes of poverty-stricken folk, there were crowds of sturdy rogues and vagabonds using subtle craft and unlawful games or plays, feigning themselves to have knowledge in physiognomy, palmistry, or other abused sciences; fencers, bearwards, common players in interludes, minstrels, jugglers, pedlars, tinkers, and petty chapmen, who wandered about without due license from two justices of the peace.

How did the sapient authorities deal with this appalling mass of vagrancy and mendicancy? The Acts of Parliament tell us. All vagrants " being whole and mighty in body and able to labour" were condemned to be tied to the end of a cart naked, and beaten with whips through the nearest market-town, till their bodies be bloody by reason of such whipping; then sent back to their native town with a certificate of their whipping; and then put to labour as a true man oweth to do. Even this severe Act did not seem to stem the tide of vagrancy, and it was followed by one of the most barbarous decrees ever invented by English law-makers. Any one found loitering without any visible means of support might be seized and set to work by any one who would give him meat and drink; if he ran away, he was to be branded on the breast with the letter V, and made the slave of his employer for two years. Bread and water and the refuse of meat were given him for food, and he could be forced to work by beating, chaining, or other forcible methods. If he attempted to escape, he was branded on the cheek with the letter S, and became the slave of his master for ever. After any subsequent attempts to break away from his fetters, he was adjudged a felon and merited the punishment of death. Such was the hideous law enacted by the counsellors of Good Queen Bess. At length a system of Poor Law administration was evolved, and people were assessed for the relief of the poor on the same principle which has since guided our Legislature. But even under this Act vagabonds were ordered to be whipped and burnt through the gristle of the right ear with a hot iron of the compass of an inch about, while death awaited the runaway.

In spite of all these devices for the cure of the evil, vagrancy still flourished. On the confines of the Metropolis, on Maidenhead thicket, in the wilds of Somersetshire, and elsewhere bands of sturdy ruffians openly defied all law, plundered as they pleased, waylaid the packmen and the wains of the clothiers and merchants, rifled the farmsteads, threatened the magistrates, who were afraid to proceed against them, and carried ruin and devastation whithersoever they went. They were the ancestors of the Knights of the Road, of Claude Duval, Dick Turpin, the Golden Farmer, and many others, who gained renown in the seventeenth and eighteenth centuries, and plundered travellers, until at length the tall gibbets thinned their ranks, wild heaths were reclaimed, and travelling lost its danger and excitement.

CHAPTER XIV

MEMORABLE SIEGES OF GREAT TOWNS

In time of war—Exeter sieges—Alfred and the Danes—Exeter and the Conqueror—A siege in mediæval times—Perkin Warbeck—"Semper fidelis"—The siege of Gloucester—Colchester—The death of heroes.

IN our peaceful country, where for so many years war has been unknown, it is difficult to go back in imagination to the days when our towns had walls and ramparts, which had to be kept in constant repair, and when at any time the citizens might be summoned to the battlements to protect their hearths and homes from ruin and desolation. Fearful was the fate of a conquered town, when, according to the usage of mediæval warfare, it was handed over to the soldiers for a two or three days' pillage, when life, honour, and property were entirely at the mercy of a band of lawless men.

In Saxon times, when the Danes were ravaging the country, sailing up the rivers, and burning and destroying as they pleased, there was hardly a town which was not taken and retaken by the opposing armies. Well might the English chroniclers lament over the evils of those days when corn was scarce and the land barren, and ruined homesteads marked the course of the invaders.

Of all English towns, Exeter seems to have been most often exposed to a siege. It was originally a British hill fort protected by earthworks, and was probably stubbornly defended by the brave Britons when the Saxon hosts bore down upon it. The city walls followed the course of the earthworks, and ran round the crest of the hill, one point going down to the river to admit commerce into the city, which was one of the richest in England. In the days of Alfred, during the war with the Danes, Exeter was often taken and retaken by the King and his foes. Here is an account of the earliest siege of Exeter, taken from Asser's "Life of Alfred":—"The King went to Exeter, where the pagans were wintering, and, having shut them up within the walls, laid siege to the town. He also gave orders to his sailors to prevent them from obtaining any supplies by sea; and his sailors were encountered by a fleet of a hundred and twenty ships full of armed soldiers who were come to help their countrymen. As soon as the King's men knew that they were fitted with pagan soldiers they leaped to their arms and bravely attacked those barbaric tribes. But the pagans, who had now for almost a month been tossed and almost wrecked among the waves of the sea, fought vainly against them; their bands were discomfited in a moment, and all were sunk and drowned in the sea at a place called Suanewic (Swanwick)." In the days of Ethelred, Exeter was taken by storm through the cowardice or treachery of the "French churl Hugh," who had been appointed steward by Emma Elfgive, daughter of Richard of Normandy. But the greatest interest is attached to the siege of Exeter by the Conqueror William. For a long time the Western capital held its own, and refused to acknowledge a Frenchman as King of England. William marched with an army to subdue the bold citizens, but he found Exeter a harder nut to crack than he expected. With consummate bravery, for eighteen days they defied the full power of the Conqueror. When we read of the exploits of Hereward the Wake and the gallantry of these brave men of Devon, who fought so determinedly for their liberty, we Englishmen cannot help feeling profound sympathy with them, although perhaps it was better for England that Exeter, York, Ely, and Durham, which were all gallantly defended, should have been subdued, in order that the kingdom might be a united one, and not made up of independent cities and states. In the time of Stephen, also, when "there was all discord, and evil-doing, and robbery," many powerful men rose up against the King, amongst whom the first was Baldwin de Redvers, "who held Exeter against the King, and Stephen besieged him, and afterwards Baldwin made terms with him."

How was it possible, before the days of gunpowder, for men to capture a strongly fortified town or castle, defended by huge walls eighteen feet thick, by moats and portcullises, and by brave and well-armed burghers? The mode of direct attack was first to discharge a flight of arrows at the besieged, so as to compel them to seek shelter behind the battlements, then to throw planks across the moat, along which the besiegers ran and placed scaling-ladders against the walls. Instantly the soldiers begin to ascend, holding above their heads their shields against arrows and stones. In this manner a band of men would try to reach the summit of the walls, and guard the way for others, until a sufficient number of men were assembled to overcome the besieged. But sometimes the ladders were thrown down, or the assailants overpowered. There is generally a space between the battlements and the wall, through which missiles and darts can be hurled on those who attempt this method of attack. Then other devices have to be adopted, such as that of the "cat," which is a covered shed wherein the soldiers can work and dig under the foundations of the walls. They make a mine, and support the roof of it with wooden props, and when the mine is well under the wall, they burn the props, and the wall falls in, forming a breach through which the soldiers can fight their way. Then there were several military engines, such as the *trebuchet*, the *mangonel*, and the *catapult*, different names for the same kind of machine for casting stones; large movable shields, behind which the soldiers could shelter themselves when within range of the bowmen on the walls; and often a large movable tower was brought into use, which placed the besiegers on a level with the besieged, and from which a drawbridge was let down upon the town walls, so that the attacking force could rush across it and gain the ramparts. Then a hand-to-hand fight ensued; swords flashed, and shields rattled with blows, while from every loophole showers of arrows flew, until the fortune of war decided the issues of the fight. Such was the way in which these apparently impregnable places were captured before villainous saltpetre was invented.

In the time of Henry VII. the impostor Perkin Warbeck besieged Exeter, and there is a very spirited account of his attack upon the ancient city by an old chronicler:—" Lacking ordnance to make a battery to raze and deface the walls, he studied all the ways possible how to break and infringe the gates; and what with casting of stones, heaving with iron bars, and kindling of fire under the gates, he omitted nothing which could be devised for the furtherance of his ungracious purpose. The citizens taking to themselves lusty hearts and manly courage, determined to repulse fire by fire, and caused faggots to be brought to the inward part of the posts and posterns, and set them all on fire, to the intent that the fire being inflamed on both sides of the gates, might as well exclude their enemies from entering, as include the citizens from running or flying out; and that they in the mean season might make trenches and rampires to defend their enemies instead of gates and bulwarks. And when Perkin assaulted the town in divers weak places, and set up ladders to climb over the walls, the citizens like valiant champions, defended them, and slew two hundred of his seditious soldiers." Thus Exeter was defended, and Perkin was forced to retire. The King entered the city in triumph, and praised the worthy citizens for their gallant defence. Queen Elizabeth gave the city its motto—*Semper Fidelis* (always faithful)—on account of the bravery of the burghers in resisting the insurrection of 1549, called "the Devonshire commotion," which was created by those who objected to the changes in religious worship produced by the Reformation. One more siege did the "faithful" city endure during the Great Rebellion, when it did not sustain fully its loyal character, and then its military annals were ended. The siege of Gloucester during the Rebellion is remarkable; for the stubborn resistance of the citizens seems to have turned the fate of the war, and proved a severe blow to the Royalists. The women and maids of the city wrought with the men in repairing the walls, and for three long months the siege continued, until the London train-bands, composed of the burghers of that city (still existing as the London Militia), marched to their relief.

Another memorable siege of the same period was that of Colchester, which, from the time when brave Boadicea took the town, has frequently been an object of attack. At the commencement of the war Colchester had espoused the cause of the Parliament against the King, but the inhabitants afterwards repented of their disloyalty, made a treaty with the Royalists, and received them into the town. The Great Parliamentarian, General Fairfax, besieged it, and a close blockade for eleven weeks ensued, during which the people bravely endured great want and suffering. But when the Scottish army had been defeated, and the royal cause seemed hopelessly lost, the townspeople yielded, and the memory of Fairfax is stained by his cruelty to two of the officers, Sir Charles Lucas and Sir George Lisle, who were shot under the walls of the castle. The former tore open his doublet, and exclaimed to the soldiers, "Fire, rebels!" and instantly fell. Lisle ran to him, kissed his dead body, and told the soldiers to come nearer.

One replied, "Fear not, sir; we shall hit you."

"My friends," he answered, "I have been nearer when you have missed me."

But the rebel bullets did not miss their mark, and the gallant Lisle was slain. Happily for England, wars have not been so incessant as on the Continent, and our towns have known little of the horrors of a protracted siege, when the stores began to run short, and all the cattle were killed, and when plague followed in the footsteps of famine, and daily diminished the strength of the defenders. Death by starvation, or pestilence, or at the hands of the victorious pillagers, was in most cases inevitable; and the canvas of a well-known painter (M. de Vertz) depicts a scene which has occasionally occurred, when madness has destroyed all maternal instinct and affection, and mothers have killed their own children in order to appease the pangs of hunger. Happily such horrors have never been enacted on English land.

CHAPTER XV

UNIVERSITY TOWNS

Oxford v. Cambridge—Mythical founders—The History of Oxford—Massacre of the Danes—Saxon palace—Norman castle—The flight of the Empress Maud—Old college life—First colleges at Oxford and Cambridge—The battles of scholars—Effect of the dissolution of monasteries—Begging scholars—Destruction of college libraries—Oxford in the Civil War—The homes of learning.

WITHOUT exception, the most interesting towns in England are those which are the homes of our ancient Universities, the centres of "light and leading," Oxford and Cambridge. Here have lived many of England's most illustrious sons; here they have laid the foundation of their greatness and acquired that learning, knowledge, and culture which have raised them above their fellows, and the shades of the great scholars which seem to haunt the old college buildings put to shame all modern pretensions. The recollection, too, of the part which our Universities have played in the nation's history, the architectural beauty and venerable appearance of the old colleges, the old associations which cling to those time-worn walls, all increase our veneration for these ancient abodes of learning, and make us love them exceedingly.

There has always been a certain rivalry between the two Universities as to which can claim the greater antiquity. When Queen Elizabeth visited Cambridge, she was greeted by the public orator with a Latin speech, in which the superior dignity and antiquity of that University were set forth, and the statement made that Oxford and Paris owed their origin to the famous University on the banks of the Cam. When the Oxford scholars heard of this bold assertion, they naturally were greatly surprised and enraged, and a learned controversy ensued, the champions of each University vying with each other in their endeavours to maintain the greater antiquity and dignity for their respective scholastic abodes. I am not sure that their imaginations did not fly back as far as the Trojan war and Noah's flood.

The mythical history of Oxford, which was first propounded by a certain John Rous, states that it was founded by a king named Mempric, who lived when Samuel was judge in Israel, B.C. 1009, and was torn to death by a pack of wolves.

He established a colony of philosophers learned in Greek at Greeklade, or Cricklade, which was soon removed to the banks of the Isis. Such is the legend, which is quite as true as that of Cantaber, the Spanish prince, who was driven from his country and hospitably received by King Gurguntius, married the Princess Guenolena, imported a company of Greek scholars from Athens, and founded Cambridge. Disregarding all other myths, and even venturing to assert that the legend of Alfred being the founder of University College at Oxford is as mythological as Mempric or Gurguntius, we may say that the University at Oxford first attained fame at the close of the twelfth century.

Paris and Bologna were the mothers of Universities, after the models of which all others seem to have been founded. The University of Paris enjoyed a world-wide prestige; the fame of its schools extended far and wide; it was the centre of intellectual life, its teachers wandered into other lands, and Oxford probably owes its origin to a migration of students from that seat of learning in the year 1167. John of Salisbury says that in that year France expelled her alien scholars, and although it is not known whither they fled, the sudden large increase in the number of students at Oxford, and the importance which the schools then attained, make it probable that a large portion of these alien students from Paris came to Oxford and laid the foundation of her greatness. Before the year 1167 there were schools and scholars at Oxford, and some famous teachers, such as Theobaldus Stampensis, Robert Pullein, and possibly Vacarius, but it was not until the close of the twelfth century that the University commenced its real existence. Cambridge never attained to high rank in mediæval times, and owes its origin to a migration from Oxford in 1209. Its glories begin with the days of the New Learning, when Fisher, Erasmus, and Ascham were its *socii*, and made Cambridge a formidable rival to the older University.

But both places have a history before any of the colleges began to spring up, and that of Oxford is the more remarkable. Every one is familiar with the great mound which the visitor passes on the road from the railway station. This great earthwork was constructed in 912 A.D. to prevent the inroads of the Danes, who sailed up the Thames, burnt the towns, and ravaged the country. Ninety years later, when the Danes and Saxons were living side by side, Ethelred the

Unready, the Saxon king, ordered that all the Danes in England should be massacred. This shameful edict was eagerly obeyed by the Saxons in Oxford; their Danish neighbours fled for refuge into the church of the monastery of St. Frideswide, and claimed the right of sanctuary, which forbade any one to slay a man who sought shelter in a sacred building. But in vain their flight. The Saxons set fire to the church, and the Danes in Oxford were killed. In revenge for this cruel deed, a body of Danes sacked and burned the town seven years later. But it was at Oxford that peace was established between the two peoples; for at a Gemot, or council, summoned by Canute 1018 A.D., it was resolved by the unanimous vote of both parties that the old laws of the country should be retained, and " Edgar's law " should be binding on English and Danes alike. In the old royal residence of the Saxon kings, which stood upon the site of the present jail, and which witnessed the murder of King Edmund, the treacherous slaughter of Sigefrith and Mortcar, after a great banquet in the hall—in that same palace was this peace restored to the rival factions. Above the mound arose the Norman castle built by William, to keep in check his new subjects; moreover he could command the services of twenty burgesses whenever he went on an expedition. The Domesday Survey shows that it was then a place of importance, as it contained seven hundred houses, but war had dealt so hardly with them that four hundred and seventy-eight were in ruins and could pay no dues. Here the Empress Maud, driven from London, found a refuge; here she was besieged for many a long day; till, dressed in white, with three faithful knights, she fled in the depth of winter across the frost-bound river by night to Wallingford Castle, and escaped her foes.

Before colleges were founded at either University, the students lived at their own expense in halls, inns, or hostels, which were presided over by a Principal; but by degrees, by the benefactions of pious founders, colleges were built and endowed, and the old hostels gradually disappeared. The colleges were originally homes for graduates, where they lived a life in common, studied and prayed, and found within the college walls havens of rest for peaceful studies. By degrees undergraduates were admitted, and thus a great improvement was effected in University discipline. Peterhouse was the first college in Cambridge, founded by Hugh de Balsam, subprior of Ely, in 1284; and University College at Oxford claims for its founder King Alfred, but it has no documents to prove that it is older than Merton, which was founded in 1264 by Walter de Merton, Chancellor of England and Bishop of Rochester. At both Universities the students in olden times ever loved a riot, and quarrels frequently arose between the townsfolk and the gownsmen. At Oxford, in 1354, several combatants on both sides were killed, and the townsmen were compelled to pay a yearly fine to the University for their offence. Frequently the scholars fought among themselves, English against Scotchmen, Irish against Welsh. On one occasion they helped a mob to pillage the monastery at Abingdon, and feared not the wrath of the Pope's legate, whose brother was slain. The townsfolk of Cambridge, jealous of the privileges conferred on the University, in 1381 mustered their men and made a great riot, broke open college gates, burned charters in the market-place, but were reduced to submission by Spencer, the warlike Bishop of Norwich. University life had its excitements in the fourteenth century!

In the time of Edward III. Oxford was the most famous seat of learning in Europe, and is said to have possessed 300 halls and 30,000 students, many of whom were foreigners. Wandering scholars, knight-errants of learning, who after the fashion of those times went about from university to university, came hither from beyond seas. The universal use of Latin in all centres of learning enabled these roving scholars to enjoy the privileges of any university whither they chose to go, and the fame of Oxford attracted very many. The number of the students probably did not, however, exceed three or four thousand. In spite of the disturbances wrought by Wiclif's teaching and by the Wars of the Roses, it continued to flourish until the dissolution of monasteries, which was very injurious to both Universities. Poor scholars were sent by the monasteries to Oxford and Cambridge, and their expenses provided for by them; but when the religious houses ceased to exist, there was no one to pay these college bills, the halls and hostels became almost empty, poor scholars and monks went a-begging with wallets on their shoulders, and the cause of learning seemed ruined.

The men of modern Oxford will find some difficulty in realising that their predecessors were such importunate beggars that they were classed with fortune-tellers and various other suspicious characters; and unless they could prove by documentary evidence that they were licensed to beg by the authorities of the University, they were liable to be tied to the tail of a cart and beaten with whips in the market-place until their backs were bloody by reason of such whipping. Here are the words of the Act: "Scholars of the Universities of Oxford and Cambridge that go about begging, not being authorised under the seal of the said Universities by the commissary, chancellor, or vice-chancellor of the same, as well as fortune-tellers and various other suspicious characters, shall, on conviction before two justices of the peace, be punished by whipping after the manner before rehearsed."

But then as now all classes were represented at the University. Besides the importunate beggar class, who were licensed to beg, and lived on bread and porridge, there was the middle-class "clerk of Oxenford" described by Chaucer:—

> "As leanë was his horse as is a rake,
> And he was not right fat, I undertake;
> But looked hollow and thereto soberly.
> Full threadbare was his overest courtessy,
> For he had gotten him yet no benefice,
> He was not worldly to have an office.
> For him was lever have at his bed's head
> Twenty bookës, clothed in black or red,
> Of Aristotle and his philosophy,
> Than robës rich, or fiddle, or psalt'ry."

And there were also men of good family, who lived at their own hostels and had many servants withal. The life of the students in mediæval times would certainly seem curious to the men of modern Oxford. The Latin tongue was heard everywhere in hall and lecture-room, and a *lupus* was often employed to spy upon undergraduates and discover the culprits who dared to converse in the vulgar tongue. Lectures began at 6 A.M., and often lasted three hours. The students dined at 10 A.M., and supped at five o'clock. Four or five men shared a bed-room in which there was no fire, and two usually occupied one bed. Such "insolent pursuits" as bat and ball were things forbidden, as also dancing in chapel or playing dice on the Cathedral altar, or marbles on the steps of St. Mary's Church. In the long evenings the student was admonished to read poems sitting at the fire in the hall, and was not allowed to go out of college, unless accompanied by a Master of Arts. Moreover, if he broke the rules of the college he was birched in the hall with a birch composed of nine rods, one for each of the muses.

The hardships of a college student were as luxuries compared with the conditions of his unattached neighbour in the hostels or lodgings.

The latter certainly enjoyed greater freedom, or which he made frequent use. He dearly loved a riot; to bait a Jew, to stir up a brawl with the townsmen, to fight his rival "nation," whether Scotch or Irish, to quarrel with monks or insult the proctors, to poach deer or rob a packman's wallet, these were the amusements which added zest to his life, and consoled him for hard fare and many discomforts. The street-life of Oxford in mediæval times was certainly extraordinary, and yet amidst all this confusion and riot, how many attained to learning and led pious and devout lives, in spite of all discouragements! What burning questions and controversies raged and disturbed the minds of the learned, when Wiclif propounded his doctrines, when the New Learning asserted its sway and Scholasticism died, or when King and Pope were at deadly enmity, and the stormy period of the Reformation dawned on England!

Terrible destruction was wrought also in the college libraries, the chief glory of the Universities. Commissioners were appointed to examine and burn all superstitious and Romish books and manuscripts. Ruthlessly did these ignorant and intolerant men carry on biers to the market-place and burn cartloads of valuable MSS., which contained nothing more iniquitous than red-lettered titles or mathematical signs and figures.

Mary's reign witnessed a still more disgraceful burning, when the great leaders of the Protestant party, Cranmer, Ridley, and Latimer, suffered martyrdom near St. Mary Magdalen's Church, where the Martyrs' Memorial now stands. But strange times dawned upon Oxford when the civil war broke out, and Charles I. held his court in the faithful city, making it the headquarters of his army. College caps were thrown away, and students and doctors donned helmets; the halls were turned into barracks; the college authorities, true to their King, melted down their stores of silver plate to supply him with money. All studies were abandoned; in Merton College the Queen held her court; in St. John's Hall plays were acted for the amusement of the royal guests; Rupert's trumpet-call sounded in the gardens of New College; gay cavaliers thronged the streets, and the quiet existence of the University was strangely disturbed. When the Puritans gained the day, little mercy was shown to the loyalists, who were ejected from their colleges, and the destruction which had been commenced by the commissioners was carried on with renewed vigour. Beautiful windows, stone figures, pictures, altars, and crosses, were all sacrificed as monuments of superstition, and scarcely a building in Oxford does not bear traces of this heedless and miserable fanaticism.

The history of these University towns is, indeed, the history of learning in England. To trace this history, to describe its colleges, to tell of the great men who lived and taught and worked within their walls, to summon again the shades of Erasmus or Milton at Cambridge, of Raleigh, Butler, Ben Jonson, Johnson, and a host of others, at Oxford—all this is beyond our purpose. We have sketched rapidly the most important eras in the history of our ancient Universities, which have been the centres of learning in England for nigh seven hundred years, which have produced most of the greatest scholars, divines, poets, and leaders of men in every rank and profession; and it is satisfactory to know that they have never played a more vigorous part in the life of the nation than at the present time. Carlyle asserted that the university of the future would be the library of books, where the scholar would roam and read at will; but his prophecy is in no danger of being fulfilled. Oxford and Cambridge, and the younger Universities, which cannot boast of so high a lineage, have never attracted to themselves more students, and their influence makes itself felt in all departments of education. They have adapted themselves to the needs of modern times, and, in spite of their antiquity, have still a great future before them.

CHAPTER XVI

CINQUE PORTS AND HARBOURS

Special privileges of the Cinque Ports—The fickleness of the sea—The navy in olden times—Old Sandwich—The troubles of Hythe—Rye and Winchelsea—The Armada—Drake and the "Golden Hind"—Feuds and piracies—Smuggling days.

WE will now journey to the sea, over whose waves Britannia is said to rule, and visit some of those old ports and harbours whence her navies sailed to discover new worlds, and lay the foundation of England's colonial greatness. The most important of these were the old Cinque Ports upon the coast of Sussex and Kent, to which William the Conqueror granted important privileges and rights, freedom from tolls and customs, the right of fishing along the coast of Norfolk, on condition that they supplied the King with fifty-seven ships, containing twenty-one men and a boy in each ship, for fifteen days, whenever he should require their service. The

Cinque Ports were Sandwich, Romney, Hastings, Hythe, and Dover, with which twelve neighbouring ports were incorporated. They were governed by a Warden, an office which still remains, although the glory of the Cinque Ports has passed away, and banks of sand fill the harbours wherein the pride of England's navy used to congregate. The old Hythe is now one mile inland; Romney is a mile from the sea, without a single creek to connect her with it; old Winchelsea lies beneath the waves, which have engulfed her; Rye and Sandwich can only receive small ships, and Hastings has no harbour. Such disastrous changes has time wrought on these once flourishing towns; the sea, wearied of their supremacy, has cast them off, and conferred her favours elsewhere.

Before the reign of Henry VII. the King had no royal navy, and in time of war relied upon the ships which were furnished by the Cinque Ports, and, in case of need, could order merchants in other towns on the sea-coast to supply vessels for his use; but it was not until the reign of Charles II. that the last service was required of them. The present state of Sandwich, with its ruined gate-house, its sand-bound haven, its dilapidated houses and disfigured churches, contrasts strangely with that prosperous town in whose harbour the Cinque Ports' navy used to assemble, and from which the armies of England passed on their way to fight the French, or the Saracens in the Holy Land, and where the Black Prince landed with his royal captives, and doubtless returned thanks for his victories in the church of St. Clement. Decayed towns have always a mournful aspect, and inspire melancholy thoughts. When walking through the moss-grown streets and deserted market-places, it is sad to reflect upon the glories of the past and recall the gorgeous spectacles of pomp and magnificence which once took place there. We see again the streets thronged with knights, bearing the red cross on their arms; we hear the cheers of the spectators as they marched along; and when our lion-hearted King Richard returned from the Crusades, after being imprisoned so long on his way, we see him landing here at Sandwich, and hear the enthusiastic shouts of his subjects as they welcomed him again. But departed is all its glory now, and the streets are as silent as those of the inland decayed towns through which, in old coaching days, kings and queens, statesmen and nobles, passed, or stayed the night,

CINQUE PORTS AND HARBOURS

and which the railways left high and dry, and their inns deserted.

The history of the decline and fall of most of these south-country ports is very similar—the fickleness of the sea and the plunder of foes. Old Hythe suffered from a variety of misfortunes: its fleet of five vessels was destroyed at sea with all the sailors; two hundred of its houses were burnt; a plague carried off nearly all its inhabitants, and the sea receded in the reign of Henry IV. But as the old or West Hythe decayed, the new Hythe sprang up nearer the sea, became a Cinque Port, and contained a fair abbey and four parish churches. The churches were destroyed even in Leland's time, and long ago it ceased to be a port.

Rye, although it has not fared quite so badly as its fellows, was in the fourteenth century repeatedly taken by the French, and its Mayors were indeed between the devil and the deep sea, for their gentle sovereign caused them to be hanged and quartered for not making a better defence. Most of these ports have suffered from having too little sea, but old Winchelsea had too much, and was entirely submerged in 1287. Henry III. planted the new town on higher ground; he built strong walls and noble gatehouses, laid out

s

the streets, and erected a magnificent church. But, although it was fairly prosperous, and Elizabeth deigned to call it "Little London," it never realised the expectations of its founder. The sea deserted it, and it is now a small village, with a few hundred inhabitants.

Dover, from its nearness to the French coast, still maintains its importance as a great military station, and its fortifications are as strong as the modern arts of war can make them. It was an important place in the days of the Conqueror. Domesday states that it supplied the King with twenty ships for fifteen days in the year, and each ship was manned by twenty-one sailors.

Many are the services which these old towns have rendered to the country, and very dignified were the freemen of the Cinque Ports, who were called barons, ranked with peers, and bore canopies over the King at his coronation.

Animated was the scene at all these ports on the south coast, from Plymouth to Dover, when the news came that the Spaniards intended to pay us a visit, and to reduce our country to a Spanish dependency. The English fleet was assembled at Plymouth when—

"About the lovely close of a warm summer day,
 There came a gallant merchant-ship full sail to Plymouth Bay."

Her crew had seen the proud fleet of the Spaniards sailing toward our shores, but our great Admiral, Sir Francis Drake, calmly finished his game of bowls before he proceeded to beat the Spaniards.

Every one knows the story of the Armada; how the small, well-handled English barks hung on the course of the stately galleys of the foe, fired their broadsides into the great ships and were off again before their formidable-looking enemies could reply. Our sailors then showed that contempt of danger and that "pluck" which has long characterised the mariners of England. Every one knows of the fire-ships at Calais, the storm, the ignominious retreat of the Spaniards round the coast of Scotland, and the return of a few shattered barks to Spain. All this is a thrice-told tale. The skill which our sailors displayed had been acquired by many a bold voyage in unknown seas, by many wild expeditions in search of plunder, when "to singe the beard of the King of Spain," to ransack his towns, and burn his galleys laden with gold and treasure, was considered perfectly legitimate and right. Who has not heard of the fame of Drake, who, with five ships and one hundred and sixty men, crossed the Atlantic to the shores of Brazil, fought and plundered, as was his wont, and then, when all the Spanish fleet were watching for his return, he boldly crossed the Pacific Ocean, and, after dangers and adventures innumerable, he doubled the Cape of Good Hope, and, after three years' absence, reached the shores of England, the first man who had sailed round the world? Only one ship survived the adventurous voyage, called the *Golden Hind*, and it was well worthy of its name, for it brought back treasure to the amount of £800,000. At Deptford his famous ship was moored after its adventures, the object of the admiration of the crowds of visitors who flocked to hear the stories of the strange lands and the rich prizes which were in store for brave England's sons. To the same school of intrepid mariners belonged Sir John Hawkins, Sir Walter Raleigh, Frobisher, Cavendish, and many others who made the name of England feared in every sea; and there were scores of other men who, animated by the same love of adventure, fitted out ships and completed the discoveries which these heroes of the sea had begun. They laid the foundations of that commerce which has made our country so great and prosperous.

In the thirteenth and fourteenth centuries there were many feuds existing between the Cinque

Ports and other ports along the coast. The men of Southampton, Weymouth, Poole, Lyme, and other towns often quarrelled with the men of the Cinque Ports; hence arose a great deal of depredation, ship-burning, bloodshed, and the like, and Edward II. tried to put an end to these disorders by issuing a proclamation. Sometimes, too, piracy was openly carried on; the ships of other countries were regarded as legitimate prey, in spite of treaties and laws to the contrary. An outlawed nobleman in 1242 established himself on Lundy Island, and plundered all the merchant-vessels he could capture. The mariners of St. Malo, in Brittany, a bold and fearless race, carried on the same trade, and frequently attacked our coasts and plundered the towns. The rich merchants of London and Bristol sometimes fitted out expeditions to punish these marauders, and performed the duty of protecting the traffic on the seas, for in those days there was no royal navy.

Very exciting scenes used to be seen in these old coast towns in the old smuggling days. The Isle of Wight and the coast near Lydd were favourite landing-places for contraband goods, and sometimes as many as two hundred men would be engaged in landing the spirits. Every one in the place was more or less connected with the traffic, and countless were the means adopted for disposing of the barrels. Smugglers' caves abound, and the old houses at Douglas, in the Isle of Man, were honeycombed with cellars, so that when a cargo of barrels was landed, and the barrels rolled up the streets, they would disappear as in a moment down these endless cellars. When the Government took severer measures to repress the traffic, the men of Lydd had a band of men armed with heavy clubs called "bats," and woe to the Custom-House officers who came in contact with these formidable batsmen! Desperate fights occurred, and many lives were lost; but happily smuggling and piracy are things of the past.

CHAPTER XVII
PALATINATE TOWNS AND CATHEDRAL CITIES

Mighty Durham—Its days of splendour—Lancaster and its Duke—Old county towns—Ely and its Palatinate—Chester and its memories—Cathedral towns and their associations — Wells and Salisbury — Her bishop and canons.

ANOTHER class of towns possess features of peculiar interest, and had special rights and privileges bestowed upon them, viz., the chief towns of Counties Palatine. Such were Durham, Chester, Lancaster, and Ely. The word Palatine is connected with Palace, and a County Palatine is one possessing royal privileges. The powerful Palatinate of Durham existed from time immemorial until the year 1836, and was presided over by the Bishop of Durham. It comprised within the limits of its jurisdiction the whole county of Durham, and its possession made the Bishop, next to the King, the most powerful prince in England. He had his courts of

Chancery, Common Pleas, and Exchequer. He had the power to levy taxes for the defence and service of his Palatinate; to make truce with his enemies; to raise troops and impress ships in time of war. He sat in judgment of life and death, and could inflict capital punishment. He could create barons of his Palatinate, and summon them to his councils, and he could confiscate their lands for treason against himself. He possessed all manner of royal jurisdictions and rights; could coin money, grant licences to establish castles, churches, hospitals, or other charities; could create corporations and grant markets or fairs. In short, every source of profit and every post of honour or service was at his disposal. The sovereign could not interfere with him, nor could the sovereign's officers enter the Palatinate without his sanction. It was no wonder, then, that when an arbitrary bishop had to deal with an arbitrary king, quarrels frequently ensued, and the Pope was often appealed to to settle differences.

Truly a mighty city was old Durham, ruled over by mighty prelates who within the limits of the Palatinate owned no earthly superior; and splendid were the entertainments which were given by these magnates to their royal and noble guests. Durham was often the headquarters of English troops when expeditions were in progress against the patriotic Scotch, and the place where negotiations were concluded, or heads struck off from rebel shoulders. After the rebellion under the Nevilles, in the reign of Queen Elizabeth, sixty-six unfortunate people were executed in the city. Edward III. often stayed here and was splendidly entertained by the Bishop, named Bury. In 1424, on the liberation and marriage of James I. of Scotland, the place was crowded with nobility, who, after their wonted manner, amused themselves with splendid tournaments, and the city was very gay with the sights of mediæval pageantry and chivalry. Charles I. also, and his retinue, before his days of sorrow came, were royally entertained by Bishop Morton for three days, at the daily expense of £1500. Such were some of the scenes, varied by dreadful plagues and Scotch invasions, which this old city witnessed. It owes its origin to the monks of Lindisfarne, who, driven by ruthless Danes from their quiet rest in Holy Island, chose this spot for the resting-place of St. Cuthbert's bones, after their many wanderings. The castle of Durham, built by the Conqueror, according to his usual custom, to overawe the English, was the residence of the powerful Prince-Bishops of Durham, and is now used as the University buildings. Bishop Van Mildert, the last of the Palatine Bishops, was the founder of the University. The sovereignty of the Bishops of Durham was curtailed by Henry VIII., but it was not until 1836 that palatine jurisdiction was transferred to the Crown.

The same sovereign power was held by the House of Lancaster. In reward for his signal services in the French wars, when the Duke of Lancaster carried all before him and conquered no less than fifty-six towns, Edward III. delighted to heap honours upon him, and raised the county of Lancaster to the rank of a Palatinate. He was called the "good Duke of Lancaster"; he lived in princely style, and when he married, as his second wife, Constance, the daughter of the King of Castile, and returned to Lancaster with his wife's dowry in 1389, he had forty-seven mules laden with chests of gold. When the King's son, John of Gaunt, married Blanche, the daughter of this duke, the wealthiest heiress in England, a very brilliant period dawned upon the famous town upon the Lune, where John held his ducal court. But sad times were in store for the old town, when in 1322 and 1389 the Scots came and burnt and plundered it; and true till death to the fortunes of the illustrious House of Lancaster during the Wars of the Roses, it suffered so severely that hardly a man was left in the old town. Again, Cromwell's cannon battered down the walls, and his Roundheads committed much mischief and wanton destruction. Fire, too, at the end of the seventeenth century wrought havoc amongst the old houses; and, ever true to the fortunes of the rulers they loved, the inhabitants clung to the fallen House of Stuart, and many of them fought in the Jacobite rising of 1745.

In many of these old county towns like Lancaster there are numerous noble mansions, once the town residences of noblemen and county gentry. To country manor-houses there were often attached town residences, whither the owner used to go to transact business connected with the management of his estates, for county meetings, and the like. Now people go to London for the "season," but a century or two ago each county town used to have "its season," whither the great folk flocked, and the place was alive with its *fêtes*, and balls, and concerts. But railroads have changed all this. Now every one flocks to London, and the old town-houses of noblemen have lost their grandeur, and are inhabited by doctors and tradespeople, and others whose occupations compel them to be stationary. All this has led to the decay of the prosperity of our county towns.

The little city of Ely, with only a few thousand inhabitants, was once the centre of a County Palatine, and its Bishop possessed sovereign rights like the Lord Bishop of Durham or the Duke of Lancaster. The monastery founded amid the fens by Ethelreda, enlarged by Ethelwold of Winchester, and favoured by Canute and Edward the Confessor, was the centre of the stirring scenes in the life of Hereward, where the gallant English made their last stand against the hated Norman, and the pride of Norman chivalry was engulfed in black mud of the Fens. But the monks "did after their kind," as Kingsley writes, and yielded themselves to William, who appointed a French-speaking Norman abbot to rule over them and bring them into subjection. The bishopric was founded in 1107, and the first bishop, Hervey, driven from the see of Bangor by the Welsh, who did not love these Norman prelates, was invested by Henry I. with sovereign rights over the Isle of Ely, and these palatinate rights continued until Henry VIII. took the power into his own hands.

Than Chester, the only English town which retains its walls in a complete state, whose palatinate rights were granted by the Conqueror to his nephew Hugh, Earl of Chester, few cities are more interesting. The Briton, Roman, Saxon, Dane, and Norman successively held it, and the place is full of memories of past heroes. Leaving aside the mythical Leon Gaur, who made caves and dungeons for unhappy wanderers, or the equally legendary King Lear, who—

"A Briton stout and valiant,
Was founder of the city by pleasant dwellings,"

we recall the might of Saxon Edgar, who made eight kings do homage, and, "forcing them on board a vessel, he compelled them to row him as he sat at the prow: thus displaying his regal magnificence who held so many kings in subjection." The wild tribes of Welsh, in the early Norman times, often made inroads and incursions upon Chester, and so often fired the suburbs of Hanbrid beyond the bridge that they call it Treboeth, or Burnt Town. A long wall of Welshmen's skulls is said by Camden to have been erected. From the Phœnix Tower, on the city wall, Charles I. watched the battle of Rowton Heath. Chester is remarkable for its fine, old-fashioned, quaint, half-timber houses, enriched with carving. One of the most interesting has, I fear, disappeared; it was called "God's Providence House," because, when a terrible plague raged in the city, the inhabitants of this house were spared the dread infection. Of Chester "Rows" we have already spoken, and gay the city must have been in the old days of pageants and spectacles, which the Chester folk dearly loved, when old and young crowded the "Rows" to witness the pageant pass along, "according to ancient custom," with "the four giants, and the unicorn, and the dromedary; the luce, the camel, the ass, snap-the-dragon, the four hobby-horses, and sixteen cupids."

The merry diversions which took place on the Roodeye, the football match, which was attended by the Mayor in state, the archery and athletic contests, and races, which were substituted for the old game on account of its roughness and violence—all these have had their chroniclers, and formed interesting features in the life of this ancient city. In bidding farewell to Chester, we will conclude with the words of honest old Fuller, who, in speaking of the city and its

"Rows,"[1] observes : "It is worth their pains who have money and leisure to make their own eyes the expounders of it, the like being said not to be seen in all England: no, nor in all Europe again."

Nowhere is the old-world life of England more clearly reflected than in these ancient cathedral cities. In the dim, mysterious aisles of the grand church, beneath the shades of the quiet cloister, we love to linger, to read the story which the old walls tell us, to mark the varied styles and periods of their architecture, and to associate with them the names of the Church's heroes of bygone times who loved to dedicate their riches, their labour, and their life to the service of the sanctuary. The quietude of a cathedral close, the unchanged aspect of the tranquil scene, the silence of the streets, the old houses of the canons, all these have a charm that is all their own. An American writer thus expresses his reflections when first he experienced the fascination of which we speak :—

"Wells is lovely in itself, and it stands on a broad expanse of lawn surrounded by old ecclesiastical buildings which escaped the destroyer, and

[1] These "Rows" were probably built for purposes of defence against the wild Welsh who frequently attacked the city.

present a picture of old cathedral life. Wells and Salisbury are perhaps the two best specimens of the cathedral close, that haven of religious calm amidst this bustling world, in which a man tired of business and contentious life might delight, especially if he has a taste for books, to find tranquillity, with quiet companionship, in his old age. Take your stand on the Close of Salisbury or Wells on a summer afternoon when the congregation is filing leisurely out from the service and the sounds are still heard from the cathedral, and you will experience a sensation not to be experienced in the New World."

In these centres of religious life for many hundreds of years has been maintained age after age a perpetual round of services, as models for the worship of the diocese. The cathedral ever was the seat of the bishop, from which he sent forth his clergy to minister to the scattered congregations in his diocese, and where he educated young men for the ministry in his theological school. The canons were the bishop's agents, his companions and advisers, whose duty it was to meet in the chapter-house and consult with the bishop with regard to important affairs concerning the welfare of the diocese, to provide for the continual round of services in the cathedral, and to go forth as missionaries to the different parishes in the diocese, teaching everywhere the principles of the faith. Besides the canons there were other ecclesiastical officers, such as the dean, the precentor, and the chancellor.. The canons were what were called "secular canons"; *i.e.*, they were not monks, but lived in their own houses, and were not bound by the usual monastic vows. Such was the community which presided over the affairs of an ancient cathedral.

The history of the cathedrals of England is, indeed, the history of the Church, oftentimes persecuted and oppressed by rapacious kings and godless Ministers of State, robbed of their wealth, and defaced by sacrilegious hands, sometimes neglected in sad times of spiritual lethargy and irreligion, but always preserved by the good providence of God, to whose service they are devoted.

CHAPTER XVIII

MODERN CHANGES AND SURVIVALS

Contrasts — Changes in the appearance of manufacturing towns — Changed industries — The old town-halls — The market-cross — Scenes in the market-place — Burning witches — Norwich riots — Birmingham riots — Nottingham and the framework knitters — The parish church — Old windows — Desecrations — Preservation of ancient features of the church — Old inns — " The Bull" Inn at Coventry — Ancient hostels — Curious signs — Conclusion.

A GREAT gulf yawns between the England of to-day and that strange, vigorous, youthful England which is so far removed from us, not so much by the lapse of years, but by the mighty changes, social and political, which time has wrought. Old beliefs, old desires, old-world notions and convictions have passed away never to return; and in their place are seen a restless, shifting mass of human thought and working, o'er which wild

" Chaos umpire sits,
And by decision more embroils the fray
By which he reigns ; next him, high arbiter,
Chance governs all."

Milton's grand description of Chaos and old Night holding eternal anarchy, amidst the noise of endless wars and by confusion standing, not unfitly depicts the modern turmoil of conflicting thought and the warring winds of agitation and unrest. We cannot cross the gulf that separates the old world and the new, and can only dimly imagine what kind of men they were who laid the foundations of our mighty empire, and ruled and worked and strove where we strive now. "Only among the aisles of the cathedrals, only as we gaze upon their silent figures sleeping on their tombs, some faint conceptions float before us of what these men were when they were alive; and perhaps in the sound of church bells, that peculiar creation of mediæval age, which falls upon the ear like the echo of a vanished world" (Froude).

Yes—rapid have been the changes in many of our old towns. We see the vast commercial towns and cities of the North, where trade and manufacture have increased so enormously, and steam has revolutionised everything. We see the countless factories, with their tall chimneys belching forth their clouds of smoke, the endless dull streets of cottages, the great coal-pits, and all the vast developments of modern skill and industry. We see the port at Liverpool crowded with the ships of all nations, when 150 years ago a few score of vessels alone belonged to that famous harbour; and even the sea has been conveyed inland and Manchester made a seaport. Small villages have rapidly grown into large and important places, and these Lancashire and Yorkshire towns are indeed the "workshops of England."

Changes, too, there have been in the industry of many of our old-fashioned towns. Many of them have lost the trades for which they were once famous; some have become decayed and ruined; the Mayor survives, also a ruined town-hall, with stocks and ducking-stool, and other relics of departed greatness; but the town perished with its industry, and nothing remains but ruin and death. Other decayed towns have wisely adopted new industries to supply the place of the old; thus Coventry has lost its silks and taken to bicycles; Reading has long ceased to produce cloth, and has adopted biscuits and seeds. There, too, bell-founders flourished, and also at Wokingham, but their works have long since disappeared. Norwich has lost its silks, once the pride of East Anglian dames; and the trade in cloth, which the monks taught the people of Bath to weave, and made it in the fourteenth century one of the chief centres of that industry, has long since vanished from the city of the hot springs.

But in spite of all the changes time has wrought, there are still some old features left of our ancient towns, and these it behoves us to cherish and protect from injury and destruction. The old town-hall, probably once the hall of the Merchant Guild, still stands in many places, an important building which has witnessed many changes in its long career. Several of these fifteenth and sixteenth century halls remain at Salisbury, Guildford, Leicester, Lincoln, and elsewhere. Sometimes they stand over one of the town gates, as at Southampton and Lincoln. The buildings usually consist of a long room for the transaction of municipal business, trying prisoners, and holding feasts. There is in many cases an open colonnade beneath the hall for the accommodation of the market-folk.

In front of the town-hall is the market-place, and in the centre stands the old market-cross, unless fanatical Puritans have pulled it down on account of the Holy Cross which adorned it. Chichester and Salisbury still retain their crosses, and a few towns still possess those erected in memory of Queen Eleanor. The beloved wife of Edward I. died at Hardby, near Lincoln. Holinshed wrote: "She was a Godlie and a modest Princesse full of pitie, and one that shewed much favour to the English nation, readie to relieve everie man's grief that sustained wrong, and to make them friends that were at discord so far as in her laie. In every town and place where the corps rested by the waie, the King caused a cross of cunning workmanship to be erected in remembrance of her, and in the same was a picture of her engraven. Two of the like crosses were set up at London, one at Charing, and the other in West Cheap." The other towns so honoured were Lincoln, Grantham, Stamford, Geddington, Stony Stratford, Woburn, Dunstable, St. Albans, Waltham, and Tottenham. There is a modern cross opposite Charing Cross Station, erected in 1863 after the ancient pattern, near the spot where the old cross once stood.

Many terrible sights have these old market-places witnessed, such as the burning of old dames who were supposed to be witches, the execution of criminals or conspirators, or the savage conflicts of townsfolk and soldiers in times of rioting and unrest. The good citizens of Norwich used to add considerably to the excitement of the place by their turbulence and eagerness for fighting. In 1272 they burned the cathedral and monastery, for which act the ringleaders were executed. Often and often did they fight; in 1549 a great riot took place, which was chiefly directed against the religious reforms and change of worship introduced by the first Prayer-Book of Edward VI. Parker, afterwards Archbishop of Canterbury, addressed the rioters from a platform, under which stood the spearmen of Kett, the leader of the riot, who amused themselves by pricking the feet of the orator with their spears as he poured forth his impassioned eloquence. Notable, too, were the Birmingham Riots of 1791, when the people rose, and burnt, plundered, and destroyed the houses of Dr. Priestley and his friends, who were supposed to be in favour of the views of the French Revolutionists. And at Nottingham, too, in 1811, the half-starved framework knitters wrought destruction, stormed factories, fought, and destroyed wholesale the machines upon which their livelihood depended. For five long years this terrible strife continued, till Nottingham was half ruined by their excesses. Indeed, in not very remote times scarcely a parliamentary election took place without a riot, and many of us can remember the old hustings days, and the free fights which followed those tumultuous meetings.

The parish church still stands, firm and sure as in the olden days, a witness of the continuity and strength of the Church of England. Sacrilegious hands have wrought havoc with the fabric in past times, pulled down altars and rood-screens, and wantonly defaced beautiful brasses and broken the magnificent windows; but, in times of disturbance, the Church's faithful sons have often rescued whatever they could from the hands of the fanatical zealots, and buried the beautiful stained glass, until the fury of the storm was past and the windows could be replaced with safety. It is said that the splendid windows in Fairford Church, Gloucestershire, were so saved from destruction during the troubled times of the great Civil War.

In spite of the rage of ignorant zealots, the lawlessness of Cromwell's soldiers, who pillaged them and broke the carvings and ornaments; in spite of the intemperate zeal of modern "restorers," our churches remain the least changed of any of our buildings. There is the old pulpit, with richly carved canopies upheld by figures of angels or holy men, and a cunningly wrought stand for the hour-glass; the monuments of illustrious men, knights in armour with their heraldic devices; the choir-stalls carved with curious grotesque figures, the hagioscope, consecration crosses, altar and font, all much the same as they were three hundred years ago. Then there are the register books, and account books, full of quaint scraps of personal and local history, the church plate, and in the belfry hangs the great "Thalebot" or the "Bretun," as at Rochester, and other noted bells bearing the names of the Church's heroes, St. Dunstan, Paulinus, and others. In the churchyard stands the old weather-beaten yew-tree, five or six hundred years old, looking like a sentinel keeping watch over the graves of our forefathers. In the last century men thought fit to cover up the beautiful old oaken roofs and make low, flat ceilings. They put up hideous galleries and "three-deckers," and high pews, and quite disfigured the old church. Happily most of these unsightly structures have been removed; and although great harm has been done to the old features of many churches by so-called "restoration," carried out by men ignorant of architecture and antiquity, the general appearance of our churches is now usually made to approximate, as nearly as possible, to its original form. Most towns which have not expanded in modern times once had many more churches than at present. Wallingford had twelve parish churches, where now there are only three. Some of the disused churches have had strange histories. At the dissolution of monasteries the monastic churches were sold to the authorities of the town or to private individuals. The old Greyfriars' Church at Reading has been used for a guildhall, a prison, and is now happily a church again.

Many of our old inns, too, remain to remind us of the old coaching days, when kings and queens, poets and generals, statesmen and highwaymen, grooms, conspirators, and coachmen, thronged their doors, rejoiced in the good fare, and slept in the comfortable beds, hung with silk and smelling of lavender. Now grass grows in the courtyard, once so busy with the tread of the hurrying feet of a strangely assorted company; and where once the merry sound of the post-horn was heard and all was life and animation, now all is silence and desolation. Great historical events have taken place in some of these noted inns, such as "The Bull" Inn at Coventry. Here Henry VII. was entertained on the night before he won the English crown at the battle of Bosworth Field. Here Mary, Queen of Scots, was detained by order of Queen Elizabeth. Here the conspirators of the Gunpowder Plot met to devise their scheme for blowing up the Houses of Parliament. And when the citizens refused to open their gates to Charles I. and his soldiers, no doubt there were great disputings among the frequenters of "The Bull" as to the possible results of their disloyal refusal.

Before the destruction of monasteries there were few inns, as the entertainment of strangers was regarded by the monks as part of their duties, and guests always found accommodation in the *hospitium*. However, in the fifteenth century inns began to spring up, the burghers being on not very good terms with the monks, and caring not to depend upon them for hospitality. Sometimes the worthy citizens used to receive travellers into their houses and accept payment for entertaining them; but there were also regular inns, which were usually distinguished by the sign of the landlord, with a bush attached to it. The proverb "Good wine needs no bush" was probably derived from this distinguishing mark of an innkeeper's trade. Many of these signs are very curious, chiefly derived from the

INDEX

Chester, plays at, 135, 192
,, Roman colony, 55
,, "Rows" at, 287
Chesterfield, Roman colony, 55
Chun Castle, Cornwall, 51
Church, ale, 236
,, influence of the, 106
,, towns, 93
Churches, numerous in early times, 105
,, plays in, 194
,, spoliation of, 234, 296
Churchyards, fairs in, 204
Cinque Ports, 270 &c.
Cirencester, Roman city, 56
Colchester, early history of, 90
,, mythical origin of, 47
,, Roman colony, 55
,, siege of, 254
Confederation of Danish towns, 89
Conquest, effect of Norman, 86, 110
Contrast between ancient and modern towns, 290
Corfe Castle, 117
Corpus Christi Day, 189
County towns, 283
Coventry, houses at, 177
,, pageants at, 188
Craft guilds, 152
Crosby Hall, London, 173

DANES at Oxford, 259
Danish towns, confederation of, 89
,, wars, effects of, 81
De la Poles at Hull, 170
Devizes, castle built at, 104
Diodorus Siculus on British towns, 51
Dover, a cinque port, 274
Dunbarton, Roman city, 55
Durham, its former greatness, 279

EARTHWORKS, British, 45
Eleanor crosses, 294
Elizabeth, Queen, in the days of, 231

Ely, County Palatine, 284
"England, Merrie," 231
English and Foreign towns compared, 36
,, towns, 31
"Evil May-day," 152
Exeter, guild at, 137
,, sieges of, 248

FAIR at Winchester, 144
Fairs, 200 &c.
Fire of London, 228
Fitz-Stephen's London, 119
Flemings, great mediæval manufacturers, 215
Foreign and English towns compared, 36
,, towns, 32
,, traders, 179 &c.
"Foreigners," 152
Freedom and progress due to towns, 41
,, of the townsman, 83, 139
Frith Guild, 138

GEOFFREY of Monmouth's "British History," 50
Ghent, 32, 215
Gloucester, mythical origin of, 49
,, siege of, 253
Green, Professor, on effects of Danish war, 82
,, ,, towns, 41
Greenstead, Essex, wooden church at, 84
Guildhalls, 146
Guilds, the, 126 &c.
,, ,, tyranny of, 148 &c.

HAUSE merchants, 180
Herefordshire Beacon, 51
Hexham, description of early church built by Wilfrid, 84
Highwaymen, 246
Hocking, 238
Houses of craftsmen, 178

INDEX

Houses of merchants, 174
  „ tradesmen, 177
Hull, foundation of, 170
  „ merchant-princes of, 173
  „ plays at, 136
Hythe, a cinque port, 273

INDUSTRIES, changes in, 292
Inns, old, 298
Inverness, Roman city, 55
Itinerary of Antoninus and of Richard of Cirencester, 53

JACK of Newbury, 240
Jews in London, 224

KENILWORTH Castle, pageant at, 189

LANCASTER, a County Palatine, 282
  „ its troubles from fire and sword, 283
Leicester, mythical origin of, 48
Libraries, destruction of, 266
Lickpenny in London, 195
Lincoln, decay of, 71
  „ its early history, 88 &c.
  „ Roman colony, 55
Lombard merchants, 179
London, Crosby Hall, 173
  „ described by Fitz-Stephen, 119
  „ description of Roman, 71
  „ Guildhall, 146
  „ guilds at, 136, 159
  „ Great metropolis, 218 &c.
  „ Lickpenny, 195
  „ Livery Companies, 183 &c.
  „ mythical origin of, 46
  „ palaces of old, 223
  „ Roman colony, 55
  „ walls of, 220
Lud, mythical founder of London, 46

MARINERS of England, 275
Markets, 207
Market-places, 293
May-day in the days of Queen Elizabeth, 241
Mediæval towns, 169
Mercers' Company of London, 184
Merchant guilds, 140, 158
  „ „ aristocracy of, 153
Merchants of England, 111
Mitford, Miss, and "Belford Regis," 37 &c.
Miracle plays, 135
Modern changes and survivals, 290
  „ disfigurements of towns, 40
Monastic towns, 93 &c.
Monks, disappearance of, 232
  „ orders, 174
  „ orders of, 94
Municipal history, attention to, 40
Mythical origin of towns, 44 &c.

NEWCASTLE, guild at, 165, 167
Norman castles, 112
Norman conquest, effects of, 86, 91, 110
Norwich, Flemish weavers at, 216
  „ mythical origin of, 47
  „ pageant at, 243
  „ riot at, 294
Northern England, its glories, 87
Nottingham, 117
  „ riot at, 295

ORIGIN of towns, 34
Origins, mythical, of towns, 44 &c.
Oxford, early history of, 259
  „ foundation of, 258
  „ mythical history of, 257
  „ scenes at, 261
  „ v. Cambridge, 257

PAGEANTS, 184, 242
Palatinate towns, 279 &c.

U

Palgrave, Sir Francis, on Roman towns, 53
Paris, University of, 258
Parliament, representation in, 214
Perth, Roman city, 55
Peterborough, 93
"Piers Ploughman," description of monastery, 97
Pit-dwellings, 45, 51
Plague in London, 226
Plays, in churches, 194
,, miracle, 192
,, performed by guilds, 135
Poor Law established, 245
Poor parson of a town, Chaucer's description of a, 107
Preston, guild at, 160
Prosperity, growth of, 215
Punishments, ancient, 194, 244

QUEEN Bess, in the days of, 231
Quintain, 123

READING ("Belford Regis"), Miss Mitford's account of, 37 &c.
Reading, abbey at, 96
,, barbers at, 151
,, guildhall at, 146
,, plays at, 193
,, scene in abbey of, 233
Reeve, ancestor of mayor, 143
,, king's and lord's, origin of, 82
,, port, of London, 142
"Restoration" of churches, 297
Rhine, 33
Richborough, 55
Riots at Oxford and Cambridge, 262
Ripon, wakeman of, 143
"Roland," bell at Ghent, 32
Roman houses, 62 &c.
,, towns, 52, 53, 57 &c.
Rye, a cinque port, 273

SANDWICH, a cinque port, 271
Saxon burghs, 78

Saxon gleemen, 80
,, houses, 78
,, origin of "Town," 73
,, ravages, 74
,, settlements, 75
,, towns, 73 &c.
Selby, hermitage at, 104
Shaftesbury, mythical origin of, 48
Sieges of great towns, 247
Signs of inns, 299
Silchester, amphitheatre, 68
,, baths at 67
,, church at, 66
,, decay of, 69
,, description of the city, 58 &c.
,, forum at, 65
,, results of recent excavations at, 57
Smoke farthings, 236
Smuggling days, 277
Social guilds, 158
Southampton, 150
Sports dear to English race, 198
,, of London citizens, 121 &c.
Stourbridge Fair, 204
Stow on water quintain, 123
Strabo on British towns, 51
Street scenes, 182 &c.

TAVERNER, John, of Hull, 173
Tournaments, 123
Town halls, 293
Towns, American, 35
,, armorial bearings of, 212
,, Bishops', 103
,, British, 44
,, castle, 109
,, church, 93
,, Danish, 81
,, English, 31
,, foreign, 32
,, mediæval, 169
,, monastic, 94
,, mythical origin of, 44
,, Palatinate, 279
,, Roman, 52, 53, 57 &c.

Towns, Saxon, 73 &c.
,,   sieges of great, 247
,,   University, 256 &c.
Trade of towns, 118
,,   ,, monks, 174
Trinity House Guild, 166
Tynwald Mound, Isle of Man, 52
Tyranny of guilds, 148 &c.

UNIVERSITY life, in Middle Ages, 261, 265
,,   of Paris, 258
,,   towns, 256 &c.

VAGRANTS, laws against, 244
Verulam, Roman city, 55

WAKEMAN, of Ripon, 143
Wallingford, charter granted to, 142

Wells, Bishop's town, 103
,,   cathedral city, 287
Whittington, Sir Richard, 171
Wilfrid, builder of churches, 84
Winchelsea, a cinque port, 273
Winchester, charter granted to, 140
,,   guilds at, 143, 145
,,   mythical origin of, 48
,,   Plague at, 227
,,   Royal, 218
Wooden Saxon churches, 83, 84
Worlebury, British town at, 45

YORK, church built by Edwin, 83
,,   decay of, 71
,,   guild at, 127
,,   mythical origin of, 49
,,   Roman city, 55, 86

THE END

UNIV. OF MICHIGAN,

DEC 10 1912

Printed by BALLANTYNE, HANSON & Co.
Edinburgh and London

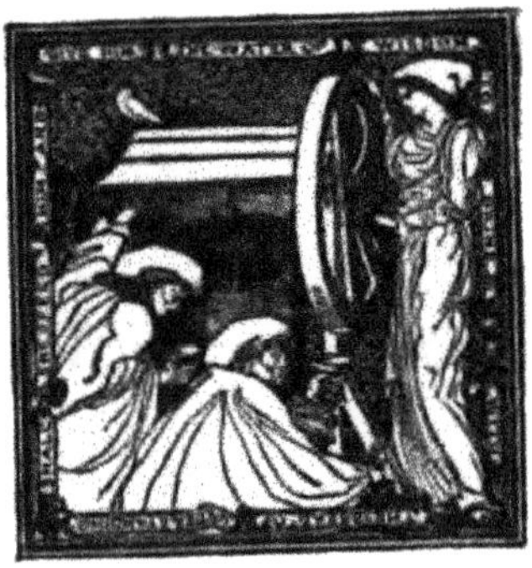

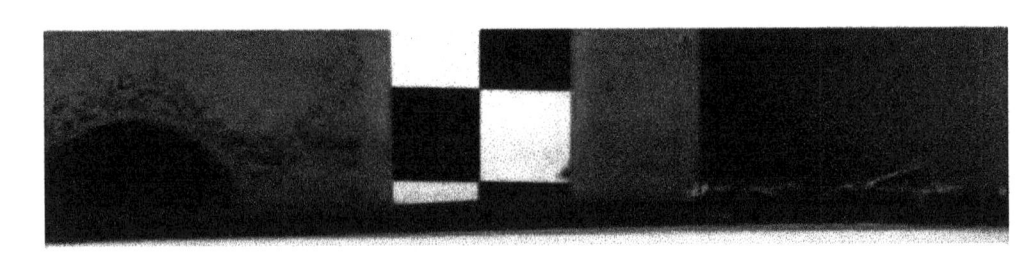

A SELECTION OF BOOKS PUBLISHED BY METHUEN AND COMPANY LIMITED 36 ESSEX STREET LONDON W.C.

CONTENTS

	PAGE		PAGE
General Literature	1	Little Library	20
Ancient Cities	15	Little Quarto Shakespeare	21
Antiquary's Books	15	Miniature Library	21
Arden Shakespeare	15	New Library of Medicine	21
Classics of Art	16	New Library of Music	22
"Complete" Series	16	Oxford Biographies	22
Connoisseur's Library	16	Romantic History	22
Handbooks of English Church History	17	Handbooks of Theology	22
		Westminster Commentaries	23
Illustrated Pocket Library of Plain and Coloured Books	17		
Leaders of Religion	18		
Library of Devotion	18	Fiction	23
Little Books on Art	19	Books for Boys and Girls	28
Little Galleries	19	Novels of Alexandre Dumas	29
Little Guides	19	Methuen's Sixpenny Books	29

OCTOBER 1910

A SELECTION OF

MESSRS. METHUEN'S
PUBLICATIONS

In this Catalogue the order is according to authors. An asterisk denotes that the book is in the press.
Colonial Editions are published of all Messrs. METHUEN's Novels issued at a price above 2s. 6d., and similar editions are published of some works of General Literature. Colonial editions are only for circulation in the British Colonies and India.
All books marked net are not subject to discount, and cannot be bought at less than the published price. Books not marked net are subject to the discount which the bookseller allows.
Messrs. METHUEN's books are kept in stock by all good booksellers. If there is any difficulty in seeing copies, Messrs. Methuen will be very glad to have early information, and specimen copies of any books will be sent on receipt of the published price plus postage for net books, and of the published price for ordinary books.
This Catalogue contains only a selection of the more important books published by Messrs. Methuen. A complete and illustrated catalogue of their publications may be obtained on application.

Addleshaw (Percy). SIR PHILIP SIDNEY. Illustrated. *Second Edition.* *Demy 8vo.* 10s. 6d. net.

Adeney (W. F.), M.A. See Bennett (W.H.).

Ady (Cecilia M.). A HISTORY OF MILAN UNDER THE SFORZA. Illustrated. *Demy 8vo.* 10s. 6d. net.

Aldis (Janet). THE QUEEN OF LETTER WRITERS, MARQUISE DE SÉVIGNÉ, DAME DE BOURBILLY. 1626-96. Illustrated. *Second Edition. Demy 8vo.* 12s. 6d. net.

Allen (M.). A HISTORY OF VERONA. Illustrated. *Demy 8vo.* 12s. 6d. net.

Amherst (Lady). A SKETCH OF EGYPTIAN HISTORY FROM THE EARLIEST TIMES TO THE PRESENT DAY. Illustrated. *A New and Cheaper Issue. Demy 8vo.* 7s. 6d.

Andrewes (Amy G.) THE STORY OF BAYARD. Edited by A. G. ANDREWES. *Cr. 8vo.* 2s. 6d.

Andrewes (Bishop). PRECES PRIVATAE. Translated and edited, with Notes, by F. E. BRIGHTMAN, Pusey House, Oxford. *Cr. 8vo.*

Anon. THE WESTMINSTER PROBLEMS BOOK. Prose and Verse. Compiled from *The Saturday Westminster Gazette* Competitions, 1904-1907. *Cr. 8vo.* 3s. 6d. net.
VENICE AND HER TREASURES. Illustrated. *Round corners. Fcap. 8vo.* 5s. net.

Aristotle. THE ETHICS OF. Edited, with an Introduction and Notes, by JOHN BURNET, M.A. *Cheaper issue. Demy 8vo.*

Bain (R. Nisbet). THE LAST KING OF POLAND AND HIS CONTEMPORARIES. Illustrated. *Demy 8vo.* 10s. 6d. net.

Balfour (Graham). THE LIFE OF ROBERT LOUIS STEVENSON. Illustrated. *Fifth Edition in one Volume. Cr. 8vo. Buckram,* 6s.

Baring (The Hon. Maurice). WITH THE RUSSIANS IN MANCHURIA. *Third Edition. Demy 8vo.* 7s. 6d. net.
A YEAR IN RUSSIA. *Second Edition. Demy 8vo.* 10s. 6d. net.
RUSSIAN ESSAYS AND STORIES. *Second Edition. Cr. 8vo.* 5s. net.
LANDMARKS IN RUSSIAN LITERATURE. *Cr. 8vo.* 6s. net.

Baring-Gould (S.). THE LIFE OF NAPOLEON BONAPARTE. Illustrated. *Second Edition. Wide Royal 8vo.* 10s. 6d. net.
THE TRAGEDY OF THE CÆSARS: A STUDY OF THE CHARACTERS OF THE CÆSARS OF THE JULIAN AND CLAUDIAN HOUSES. Illustrated. *Seventh Edition. Royal 8vo.* 10s. 6d. net.
A BOOK OF FAIRY TALES. Illustrated. *Second Edition. Cr. 8vo. Buckram.* 6s. Also *Medium 8vo.* 6d.
OLD ENGLISH FAIRY TALES. Illustrated. *Third Edition. Cr. 8vo. Buckram.* 6s.
THE VICAR OF MORWENSTOW. Revised Edition. With a Portrait. *Third Edition. Cr. 8vo.* 3s. 6d.
OLD COUNTRY LIFE. Illustrated. *Fifth Edition. Large Cr. 8vo.* 6s.
A GARLAND OF COUNTRY SONG: English Folk Songs with their Traditional Melodies. Collected and arranged by S. BARING-GOULD and H. F. SHEPPARD. *Demy 4to.* 6s.
SONGS OF THE WEST: Folk Songs of Devon and Cornwall. Collected from the Mouths of the People. By S. BARING-GOULD, M.A., and H. FLEETWOOD SHEPPARD, M.A. New and Revised Edition, under the musical editorship of CECIL J. SHARP. *Large Imperial 8vo.* 5s. net.
STRANGE SURVIVALS: SOME CHAPTERS IN THE HISTORY OF MAN. Illustrated. *Third Edition. Cr. 8vo.* 2s. 6d. net.
YORKSHIRE ODDITIES: INCIDENTS AND STRANGE EVENTS. *Fifth Edition. Cr. 8vo.* 2s. 6d. net.
A BOOK OF CORNWALL. Illustrated. *Second Edition. Cr. 8vo.* 6s.
A BOOK OF DARTMOOR. Illustrated. *Second Edition. Cr. 8vo.* 6s.
A BOOK OF DEVON. Illustrated. *Third Edition. Cr. 8vo.* 6s.
A BOOK OF NORTH WALES. Illustrated. *Cr. 8vo.* 6s.
A BOOK OF SOUTH WALES. Illustrated. *Cr. 8vo.* 6s.

A BOOK OF BRITTANY. Illustrated. *Second Edition. Cr. 8vo.* 6s.
A BOOK OF THE RHINE: From Cleve to Mainz. Illustrated. *Second Edition. Cr. 8vo.* 6s.
A BOOK OF THE RIVIERA. Illustrated. *Second Edition. Cr. 8vo.* 6s.
A BOOK OF THE PYRENEES. Illustrated. *Cr. 8vo.* 6s.

Barker (E.), M.A., (Late) Fellow of Merton College, Oxford. THE POLITICAL THOUGHT OF PLATO AND ARISTOTLE. *Demy 8vo.* 10s. 6d. net.

Baron (R. R. N.), M.A. FRENCH PROSE COMPOSITION. *Fourth Edition. Cr. 8vo.* 2s. 6d. Key, 3s. net.

Bartholomew (J. G.), F.R.S.E. See Robertson (C. G.).

Bastable (C. F.), LL.D. THE COMMERCE OF NATIONS. *Fourth Edition. Cr. 8vo.* 2s. 6d.

Bastian (H. Charlton), M.A., M.D., F.R.S. THE EVOLUTION OF LIFE. Illustrated. *Demy 8vo.* 7s. 6d. net.

Batson (Mrs. Stephen). A CONCISE HANDBOOK OF GARDEN FLOWERS. *Fcap. 8vo.* 3s. 6d. net.
THE SUMMER GARDEN OF PLEASURE. Illustrated. *Wide Demy 8vo.* 15s. net.

Beckett (Arthur). THE SPIRIT OF THE DOWNS: Impressions and Reminiscences of the Sussex Downs. Illustrated. *Second Edition. Demy 8vo.* 10s. 6d. net.

Beckford (Peter). THOUGHTS ON HUNTING. Edited by J. OTHO PAGET. Illustrated. *Second Edition. Demy 8vo.* 6s.

Begbie (Harold). MASTER WORKERS. Illustrated. *Demy 8vo.* 7s. 6d. net.

Behmen (Jacob). DIALOGUES ON THE SUPERSENSUAL LIFE. Edited by BERNARD HOLLAND. *Fcap. 8vo.* 3s. 6d.

Bell (Mrs. Arthur G.). THE SKIRTS OF THE GREAT CITY. Illustrated. *Second Edition. Cr. 8vo.* 6s.

Belloc (H.), M.P. PARIS. Illustrated. *Second Edition, Revised. Cr. 8vo.* 6s.
HILLS AND THE SEA. *Third Edition. Fcap. 8vo.* 5s.
ON NOTHING AND KINDRED SUBJECTS. *Third Edition. Fcap. 8vo.* 5s.
ON EVERYTHING. *Second Edition. Fcap. 8vo.* 5s.
MARIE ANTOINETTE. Illustrated. *Third Edition. Demy 8vo.* 15s. net.
THE PYRENEES. Illustrated. *Second Edition. Demy 8vo.* 7s. 6d. net.

Bellot (H. H. L.), M.A. See Jones (L. A. A.).

Bennett (Joseph). FORTY YEARS OF MUSIC, 1865-1905. Illustrated. *Demy 8vo.* 16s. *net.*

Bennett (W. H.), M.A. A PRIMER OF THE BIBLE. *Fifth Edition. Cr. 8vo.* 2s. 6d.

Bennett (W. H.) and Adeney (W. F.). A BIBLICAL INTRODUCTION. With a concise Bibliography. *Fifth Edition. Cr. 8vo.* 7s. 6d.

Benson (Archbishop). GOD'S BOARD. Communion Addresses. *Second Edition. Fcap. 8vo.* 3s. 6d. *net.*

Benson (R. M.). THE WAY OF HOLINESS. An Exposition of Psalm cxix. Analytical and Devotional. *Cr. 8vo.* 5s.

Bensusan (Samuel L.). HOME LIFE IN SPAIN. Illustrated. *Demy 8vo.* 10s. 6d. *net.*

Berry (W. Grinton), M.A. FRANCE SINCE WATERLOO. Illustrated. *Cr. 8vo.* 6s.

Betham-Edwards (Miss). HOME LIFE IN FRANCE. Illustrated. *Fifth Edition. Cr. 8vo.* 6s.

Bindley (T. Herbert), B.D. THE OECUMENICAL DOCUMENTS OF THE FAITH. With Introductions and Notes. *Second Edition. Cr. 8vo.* 6s. *net.*

Binyon (Laurence). See Blake (William).

Blake (William). ILLUSTRATIONS OF THE BOOK OF JOB. With General Introduction by LAURENCE BINYON. Illustrated. *Quarto.* 21s. *net.*

Body (George), D.D. THE SOUL'S PILGRIMAGE: Devotional Readings from the Published and Unpublished writings of George Body, D.D. Selected and arranged by J. H. BURN, D.D., F.R.S.E. *Demy 16mo.* 2s. 6d.

Boulting (W.). TASSO AND HIS TIMES. Illustrated. *Demy 8vo.* 10s. 6d. *net.*

Bovill (W. B. Forster). HUNGARY AND THE HUNGARIANS. Illustrated. *Demy 8vo.* 7s. 6d. *net.*

Bowden (E. M.). THE IMITATION OF BUDDHA: Being Quotations from Buddhist Literature for each Day in the Year. *Fifth Edition. Cr. 16mo.* 2s. 6d.

Brabant (F. G.), M.A. RAMBLES IN SUSSEX. Illustrated. *Cr. 8vo.* 6s.

Bradley (A. G.). ROUND ABOUT WILTSHIRE. Illustrated. *Second Edition. Cr. 8vo.* 6s.
THE ROMANCE OF NORTHUMBERLAND. Illustrated. *Second Edition. Demy 8vo.* 7s. 6d. *net.*

Braid (James). Open Champion, 1901, 1905 and 1906. ADVANCED GOLF. Illustrated. *Fifth Edition. Demy 8vo.* 10s. 6d. *net.*

Braid (James) and Others. GREAT GOLFERS IN THE MAKING. Edited by HENRY LEACH. Illustrated. *Second Edition. Demy 8vo.* 7s. 6d. *net.*

Brailsford (H. N.). MACEDONIA: Its RACES AND THEIR FUTURE. Illustrated. *Demy 8vo.* 12s. 6d. *net.*

Brodrick (Mary) and Morton (A. Anderson). A CONCISE DICTIONARY OF EGYPTIAN ARCHÆOLOGY. A Handbook for Students and Travellers. Illustrated. *Cr. 8vo.* 3s. 6d.

Brown (J. Wood), M.A. THE BUILDERS OF FLORENCE. Illustrated. *Demy 4to.* 18s. *net.*

Browning (Robert). PARACELSUS. Edited with Introduction, Notes, and Bibliography by MARGARET L. LEE and KATHARINE B. LOCOCK. *Fcap. 8vo.* 3s. 6d. *net.*

Buckton (A. M.). EAGER HEART: A Mystery Play. *Eighth Edition. Cr. 8vo.* 1s. *net.*

Budge (E. A. Wallis). THE GODS OF THE EGYPTIANS. Illustrated. *Two Volumes. Royal 8vo.* £3 3s. *net.*

Bull (Paul), Army Chaplain. GOD AND OUR SOLDIERS. *Second Edition. Cr. 8vo.* 6s.

Bulley (Miss). See Dilke (Lady).

Burns (Robert), THE POEMS. Edited by ANDREW LANG and W. A. CRAIGIE. With Portrait. *Third Edition. Wide Demy 8vo.* gilt top. 6s.

Bussell (F. W.), D.D. CHRISTIAN THEOLOGY AND SOCIAL PROGRESS (The Bampton Lectures of 1905). *Demy 8vo.* 10s. 6d. *net.*

Butler (Sir William), Lieut.-General, G.C.B. THE LIGHT OF THE WEST. With some other Wayside Thoughts, 1865-1908. *Cr. 8vo.* 5s. *net.*

Butlin (F. M.). AMONG THE DANES. Illustrated. *Demy 8vo.* 7s. 6d. *net.*

Cain (Georges), Curator of the Carnavalet Museum, Paris. WALKS IN PARIS. Translated by A. R. ALLINSON, M.A. Illustrated. *Demy 8vo.* 7s. 6d. *net.*

Cameron (Mary Lovett). OLD ETRURIA AND MODERN TUSCANY. Illustrated. *Second Edition. Cr. 8vo.* 6s. *net.*

Carden (Robert W.). THE CITY OF GENOA. Illustrated. *Demy 8vo.* 10s. 6d. *net.*

General Literature

Carlyle (Thomas). THE FRENCH REVOLUTION. Edited by C. R. L. FLETCHER, Fellow of Magdalen College, Oxford. *Three Volumes. Cr. 8vo. 18s.*
THE LETTERS AND SPEECHES OF OLIVER CROMWELL. With an Introduction by C. H. FIRTH, M.A., and Notes and Appendices by Mrs. S. C. LOMAS. *Three Volumes. Demy 8vo. 18s. net.*

Celano (Brother Thomas of). THE LIVES OF FRANCIS OF ASSISI. Translated by A. G. FERRERS HOWELL. Illustrated. *Cr. 8vo. 5s. net.*

Chambers (Mrs. Lambert). Lawn Tennis for Ladies. Illustrated. *Crown 8vo. 2s. 6d. net.*

Chandler (Arthur), Bishop of Bloemfontein. ARA CŒLI: AN ESSAY IN MYSTICAL THEOLOGY. *Third Edition. Cr. 8vo. 3s. 6d. net.*

Chesterfield (Lord). THE LETTERS OF THE EARL OF CHESTERFIELD TO HIS SON. Edited, with an Introduction by C. STRACHEY, with Notes by A. CALTHROP. *Two Volumes. Cr. 8vo. 12s.*

Chesterton (G. K.). CHARLES DICKENS. With two Portraits in Photogravure. *Sixth Edition. Cr. 8vo. 6s.*
ALL THINGS CONSIDERED. *Sixth Edition. Fcap. 8vo. 5s.*
TREMENDOUS TRIFLES. *Fourth Edition. Fcap. 8vo. 5s.*

Clausen (George), A.R.A., R.W.S. SIX LECTURES ON PAINTING. Illustrated. *Third Edition. Large Post. 8vo. 3s. 6d. net.*
AIMS AND IDEALS IN ART. Eight Lectures delivered to the Students of the Royal Academy of Arts. Illustrated. *Second Edition. Large Post 8vo. 5s. net.*

Clutton-Brock (A.) SHELLEY: THE MAN AND THE POET. Illustrated. *Demy 8vo. 7s. 6d. net.*

Cobb (W. F.), M.A. THE BOOK OF PSALMS: with an Introduction and Notes. *Demy 8vo. 10s. 6d. net.*

Cockshott (Winifred), St. Hilda's Hall, Oxford. THE PILGRIM FATHERS, THEIR CHURCH AND COLONY. Illustrated. *Demy 8vo. 7s. 6d. net.*

Collingwood (W. G.), M.A. THE LIFE OF JOHN RUSKIN. With Portrait. *Sixth Edition. Cr. 8vo. 2s. 6d. net.*

Colvill (Helen H.). ST. TERESA OF SPAIN. Illustrated. *Second Edition. Demy 8vo. 7s. 6d. net.*

*****Condamine (Robert de la).** THE UPPER GARDEN. *Fcap. 8vo. 5s. net.*

Conrad (Joseph). THE MIRROR OF THE SEA: Memories and Impressions. *Third Edition. Cr. 8vo. 6s.*

Coolidge (W. A. B.), M.A. THE ALPS. Illustrated. *Demy 8vo. 7s. 6d. net.*

Cooper (C. S.), F.R.H.S. See Westell (W.P.)

Coulton (G. G.). CHAUCER AND HIS ENGLAND. Illustrated. *Second Edition. Demy 8vo. 10s. 6d. net.*

Cowper (William). THE POEMS. Edited with an Introduction and Notes by J. C. BAILEY, M.A. Illustrated. *Demy 8vo. 10s. 6d. net.*

Crane (Walter), R.W.S. AN ARTIST'S REMINISCENCES. Illustrated. *Second Edition. Demy 8vo. 18s. net.*
INDIA IMPRESSIONS. Illustrated. *Second Edition. Demy 8vo. 7s. 6d. net.*

Crispe (T. E.). REMINISCENCES OF A K.C. With 2 Portraits. *Second Edition. Demy 8vo. 10s. 6d. net.*

Crowley (Ralph H.). THE HYGIENE OF SCHOOL LIFE. Illustrated. *Cr. 8vo. 3s. 6d. net.*

Dante (Alighieri). LA COMMEDIA DI DANTE. The Italian Text edited by PAGET TOYNBEE, M.A., D.Litt. *Cr. 8vo. 6s.*

Davey (Richard). THE PAGEANT OF LONDON. Illustrated. *In Two Volumes. Demy 8vo. 15s. net.*

Davis (H. W. C.), M.A., Fellow and Tutor of Balliol College. ENGLAND UNDER THE NORMANS AND ANGEVINS: 1066-1272. Illustrated. *Demy 8vo. 10s. 6d. net.*

Deans (R. Storry). THE TRIALS OF FIVE QUEENS: KATHARINE OF ARAGON, ANNE BOLEYN, MARY QUEEN OF SCOTS, MARIE ANTOINETTE and CAROLINE OF BRUNSWICK. Illustrated. *Second Edition. Demy 8vo. 10s. 6d. net.*

Dearmer (Mabel). A CHILD'S LIFE OF CHRIST. Illustrated. *Large Cr. 8vo. 6s.*

D'Este (Margaret). IN THE CANARIES WITH A CAMERA. Illustrated. *Cr. 8vo. 7s. 6d. net.*

Dickinson (G. L.), M.A., Fellow of King's College, Cambridge. THE GREEK VIEW OF LIFE. *Seventh and Revised Edition. Crown 8vo. 2s. 6d. net.*

Ditchfield (P. H.), M.A., F.S.A. THE PARISH CLERK. Illustrated. *Third Edition. Demy 8vo. 7s. 6d. net.*
THE OLD-TIME PARSON. Illustrated. *Second Edition. Demy 8vo. 7s. 6d. net.*

Douglas (Hugh A.). VENICE ON FOOT. With the Itinerary of the Grand Canal. Illustrated. *Second Edition. Fcap. 8vo. 5s. net.*

6 METHUEN AND COMPANY LIMITED

Douglas (James). THE MAN IN THE PULPIT. *Cr. 8vo.* 2s. 6d. net.

Dowden (J.), D.D., Late Lord Bishop of Edinburgh. FURTHER STUDIES IN THE PRAYER BOOK. *Cr. 8vo.* 6s.

Driver (S. R.), D.D., D.C.L., Regius Professor of Hebrew in the University of Oxford. SERMONS ON SUBJECTS CONNECTED WITH THE OLD TESTAMENT. *Cr. 8vo.* 6s.

Duff (Nora). MATILDA OF TUSCANY. Illustrated. *Demy 8vo.* 10s. 6d. net.

Dumas (Alexandre). THE CRIMES OF THE BORGIAS AND OTHERS. With an Introduction by R. S. GARNETT. Illustrated. *Cr. 8vo.* 6s.
THE CRIMES OF URBAIN GRANDIER AND OTHERS. Illustrated. *Cr. 8vo.* 6s.
THE CRIMES OF THE MARQUISE DE BRINVILLIERS AND OTHERS. Illustrated. *Cr. 8vo.* 6s.
THE CRIMES OF ALI PACHA AND OTHERS. Illustrated. *Cr. 8vo.* 6s.
MY MEMOIRS. Translated by E. M. WALLER. With an Introduction by ANDREW LANG. With Frontispieces in Photogravure. In six Volumes. *Cr. 8vo.* 6s. each volume.
VOL. I. 1802-1821. VOL. IV. 1830-1831.
VOL. II. 1822-1825. VOL. V. 1831-1832.
VOL. III. 1826-1830. VOL. VI. 1832-1833.
MY PETS. Newly translated by A. R. ALLINSON, M.A. Illustrated. *Cr. 8vo.* 6s.

Duncan (David), D.Sc., LL.D. THE LIFE AND LETTERS OF HERBERT SPENCER. Illustrated. *Demy 8vo.* 15s.

Dunn-Pattison (R. P.). NAPOLEON'S MARSHALS. Illustrated. *Demy 8vo.* *Second Edition.* 12s. 6d. net.
THE BLACK PRINCE. Illustrated. *Second Edition. Demy 8vo.* 7s. 6d. net.

Durham (The Earl of). A REPORT ON CANADA. With an Introductory Note. *Demy 8vo.* 4s. 6d. net.

Dutt (W. A.). THE NORFOLK BROADS. Illustrated. *Second Edition. Cr. 8vo.* 6s.
WILD LIFE IN EAST ANGLIA. Illustrated. *Second Edition. Demy 8vo.* 7s. 6d. net.
SOME LITERARY ASSOCIATIONS OF EAST ANGLIA. Illustrated. *Demy 8vo.* 10s. 6d. net.

Edmonds (Major J. E.), R.E.; D. A. Q.-M. G. See Wood (W. Birkbeck).

Edwardes (Tickner). THE LORE OF THE HONEY BEE. Illustrated. *Cr. 8vo.* 6s.
LIFT-LUCK ON SOUTHERN ROADS. Illustrated. *Cr. 8vo.* 6s.

Egerton (H. E.), M.A. A HISTORY OF BRITISH COLONIAL POLICY. *Third Edition. Demy 8vo.* 7s. 6d. net.

Everett-Green (Mary Anne). ELIZABETH; ELECTRESS PALATINE AND QUEEN OF BOHEMIA. Revised by her Niece S. C. LOMAS. With a Prefatory Note by A. W. WARD, Litt.D. *Demy 8vo.* 10s. 6d. net.

Fairbrother (W. H.), M.A. THE PHILOSOPHY, OF T. H. GREEN. *Second Edition. Cr. 8vo.* 3s. 6d.

Fea (Allan). THE FLIGHT OF THE KING. Illustrated. *New and Revised Edition. Demy 8vo.* 7s. 6d. net.
SECRET CHAMBERS AND HIDING-PLACES. Illustrated. *New and Revised Edition. Demy 8vo.* 7s. 6d. net.
JAMES II. AND HIS WIVES. Illustrated. *Demy 8vo.* 10s. 6d. net.

Fell (E. F. B.). THE FOUNDATIONS OF LIBERTY. *Cr. 8vo.* 5s. net.

Firth (C. H.), M.A., Regius Professor of Modern History at Oxford. CROMWELL'S ARMY: A History of the English Soldier during the Civil Wars, the Commonwealth, and the Protectorate. *Cr. 8vo.* 6s.

FitzGerald (Edward). THE RUBAIYAT OF OMAR KHAYYAM. Printed from the Fifth and last Edition. With a Commentary by Mrs. STEPHEN BATSON, and a Biography of Omar by E. D. ROSS. *Cr. 8vo.* 6s.

*Fletcher (B. F. and H. P.). THE ENGLISH HOME. Illustrated. *Demy 8vo.* 12s. 6d. net.

Fletcher (J. S.). A BOOK OF YORKSHIRE. Illustrated. *Demy 8vo.* 7s. 6d. net.

Flux (A. W.), M.A., William Dow Professor of Political Economy in M'Gill University, Montreal. ECONOMIC PRINCIPLES. *Demy 8vo.* 7s. 6d. net.

Foot (Constance M.). INSECT WONDERLAND. Illustrated. *Second Edition. Cr. 8vo.* 3s. 6d. net.

Forel (A.). THE SENSES OF INSECTS. Translated by MACLEOD YEARSLEY. Illustrated. *Demy 8vo.* 10s. 6d. net.

Fouqué (La Motte). SINTRAM AND HIS COMPANIONS. Translated by A. C. FARQUHARSON. Illustrated. *Demy 8vo.* 7s. 6d. net. *Half White Vellum,* 10s. 6d. net.

Fraser (J. F.). ROUND THE WORLD ON A WHEEL. Illustrated. *Fifth Edition. Cr. 8vo.* 6s.

General Literature

Galton (Sir Francis), F.R.S.; D.C.L., Oxf.; Hon. Sc.D., Camb.; Hon. Fellow Trinity College, Cambridge. MEMORIES OF MY LIFE. Illustrated. *Third Edition. Demy 8vo.* 10s. 6d. *net.*

Garnett (Lucy M. J.). THE TURKISH PEOPLE; THEIR SOCIAL LIFE, RELIGIOUS BELIEFS AND INSTITUTIONS, AND DOMESTIC LIFE. Illustrated. *Demy 8vo.* 10s. 6d. *net.*

Gibbins (H. de B.), Litt.D., M.A. INDUSTRY IN ENGLAND: HISTORICAL OUTLINES. With 5 Maps. *Fifth Edition. Demy 8vo.* 10s. 6d.
THE INDUSTRIAL HISTORY OF ENGLAND. Illustrated. *Fifteenth Edition Revised. Cr. 8vo.* 3s.
ENGLISH SOCIAL REFORMERS. *Second Edition. Cr. 8vo.* 2s. 6d.
See also Hadfield, R.A.

Gibbon (Edward). MEMOIRS OF THE LIFE OF EDWARD GIBBON. Edited by G. BIRKBECK HILL, LL.D. *Cr. 8vo.* 6s.
*THE DECLINE AND FALL OF THE ROMAN EMPIRE. Edited, with Notes, Appendices, and Maps, by J. B. BURY, M.A., Litt.D., Regius Professor of Modern History at Cambridge. Illustrated. *In Seven Volumes. Demy 8vo. Gilt Top. Each* 10s. 6d. *net.*

Gibbs (Philip.) THE ROMANCE OF GEORGE VILLIERS: FIRST DUKE OF BUCKINGHAM, AND SOME MEN AND WOMEN OF THE STUART COURT. Illustrated. *Second Edition. Demy 8vo.* 15s. *net.*

Gloag (M. R.) and Wyatt (Kate M.). A BOOK OF ENGLISH GARDENS. Illustrated. *Demy 8vo.* 10s. 6d. *net.*

Glover (T. R.), M.A., Fellow and Classical Lecturer of St. John's College, Cambridge. THE CONFLICT OF RELIGIONS IN THE EARLY ROMAN EMPIRE. *Fourth Edition. Demy 8vo.* 7s. 6d. *net.*

Godfrey (Elizabeth). A BOOK OF REMEMBRANCE. Being Lyrical Selections for every day in the Year. Arranged by E. Godfrey. *Second Edition. Fcap. 8vo.* 2s. 6d. *net.*
ENGLISH CHILDREN IN THE OLDEN TIME. Illustrated. *Second Edition. Demy 8vo.* 7s. 6d. *net.*

Godley (A. D.), M.A., Fellow of Magdalen College, Oxford. OXFORD IN THE EIGHTEENTH CENTURY. Illustrated. *Second Edition. Demy 8vo.* 7s. 6d. *net.*
LYRA FRIVOLA. *Fourth Edition. Fcap. 8vo.* 2s. 6d.
VERSES TO ORDER. *Second Edition. Fcap. 8vo.* 2s. 6d.
SECOND STRINGS. *Fcap. 8vo.* 2s. 6d.

Goll (August). CRIMINAL TYPES IN SHAKESPEARE. Authorised Translation from the Danish by Mrs. CHARLES WEEKES. *Cr. 8vo.* 5s. *net.*

Gordon (Lina Duff) (Mrs. Aubrey Waterfield). HOME LIFE IN ITALY: LETTERS FROM THE APENNINES. Illustrated. *Second Edition. Demy 8vo.* 10s. 6d. *net.*

Gostling (Frances M.). THE BRETONS AT HOME. Illustrated. *Second Edition. Demy 8vo.* 10s. 6d. *net.*

Graham (Harry). A GROUP OF SCOTTISH WOMEN. Illustrated. *Second Edition. Demy 8vo.* 10s. 6d. *net.*

Grahame (Kenneth). THE WIND IN THE WILLOWS. Illustrated. *Fourth Edition. Cr. 8vo.* 6s.

Gwynn (Stephen), M.P. A HOLIDAY IN CONNEMARA. Illustrated. *Demy 8vo.* 10s. 6d. *net.*

Hall (Cyril). THE YOUNG CARPENTER. Illustrated. *Cr. 8vo.* 5s.

Hall (Hammond). THE YOUNG ENGINEER; or MODERN ENGINES AND THEIR MODELS. Illustrated. *Second Edition. Cr. 8vo.* 5s.

Hall (Mary). A WOMAN'S TREK FROM THE CAPE TO CAIRO. Illustrated. *Second Edition. Demy 8vo.* 16s. *net.*

Hamel (Frank). FAMOUS FRENCH SALONS. Illustrated. *Third Edition. Demy 8vo.* 12s. 6d. *net.*

Hannay (D.). A SHORT HISTORY OF THE ROYAL NAVY. Vol. I., 1217-1688. Vol. II., 1689-1815. *Demy 8vo. Each* 7s. 6d. *net.*

Hannay (James O.), M.A. THE SPIRIT AND ORIGIN OF CHRISTIAN MONASTICISM. *Cr. 8vo.* 6s.
THE WISDOM OF THE DESERT. *Fcap. 8vo.* 3s. 6d. *net.*

Harper (Charles G.). THE AUTOCAR ROAD-BOOK. Four Volumes with Maps. *Cr. 8vo. Each* 7s. 6d. *net.*
Vol. I.—SOUTH OF THE THAMES.
Vol. II.—NORTH AND SOUTH WALES AND WEST MIDLANDS.

Headley (F. W.). DARWINISM AND MODERN SOCIALISM. *Second Edition. Cr. 8vo.* 5s. *net.*

Henderson (B. W.), Fellow of Exeter, College, Oxford. THE LIFE AND PRINCIPATE OF THE EMPEROR NERO. Illustrated. *New and cheaper issue. Demy 8vo.* 7s. 6d. *net.*

Henderson (M. Sturge). GEORGE MEREDITH: NOVELIST, POET, REFORMER. Illustrated. *Second Edition. Cr. 8vo.* 6s.

METHUEN AND COMPANY LIMITED

Henderson (T. F.) and Watt (Francis). SCOTLAND OF TO-DAY. Illustrated. *Second Edition. Cr. 8vo. 6s.*

Henley (W. E.). ENGLISH LYRICS, CHAUCER TO POE, 1340-1849. *Second Edition. Cr. 8vo. 2s. 6d. net.*

Heywood (W.). A HISTORY OF PERUGIA. Illustrated. *Demy 8vo. 12s. 6d. net.*

Hill (George Francis). ONE HUNDRED MASTERPIECES OF SCULPTURE. Illustrated. *Demy 8vo. 10s. 6d. net.*

Hind (C. Lewis). DAYS IN CORNWALL. Illustrated. *Second Edition. Cr. 8vo. 6s.*

Hobhouse (L. T.), late Fellow of C.C.C., Oxford. THE THEORY OF KNOWLEDGE. *Demy 8vo. 10s. 6d. net.*

Hodgetts (E. A. Brayley). THE COURT OF RUSSIA IN THE NINETEENTH CENTURY. Illustrated. *Two volumes. Demy 8vo. 24s. net.*

Hodgson (Mrs. W.). HOW TO IDENTIFY OLD CHINESE PORCELAIN. Illustrated. *Second Edition. Post 8vo. 6s.*

Holdich (Sir T. H.), K.C.I.E., C.B., F.S.A. THE INDIAN BORDERLAND, 1880-1900. Illustrated. *Second Edition. Demy 8vo. 10s. 6d. net.*

Holdsworth (W. S.), D.C.L. A HISTORY OF ENGLISH LAW. *In Four Volumes. Vols. I., II., III. Demy 8vo. Each 10s. 6d. net.*

Holland (Clive). TYROL AND ITS PEOPLE. Illustrated. *Demy 8vo. 10s. 6d. net.*

Hollway-Calthrop (H. C.), late of Balliol College, Oxford; Bursar of Eton College. PETRARCH: HIS LIFE, WORK, AND TIMES. Illustrated. *Demy 8vo. 12s. 6d. net.*

Horsburgh (E. L. S.), M.A. LORENZO THE MAGNIFICENT: AND FLORENCE IN HER GOLDEN AGE. Illustrated. *Second Edition. Demy 8vo. 15s. net.*
WATERLOO: with Plans. *Second Edition. Cr. 8vo. 5s.*

Hosie (Alexander). MANCHURIA. Illustrated. *Second Edition. Demy 8vo. 7s. 6d. net.*

Hulton (Samuel F.). THE CLERK OF OXFORD IN FICTION. Illustrated. *Demy 8vo. 10s. 6d. net.*

*Humphreys (John H.). PROPORTIONAL REPRESENTATION. *Cr. 8vo. 3s. 6d. net.*

Hutchinson (Horace G.). THE NEW FOREST. Illustrated. *Fourth Edition. Cr. 8vo. 6s.*

Hutton (Edward). THE CITIES OF UMBRIA. Illustrated. *Fourth Edition. Cr. 8vo. 6s.*
THE CITIES OF SPAIN. Illustrated. *Third Edition. Cr. 8vo. 6s.*
FLORENCE AND THE CITIES OF NORTHERN TUSCANY, WITH GENOA. Illustrated. *Second Edition. Crown 8vo. 6s.*
ENGLISH LOVE POEMS. Edited with an Introduction. *Fcap. 8vo. 3s. 6d net.*
COUNTRY WALKS ABOUT FLORENCE. Illustrated. *Fcap. 8vo. 5s. net.*
IN UNKNOWN TUSCANY With an Appendix by WILLIAM HEYWOOD. Illustrated. *Second Edition. Demy 8vo. 7s. 6d. net.*
ROME. Illustrated. *Second Edition. Cr. 8vo. 6s.*

Hyett (F. A.) FLORENCE: HER HISTORY AND ART TO THE FALL OF THE REPUBLIC. *Demy 8vo. 7s. 6d. net.*

Ibsen (Henrik). BRAND. A Drama. Translated by WILLIAM WILSON. *Fourth Edition. Cr. 8vo. 3s. 6d.*

Inge (W. R.), M.A., Fellow and Tutor of Hertford College, Oxford. CHRISTIAN MYSTICISM. (The Bampton Lectures of 1899.) *Demy 8vo. 12s. 6d. net.*

Innes (A. D.), M.A. A HISTORY OF THE BRITISH IN INDIA. With Maps and Plans. *Cr. 8vo. 6s.*
ENGLAND UNDER THE TUDORS. With Maps. *Third Edition. Demy 8vo. 10s. 6d. net.*

Innes (Mary). SCHOOLS OF PAINTING. Illustrated. *Cr. 8vo. 5s. net.*

James (Norman G. B.). THE CHARM OF SWITZERLAND. *Cr. 8vo. 5s. net.*

Jebb (Camilla). A STAR OF THE SALONS: JULIE DE LESPINASSE. Illustrated. *Demy 8vo. 10s. 6d. net.*

Jeffery (Reginald W.), M.A. THE HISTORY OF THE THIRTEEN COLONIES OF NORTH AMERICA, 1497-1763. Illustrated. *Demy 8vo. 7s. 6d. net.*

Jenks (E.), M.A., B.C.L. AN OUTLINE OF ENGLISH LOCAL GOVERNMENT. *Second Edition.* Revised by R. C. K. ENSOR, M.A. *Cr. 8vo. 2s. 6d.*

Jennings (Oscar), M.D. EARLY WOODCUT INITIALS. Illustrated. *Demy 4to. 21s. net.*

Jerningham (Charles Edward). THE MAXIMS OF MARMADUKE. *Second Edition. Cr. 8vo. 5s.*

Johnston (Sir H. H.), K.C.B. BRITISH CENTRAL AFRICA. Illustrated. *Third Edition. Cr. 4to. 18s. net.*

General Literature

*THE NEGRO IN THE NEW WORLD. Illustrated. *Demy 8vo. 16s. net.*

Jones (R. Crompton), M.A. POEMS OF THE INNER LIFE. Selected by R. C. Jones. *Thirteenth Edition. Fcap 8vo. 2s. 6d. net.*

Julian (Lady) of Norwich. REVELATIONS OF DIVINE LOVE. Edited by Grace Warrack. *Third Edition. Cr. 8vo. 3s. 6d.*

'Kappa.' LET YOUTH BUT KNOW: A Plea for Reason in Education. *Second Edition. Cr. 8vo. 3s. 6d. net.*

Keats (John). THE POEMS. Edited with Introduction and Notes by E. de Sélincourt, M.A. With a Frontispiece in Photogravure. *Second Edition Revised. Demy 8vo. 7s. 6d. net.*

Keble (John). THE CHRISTIAN YEAR. With an Introduction and Notes by W. Lock, D.D., Warden of Keble College. Illustrated. *Third Edition. Fcap. 8vo. 3s. 6d.; padded morocco. 5s.*

Kempis (Thomas à). THE IMITATION OF CHRIST. With an Introduction by Dean Farrar. Illustrated. *Third Edition. Fcap. 8vo. 3s. 6d.; padded morocco, 5s.*
Also translated by C. Bigg, D.D. *Cr 8vo. 3s. 6d.*

Kerr (S. Parnell). GEORGE SELWYN AND THE WITS. Illustrated. *Demy 8vo. 12s. 6d. net.*

Kipling (Rudyard). BARRACK-ROOM BALLADS. *96th Thousand. Twenty-eighth Edition. Cr. 8vo. 6s.* Also *Fcap. 8vo, Leather. 5s. net.*
THE SEVEN SEAS. *81st Thousand. Sixteenth Edition. Cr. 8vo. 6s.* Also *Fcap. 8vo, Leather. 5s. net.*
THE FIVE NATIONS. *69th Thousand. Seventh Edition. Cr. 8vo. 6s.* Also *Fcap. 8vo, Leather. 5s. net.*
DEPARTMENTAL DITTIES. *Eighteenth Edition. Cr. 8vo. 6s.* Also *Fcap. 8vo, Leather. 5s. net.*

Knox (Winifred F.). THE COURT OF A SAINT. Illustrated. *Demy 8vo. 10s. 6d. net.*

Lamb (Charles and Mary). THE WORKS. Edited by E. V. Lucas. Illustrated. *In Seven Volumes. Demy 8vo. 7s. 6d. each.*

Lane-Poole (Stanley). A HISTORY OF EGYPT IN THE MIDDLE AGES. Illustrated. *Cr. 8vo. 6s.*

Lankester (Sir Ray), K.C.B., F.R.S. SCIENCE FROM AN EASY CHAIR. Illustrated. *Fifth Edition. Cr. 8vo. 6s.*

Leach (Henry). THE SPIRIT OF THE LINKS. *Cr. 8vo. 6s.*

Le Braz (Anatole). THE LAND OF PARDONS. Translated by Frances M. Gostling. Illustrated. *Third Edition. Cr. 8vo. 6s.*

Lees (Frederick). A SUMMER IN TOURAINE. Illustrated. *Second Edition. Demy 8vo. 10s. 6d. net.*

Lindsay (Lady Mabel). ANNI DOMINI: A Gospel Study. With Maps. *Two Volumes. Super Royal 8vo. 10s. net.*

Llewellyn (Owen) and Raven-Hill (L.). THE SOUTH-BOUND CAR. Illustrated. *Cr. 8vo. 6s.*

Lock (Walter), D.D., Warden of Keble College. ST. PAUL, THE MASTER-BUILDER. *Second Edition. Cr. 8vo. 3s. 6d.*
THE BIBLE AND CHRISTIAN LIFE. *Cr. 8vo. 6s.*

Lodge (Sir Oliver), F.R.S. THE SUBSTANCE OF FAITH, ALLIED WITH SCIENCE: A Catechism for Parents and Teachers. *Tenth Edition. Cr. 8vo. 2s. net.*
MAN AND THE UNIVERSE: A Study of the Influence of the Advance in Scientific Knowledge upon our Understanding of Christianity. *Eighth and Cheaper Edition. Demy 8vo. 5s. net.*
THE SURVIVAL OF MAN. A Study in Unrecognised Human Faculty. *Fourth Edition. Demy 8vo. 7s. 6d. net.*

Lofthouse (W. F.), M.A. ETHICS AND ATONEMENT. With a Frontispiece. *Demy 8vo. 5s. net.*

Lorimer (George Horace). LETTERS FROM A SELF-MADE MERCHANT TO HIS SON. Illustrated. *Eighteenth Edition. Cr. 8vo. 3s. 6d.*
OLD GORGON GRAHAM. Illustrated. *Second Edition. Cr. 8vo. 6s.*

Lorimer (Norma). BY THE WATERS OF EGYPT. Illustrated. *Demy 8vo. 16s. net.*

Lucas (E. V.). THE LIFE OF CHARLES LAMB. Illustrated. *Fifth and Revised Edition in One Volume. Demy 8vo. 7s. 6d. net.*
A WANDERER IN HOLLAND. Illustrated. *Eleventh Edition. Cr. 8vo. 6s.*
A WANDERER IN LONDON. Illustrated. *Ninth Edition. Cr. 8vo. 6s.*
A WANDERER IN PARIS. Illustrated. *Fifth Edition. Cr. 8vo. 6s.*

Methuen and Company Limited

THE OPEN ROAD: A Little Book for Wayfarers. *Seventeenth Edition. Fcp. 8vo. 5s.; India Paper, 7s. 6d.*
THE FRIENDLY TOWN: a Little Book for the Urbane. *Sixth Edition. Fcap. 8vo. 5s.; India Paper, 7s. 6d.*
FIRESIDE AND SUNSHINE. *Sixth Edition. Fcap. 8vo. 5s.*
CHARACTER AND COMEDY. *Sixth Edition. Fcap. 8vo. 5s.*
THE GENTLEST ART. A Choice of Letters by Entertaining Hands. *Sixth Edition. Fcap 8vo. 5s.*
A SWAN AND HER FRIENDS. Illustrated. *Demy 8vo. 12s. 6d. net.*
HER INFINITE VARIETY: A Feminine Portrait Gallery. *Fifth Edition. Fcap. 8vo. 5s.*
LISTENER'S LURE: An Oblique Narration. *Seventh Edition. Fcap. 8vo. 5s.*
GOOD COMPANY: A Rally of Men. *Second Edition. Fcap. 8vo. 5s.*
ONE DAY AND ANOTHER. *Fourth Edition. Fcap. 8vo. 5s.*
OVER BEMERTON'S: An Easy-Going Chronicle. *Eighth Edition. Fcap. 8vo. 5s.*

M. (R.). THE THOUGHTS OF LUCIA HALLIDAY. With some of her Letters. Edited by R. M. *Fcap. 8vo. 2s. 6d. net.*

Macaulay (Lord). CRITICAL AND HISTORICAL ESSAYS. Edited by F. C. Montague, M.A. *Three Volumes. Cr. 8vo. 18s.*

McCabe (Joseph) (formerly Very Rev. F. Antony, O.S.F.). THE DECAY OF THE CHURCH OF ROME. *Second Edition. Demy 8vo. 7s. 6d. net.*

McCullagh (Francis). The Fall of Abd-ul-Hamid. Illustrated. *Demy 8vo. 10s. 6d. net.*

MacCunn (Florence A.). MARY STUART. Illustrated. *New and Cheaper Edition. Large Cr. 8vo. 6s.*

McDougall (William), M.A. (Oxon., M.B. (Cantab.). AN INTRODUCTION TO SOCIAL PSYCHOLOGY. *Third Edition. Cr. 8vo. 5s. net.*

'Mdlle. Mori'(Author of). ST. CATHERINE OF SIENA AND HER TIMES. Illustrated. *Second Edition. Demy 8vo. 7s. 6d. net.*

Maeterlinck (Maurice). THE BLUE BIRD: A Fairy Play in Five Acts. Translated by Alexander Teixeira de Mattos. *Thirteenth Edition. Fcap. 8vo. Deckle Edges. 3s. 6d. net. Also Fcap. 8vo. Paper covers, 1s. net.*

Mahaffy (J. P.), Litt.D. A HISTORY OF THE EGYPT OF THE PTOLEMIES. Illustrated. *Cr. 8vo. 6s.*

Maitland (F. W.), M.A., LL.D. ROMAN CANON LAW IN THE CHURCH OF ENGLAND. *Royal 8vo. 7s. 6d.*

Marett (R. R.), M.A., Fellow and Tutor of Exeter College, Oxford. THE THRESHOLD OF RELIGION. *Cr. 8vo. 3s. 6d. net.*

Marriott (Charles). A SPANISH HOLIDAY. Illustrated. *Demy 8vo. 7s. 6d. net.*

Marriott (J. A. R.), M.A. THE LIFE AND TIMES OF LORD FALKLAND. Illustrated. *Second Edition. Demy 8vo. 7s. 6d. net.*

Masefield (John). SEA LIFE IN NELSON'S TIME. Illustrated. *Cr. 8vo. 3s. 6d. net.*
A SAILOR'S GARLAND. Selected and Edited. *Second Edition. Cr. 8vo. 3s. 6d. net.*
AN ENGLISH PROSE MISCELLANY. Selected and Edited. *Cr. 8vo. 6s.*

Masterman (C. F. G.), M.A., M.P., TENNYSON AS A RELIGIOUS TEACHER. *Cr. 8vo. 6s.*
THE CONDITION OF ENGLAND. *Fourth Edition. Cr. 8vo. 6s.*

Mayne (Ethel Colburn). ENCHANTERS OF MEN. Illustrated. *Demy 8vo. 10s. 6d. net.*

Meakin (Annette M. B.), Fellow of the Anthropological Institute. WOMAN IN TRANSITION. *Cr. 8vo. 6s.*
GALICIA: The Switzerland of Spain. Illustrated. *Demy 8vo. 12s. 6d. net.*

Medley (D. J.), M.A., Professor of History in the University of Glasgow. ORIGINAL ILLUSTRATIONS OF ENGLISH CONSTITUTIONAL HISTORY, Comprising a Selected Number of the Chief Charters and Statutes. *Cr. 8vo. 7s. 6d. net.*

Methuen (A. M. S.), M.A. THE TRAGEDY OF SOUTH AFRICA. *Cr. 8vo. 2s. net.*
ENGLAND'S RUIN: Discussed in Fourteen Letters to a Protectionist. *Ninth Edition. Cr. 8vo. 3d. net.*

Meynell (Everard). COROT AND HIS FRIENDS. Illustrated. *Demy 8vo. 10s. 6d. net.*

Miles (Eustace), M.A. LIFE AFTER LIFE: or, The Theory of Reincarnation. *Cr. 8vo. 2s. 6d. net.*
THE POWER OF CONCENTRATION: How to Acquire it. *Third Edition. Cr. 8vo. 3s. 6d. net.*

Millais (J. G.). THE LIFE AND LETTERS OF SIR JOHN EVERETT MILLAIS, President of the Royal Academy. Illustrated. *New Edition. Demy 8vo. 7s. 6d. net.*

Milne (J. G.), M.A. A HISTORY OF EGYPT UNDER ROMAN RULE. Illustrated. *Cr. 8vo. 6s.*

GENERAL LITERATURE

Mitton (G. E.). JANE AUSTEN AND HER TIMES. Illustrated. *Second and Cheaper Edition. Large Cr. 8vo. 6s.*

Moffat (Mary M.). QUEEN LOUISA OF PRUSSIA. Illustrated. *Fourth Edition. Cr. 8vo. 6s.*

Money (L. G. Chiozza). RICHES AND POVERTY. *Ninth Edition. Cr. 8vo. 1s. net.* Also *Demy 8vo. 5s. net.*
MONEY'S FISCAL DICTIONARY, 1910. *Demy 8vo. Second Edition. 5s. net.*

Moore (T. Sturge). ART AND LIFE. Illustrated. *Cr. 8vo. 5s. net.*

Moorhouse (E. Hallam). NELSON'S LADY HAMILTON. Illustrated. *Second Edition. Demy 8vo. 7s. 6d. net.*

Morgan (J. H.), M.A. THE HOUSE OF LORDS AND THE CONSTITUTION. With an Introduction by the LORD CHANCELLOR. *Cr. 8vo. 1s. net.*

Morton (A. Anderson). See Brodrick (M.).

Norway (A. H.). NAPLES. PAST AND PRESENT. Illustrated. *Third Edition. Cr. 8vo. 6s.*

Oman (C. W. C.), M.A., Fellow of All Souls', Oxford. A HISTORY OF THE ART OF WAR IN THE MIDDLE AGES. Illustrated. *Demy 8vo. 10s. 6d. net.*
ENGLAND BEFORE THE NORMAN CONQUEST. With Maps. *Second Edition. Demy 8vo. 10s. 6d. net.*

Oxford (M. N.), of Guy's Hospital. A HANDBOOK OF NURSING. *Fifth Edition. Cr. 8vo. 3s. 6d.*

Pakes (W. C. C.). THE SCIENCE OF HYGIENE. Illustrated. *Demy 8vo. 15s.*

Parker (Eric). THE BOOK OF THE ZOO; BY DAY AND NIGHT. Illustrated. *Second Edition. Cr. 8vo. 6s.*

Parsons (Mrs. C.). THE INCOMPARABLE SIDDONS. Illustrated. *Demy 8vo. 12s. 6d. net.*

Patmore (K. A.). THE COURT OF LOUIS XIII. Illustrated. *Third Edition. Demy 8vo. 10s. 6d. net.*

Patterson (A. H.). MAN AND NATURE ON TIDAL WATERS. Illustrated. *Cr. 8vo. 6s.*

Petrie (W. M. Flinders), D.C.L., LL.D., Professor of Egyptology at University College. A HISTORY OF EGYPT. Illustrated. *In Six Volumes. Cr. 8vo. 6s. each.*

VOL. I. FROM THE EARLIEST KINGS TO XVITH DYNASTY. *Sixth Edition.*
VOL. II. THE XVIITH AND XVIIITH DYNASTIES. *Fourth Edition.*
VOL. III. XIXTH TO XXXTH DYNASTIES.
VOL. IV. EGYPT UNDER THE PTOLEMAIC DYNASTY. J. P. MAHAFFY, Litt.D.
VOL. V. EGYPT UNDER ROMAN RULE. J. G. MILNE, M.A.
VOL. VI. EGYPT IN THE MIDDLE AGES. STANLEY LANE-POOLE, M.A.
RELIGION AND CONSCIENCE IN ANCIENT EGYPT. Lectures delivered at University College, London. Illustrated. *Cr. 8vo. 2s. 6d.*
SYRIA AND EGYPT, FROM THE TELL EL AMARNA LETTERS. *Cr. 8vo. 2s. 6d.*
EGYPTIAN TALES. Translated from the Papyri. First Series, IVth to XIIth Dynasty. Edited by W. M. FLINDERS PETRIE. Illustrated. *Second Edition. Cr. 8vo. 3s. 6d.*
EGYPTIAN TALES. Translated from the Papyri. Second Series, XVIIIth to XIXth Dynasty. Illustrated. *Cr. 8vo. 3s. 6d.*
EGYPTIAN DECORATIVE ART. A Course of Lectures delivered at the Royal Institution. Illustrated. *Cr. 8vo. 3s. 6d.*

Phelps (Ruth S.). SKIES ITALIAN: A LITTLE BREVIARY FOR TRAVELLERS IN ITALY. *Fcap. 8vo. 5s. net.*

Phythian (J. Ernest). TREES IN NATURE, MYTH, AND ART. Illustrated. *Cr. 8vo. 6s.*

Podmore (Frank). MODERN SPIRITUALISM. *Two Volumes. Demy 8vo. 21s. net.*
MESMERISM AND CHRISTIAN SCIENCE: A Short History of Mental Healing. *Second Edition. Demy 8vo. 10s. 6d. net.*

Pollard (Alfred W.). SHAKESPEARE FOLIOS AND QUARTOS. A Study in the Bibliography of Shakespeare's Plays, 1594-1685. Illustrated. *Folio. 21s. net.*

Powell (Arthur E.). FOOD AND HEALTH. *Cr. 8vo. 3s. 6d. net.*

Power (J. O'Connor). THE MAKING OF AN ORATOR. *Cr. 8vo. 6s.*

Price (L. L.), M.A., Fellow of Oriel College, Oxon. A HISTORY OF ENGLISH POLITICAL ECONOMY FROM ADAM SMITH TO ARNOLD TOYNBEE. *Sixth Edition. Cr. 8vo. 2s. 6d.*

Pullen-Burry (B.). IN A GERMAN COLONY; or, FOUR WEEKS IN NEW BRITAIN. Illustrated. *Cr. 8vo. 5s. net.*

Pycraft (W. P.). BIRD LIFE. Illustrated. *Demy 8vo. 10s. 6d. net.*

Ragg (Lonsdale), B.D. Oxon. DANTE AND HIS ITALY. Illustrated. *Demy 8vo. 12s. 6d. net.*

*****Rappoport (Angelo S.).** HOME LIFE IN RUSSIA. Illustrated. *Demy 8vo. 10s. 6d. net.*

Raven-Hill (L.). See Llewellyn (Owen).

Rawlings (Gertrude). COINS AND HOW TO KNOW THEM. Illustrated. *Second Edition. Cr. 8vo. 5s. net.*

Rea (Lillian). THE LIFE AND TIMES OF MARIE MADELEINE COUNTESS OF LA FAYETTE. Illustrated. *Demy 8vo. 10s. 6d. net.*

Read (C. Stanford), M.B. (Lond.), M.R.C.S., L.R.C.P. FADS AND FEEDING. *Cr. 8vo. 2s. 6d. net.*

Rees (J. D.), C.I.E., M.P. THE REAL INDIA. *Second Edition. Demy 8vo. 10s. 6d. net.*

Reich (Emil), Doctor Juris. WOMAN THROUGH THE AGES. Illustrated. *Two Volumes. Demy 8vo. 21s. net.*

Reid (Archdall), M.B. THE LAWS OF HEREDITY. *Second Edition. Demy 8vo. 21s. net.*

Richmond (Wilfrid), Chaplain of Lincoln's Inn. THE CREED IN THE EPISTLES. *Cr. 8vo. 2s. 6d. net.*

Roberts (M. E.). See Channer (C.C.).

Robertson (A.), D.D., Lord Bishop of Exeter. REGNUM DEI. (The Bampton Lectures of 1901.) *A New and Cheaper Edition. Demy 8vo. 7s. 6d. net.*

Robertson (C. Grant), M.A., Fellow of All Souls' College, Oxford. SELECT STATUTES, CASES, AND CONSTITUTIONAL DOCUMENTS, 1660-1832. *Demy 8vo. 10s. 6d. net.*

Robertson (Sir G. S.), K.C.S.I. CHITRAL: THE STORY OF A MINOR SIEGE. Illustrated. *Third Edition. Demy 8vo. 10s. 6d. net.*

Roe (Fred). OLD OAK FURNITURE. Illustrated. *Second Edition. Demy 8vo. 10s. 6d. net.*

Royde-Smith (N. G.). THE PILLOW BOOK: A GARNER OF MANY MOODS. Collected. *Second Edition. Cr. 8vo. 4s. 6d. net.*
POETS OF OUR DAY. Selected, with an Introduction. *Fcap. 8vo. 5s.*

Rumbold (The Right Hon. Sir Horace), Bart., G. C. B., G. C. M. G. THE AUSTRIAN COURT IN THE NINETEENTH CENTURY. Illustrated. *Second Edition. Demy 8vo. 18s. net.*

Russell (W. Clark). THE LIFE OF ADMIRAL LORD COLLINGWOOD. Illustrated. *Fourth Edition. Cr. 8vo. 6s.*

St. Francis of Assisi. THE LITTLE FLOWERS OF THE GLORIOUS MESSER, AND OF HIS FRIARS. Done into English, with Notes by WILLIAM HEYWOOD. Illustrated. *Demy 8vo. 5s. net.*

'Saki' (H. Munro). REGINALD. *Second Edition. Fcap. 8vo. 2s. 6d. net.*
REGINALD IN RUSSIA. *Fcap. 8vo. 2s. 6d. net.*

Sanders (Lloyd). THE HOLLAND HOUSE CIRCLE. Illustrated. *Second Edition. Demy 8vo. 12s. 6d. net.*

*****Scott (Ernest).** TERRE NAPOLÉON, AND THE EXPEDITION OF DISCOVERY DESPATCHED TO AUSTRALIA BY ORDER OF BONAPARTE, 1800-1804. Illustrated. *Demy 8vo. 10s. 6d. net.*

Sélincourt (Hugh de). GREAT RALEGH. Illustrated. *Demy 8vo. 10s. 6d. net.*

Selous (Edmund). TOMMY SMITH'S ANIMALS. Illustrated. *Eleventh Edition. Fcap. 8vo. 2s. 6d.*
TOMMY SMITH'S OTHER ANIMALS. Illustrated. *Fifth Edition. Fcap. 8vo. 2s. 6d.*

*****Shafer (Sara A.).** A WHITE PAPER GARDEN. Illustrated. *Demy 8vo. 7s. 6d. net.*

Shakespeare (William).
THE FOUR FOLIOS, 1623; 1632; 1664; 1685. Each £4 4s. net, or a complete set, £12 12s. net.
Folios 2, 3 and 4 are ready.
THE POEMS OF WILLIAM SHAKESPEARE. With an Introduction and Notes by GEORGE WYNDHAM. *Demy 8vo. Buckram, gilt top. 10s. 6d.*

Sharp (A.). VICTORIAN POETS. *Cr. 8vo. 2s. 6d.*

Sidgwick (Mrs. Alfred). HOME LIFE IN GERMANY. Illustrated. *Second Edition. Demy 8vo. 10s. 6d. net.*

Sime (John). See Little Books on Art.

Sladen (Douglas). SICILY: The New Winter Resort. Illustrated. *Second Edition. Cr. 8vo. 5s. net.*

Smith (Adam). THE WEALTH OF NATIONS. Edited with an Introduction and numerous Notes by EDWIN CANNAN, M.A. *Two Volumes. Demy 8vo. 21s. net.*

Smith (Sophia S.). DEAN SWIFT. Illustrated. *Demy 8vo. 10s. 6d. net.*

Snell (F. J.). A BOOK OF EXMOOR. Illustrated. *Cr. 8vo. 6s.*

'Stancliffe' GOLF DO'S AND DON'TS. *Second Edition. Fcap. 8vo. 1s.*

General Literature

Stead (Francis H.), M.A. HOW OLD AGE PENSIONS BEGAN TO BE. Illustrated. *Demy 8vo. 2s. 6d. net.*

Stevenson (R. L.). THE LETTERS OF ROBERT LOUIS STEVENSON TO HIS FAMILY AND FRIENDS. Selected and Edited by SIDNEY COLVIN. *Ninth Edition. Two Volumes. Cr. 8vo. 12s.*
VAILIMA LETTERS. With an Etched Portrait by WILLIAM STRANG. *Eighth Edition. Cr. 8vo. Buckram. 6s.*
THE LIFE OF R. L. STEVENSON. See Balfour (G.).

Stevenson (M. I.). FROM SARANAC TO THE MARQUESAS. Being Letters written by Mrs. M. I. STEVENSON during 1887-88. *Cr. 8vo. 6s. net.*
LETTERS FROM SAMOA, 1891-95. Edited and arranged by M. C. BALFOUR. Illustrated. *Second Edition. Cr. 8vo. 6s. net.*

Storr (Vernon F.), M.A., Canon of Winchester. DEVELOPMENT AND DIVINE PURPOSE. *Cr. 8vo. 5s. net.*

Streatfeild (R. A.). MODERN MUSIC AND MUSICIANS. Illustrated. *Second Edition. Demy 8vo. 7s. 6d. net.*

Swanton (E. W.). FUNGI AND HOW TO KNOW THEM. Illustrated. *Cr. 8vo. 6s. net.*

*Sykes (Ella C.). PERSIA AND ITS PEOPLE. Illustrated. *Demy 8vo. 10s. 6d. net.*

Symes (J. E.). M.A. THE FRENCH REVOLUTION. *Second Edition. Cr. 8vo. 2s. 6d.*

Tabor (Margaret E.). THE SAINTS IN ART. Illustrated. *Fcap. 8vo. 3s. 6d. net.*

Taylor (A. E.). THE ELEMENTS OF METAPHYSICS. *Second Edition. Demy 8vo. 10s. 6d. net.*

Taylor (John W.). THE COMING OF THE SAINTS. Illustrated. *Demy 8vo. 7s. 6d. net.*

Thibaudeau (A. C.). BONAPARTE AND THE CONSULATE. Translated and Edited by G. K. FORTESCUE, LL.D. Illustrated. *Demy 8vo. 10s. 6d. net.*

Thompson (Francis). SELECTED POEMS OF FRANCIS THOMPSON. With a Biographical Note by WILFRID MEYNELL. With a Portrait in Photogravure. *Second Edition. Fcap. 8vo. 5s. net.*

Tileston (Mary W.). DAILY STRENGTH FOR DAILY NEEDS. *Seventeenth Edition. Medium 16mo. 2s. 6d. net.* Also an edition in superior binding, 6s.

Toynbee (Paget). M.A., D. Litt. DANTE IN ENGLISH LITERATURE: FROM

CHAUCER TO CARY. *Two Volumes. Demy 8vo. 21s. net.*
See also Oxford Biographies.

Tozer (Basil). THE HORSE IN HISTORY. Illustrated. *Cr. 8vo. 6s.*

Trench (Herbert). DEIRDRE WEDDED, AND OTHER POEMS. *Second and Revised Edition. Large Post 8vo. 6s.*
NEW POEMS. *Second Edition. Large Post 8vo. 6s.*
APOLLO AND THE SEAMAN. *Large Post 8vo. Paper, 1s. 6d. net; cloth, 2s. 6d. net.*

Trevelyan (G. M.), Fellow of Trinity College, Cambridge. ENGLAND UNDER THE STUARTS. With Maps and Plans. *Fourth Edition. Demy 8vo. 10s. 6d. net.*

Triggs (Inigo H.), A.R.I.B.A. TOWN PLANNING: PAST, PRESENT, AND POSSIBLE. Illustrated. *Second Edition. Wide Royal 8vo. 15s. net.*

Vaughan (Herbert M.), B.A. (OXON), F.S.A. THE LAST OF THE ROYAL STUARTS, HENRY STUART, CARDINAL, DUKE OF YORK. Illustrated. *Second Edition. Demy 8vo. 10s. 6d. net.*
THE MEDICI POPES (LEO X. AND CLEMENT VII.). Illustrated. *Demy 8vo. 15s. net.*
THE NAPLES RIVIERA. Illustrated. *Second Edition. Cr. 8vo. 6s.*
*FLORENCE AND HER TREASURES. Illustrated. *Fcap. 8vo. 5s. net.*

Vernon (Hon. W. Warren), M.A. READINGS ON THE INFERNO OF DANTE. With an Introduction by the REV. DR. MOORE. *Two Volumes. Second Edition. Cr. 8vo. 15s. net.*
READINGS ON THE PURGATORIO OF DANTE. With an Introduction by the late DEAN CHURCH. *Two Volumes. Third Edition. Cr. 8vo. 15s. net.*
READINGS ON THE PARADISO OF DANTE. With an Introduction by the BISHOP OF RIPON. *Two Volumes. Second Edition. Cr. 8vo. 15s. net.*

Vincent (J. E.). THROUGH EAST ANGLIA IN A MOTOR CAR. Illustrated. *Cr. 8vo. 6s.*

Waddell (Col. L. A.), LL.D., C.B. LHASA AND ITS MYSTERIES. With a Record of the Expedition of 1903-1904. Illustrated. *Third and Cheaper Edition. Medium 8vo. 7s. 6d. net.*

Wagner (Richard). RICHARD WAGNER'S MUSIC DRAMAS: Interpretations, embodying Wagner's own explanations. By ALICE LEIGHTON CLEATHER and BASIL CRUMP. *In Three Volumes. Fcap. 8vo. 2s. 6d. each.*
VOL. I.—THE RING OF THE NIBELUNG. *Third Edition.*

14 Methuen and Company Limited

Vol. II.—Parsifal, Lohengrin, and The Holy Grail.
Vol. III.—Tristan and Isolde.

Waineman (Paul). A SUMMER TOUR IN FINLAND. Illustrated. *Demy 8vo.* 10s. 6d. net.

Walkley (A. B.). DRAMA AND LIFE. *Cr. 8vo.* 6s.

Waterhouse (Elizabeth). WITH THE SIMPLE-HEARTED: Little Homilies to Women in Country Places. *Second Edition. Small Pott 8vo.* 2s. net.
COMPANIONS OF THE WAY. Being Selections for Morning and Evening Reading. Chosen and arranged by Elizabeth Waterhouse. *Large Cr. 8vo.* 5s. net.
THOUGHTS OF A TERTIARY. *Second Edition. Small Pott 8vo.* 1s. net.

Watt (Francis). See Henderson (T. F.).

Weigall (Arthur E. P.). A GUIDE TO THE ANTIQUITIES OF UPPER EGYPT: From Abydos to the Sudan Frontier. Illustrated. *Cr. 8vo.* 7s. 6d. net.

Welch (Catharine). THE LITTLE DAUPHIN. Illustrated. *Cr. 8vo.* 6s.

Wells (J.), M.A., Fellow and Tutor of Wadham College. OXFORD AND OXFORD LIFE. *Third Edition. Cr. 8vo.* 3s. 6d.
A SHORT HISTORY OF ROME. *Tenth Edition.* With 3 Maps. *Cr. 8vo.* 3s. 6d.

Westell (W. Percival). THE YOUNG NATURALIST. Illustrated. *Cr. 8vo.* 6s.

Westell (W. Percival), F.L.S., M.B.O.U., and **Cooper (C. S.),** F.R.H.S. THE YOUNG BOTANIST. Illustrated. *Cr. 8vo.* 3s. 6d. net.

*****Wheeler (Ethel R.).** FAMOUS BLUE STOCKINGS. Illustrated. *Demy 8vo.* 10s. 6d. net.

Whibley (C.). See Henley (W. E.).

White (George F.), Lieut.-Col. A CENTURY OF SPAIN AND PORTUGAL, 1788-1898. *Demy 8vo.* 12s. 6d. net.

Whitley (Miss). See Dilke (Lady).

Wilde (Oscar). DE PROFUNDIS. *Twelfth Edition. Cr. 8vo.* 5s. net.

THE WORKS OF OSCAR WILDE. *In Twelve Volumes. Fcap. 8vo.* 5s. net each volume.
I. Lord Arthur Savile's Crime and the Portrait of Mr. W. H. II. The Duchess of Padua. III. Poems. IV. Lady Windermere's Fan. V. A Woman of No Importance. VI. An Ideal Husband. VII. The Importance of being Earnest. VIII. A House of Pomegranates. IX. Intentions. X. De Profundis and Prison Letters. XI. Essays. XII. Salomé, A Florentine Tragedy, and La Sainte Courtisane.

Williams (H. Noel). THE WOMEN BONAPARTES. The Mother and three Sisters of Napoleon. Illustrated. *In Two Volumes. Demy 8vo.* 24s. net.
A ROSE OF SAVOY: Marie Adélaïde of Savoy, Duchesse de Bourgogne, Mother of Louis XV. Illustrated. *Second Edition. Demy 8vo.* 15s. net.
*THE FASCINATING DUC DE RICHELIEU: Louis François Armand du Plessis, Maréchal Duc de Richelieu. Illustrated. *Demy 8vo.* 15s. net.

Wood (Sir Evelyn), F.M., V.C., G.C.B., G.C.M.G. FROM MIDSHIPMAN TO FIELD-MARSHAL. Illustrated. *Fifth and Cheaper Edition. Demy 8vo.* 7s. 6d. net.
THE REVOLT IN HINDUSTAN. 1857-59. Illustrated. *Second Edition. Cr. 8vo.* 6s.

Wood (W. Birkbeck), M.A., late Scholar of Worcester College, Oxford, and **Edmonds (Major J. E.),** R.E., D.A.Q.-M.G. A HISTORY OF THE CIVIL WAR IN THE UNITED STATES. With an Introduction by H. Spenser Wilkinson. With 24 Maps and Plans. *Second Edition. Demy 8vo.* 12s. 6d. net.

Wordsworth (W.). THE POEMS. With an Introduction and Notes by Nowell C. Smith, late Fellow of New College, Oxford. *In Three Volumes. Demy 8vo.* 15s. net.
POEMS BY WILLIAM WORDSWORTH. Selected with an Introduction by Stopford A. Brooke. Illustrated. *Cr. 8vo.* 7s. 6d. net.

Wyatt (Kate M.). See Gloag (M. R.).

Wyllie (M. A.). NORWAY AND ITS FJORDS. Illustrated. *Second Edition. Cr. 8vo.* 6s.

Yeats (W. B.). A BOOK OF IRISH VERSE. *Revised and Enlarged Edition. Cr. 8vo.* 3s. 6d.

Young (Filson). See The Complete Series.

GENERAL LITERATURE 15

PART II.—A SELECTION OF SERIES.

Ancient Cities.
General Editor, B. C. A. WINDLE, D.Sc., F.R.S.

Cr. 8vo. 4s. 6d. net.

With Illustrations by E. H. NEW, and other Artists.

BRISTOL. By Alfred Harvey, M.B.
CANTERBURY. By J. C. Cox, LL.D., F.S.A.
CHESTER. By B. C. A. Windle, D.Sc., F.R.S.
DUBLIN. By S. A. O. Fitzpatrick.

EDINBURGH. By M. G. Williamson, M.A.
LINCOLN. By E. Mansel Sympson, M.A.
SHREWSBURY. By T. Auden, M.A., F.S.A.
WELLS and GLASTONBURY. By T. S. Holmes.

The Antiquary's Books.
General Editor, J. CHARLES COX, LL.D., F.S.A.

Demy 8vo. 7s. 6d. net.

With Numerous Illustrations.

ARCHÆOLOGY AND FALSE ANTIQUITIES. By R. Munro.
BELLS OF ENGLAND, THE. By Canon J. J. Raven. *Second Edition.*
BRASSES OF ENGLAND, THE. By Herbert W. Macklin. *Second Edition.*
CELTIC ART IN PAGAN AND CHRISTIAN TIMES. By J. Romilly Allen.
DOMESDAY INQUEST, THE. By Adolphus Ballard.
ENGLISH CHURCH FURNITURE. By J. C. Cox and A. Harvey. *Second Edition.*
ENGLISH COSTUME. From Prehistoric Times to the End of the Eighteenth Century. By George Clinch.
ENGLISH MONASTIC LIFE. By the Right Rev. Abbot Gasquet. *Fourth Edition.*
ENGLISH SEALS. By J. Harvey Bloom.
FOLK-LORE AS AN HISTORICAL SCIENCE. By G. L. Gomme.

GILDS AND COMPANIES OF LONDON, THE. By George Unwin.
MANOR AND MANORIAL RECORDS, THE. By Nathaniel J. Hone.
MEDIÆVAL HOSPITALS OF ENGLAND, THE. By Rotha Mary Clay.
OLD SERVICE BOOKS OF THE ENGLISH CHURCH. By Christopher Wordsworth, M.A., and Henry Littlehales.
PARISH LIFE IN MEDIÆVAL ENGLAND. By the Right Rev. Abbot Gasquet. *Second Edition.*
*PARISH REGISTERS OF ENGLAND, THE. By J. C. Cox.
REMAINS OF THE PREHISTORIC AGE IN ENGLAND. By B. C. A. Windle. *Second Edition.*
ROYAL FORESTS OF ENGLAND, THE. By J. C. Cox, LL.D.
SHRINES OF BRITISH SAINTS. By J. C. Wall.

The Arden Shakespeare.

Demy 8vo. 2s. 6d. net each volume.

An edition of Shakespeare in single Plays. Edited with a full Introduction, Textual Notes, and a Commentary at the foot of the page.

ALL'S WELL THAT ENDS WELL.
ANTONY AND CLEOPATRA.
CYMBELINE.
COMEDY OF ERRORS, THE.
HAMLET. *Second Edition.*
JULIUS CÆSAR.
KING HENRY V.
KING HENRY VI. PT. I.
KING HENRY VI. PT. II.
KING HENRY VI. PT. III.
KING LEAR.
KING RICHARD III.
LIFE AND DEATH OF KING JOHN, THE.
LOVE'S LABOUR'S LOST.
MACBETH.

MEASURE FOR MEASURE.
MERCHANT OF VENICE, THE.
MERRY WIVES OF WINDSOR, THE.
MIDSUMMER NIGHT'S DREAM, A.
OTHELLO.
PERICLES.
ROMEO AND JULIET.
TAMING OF THE SHREW, THE.
TEMPEST, THE.
TIMON OF ATHENS.
TITUS ANDRONICUS.
TROILUS AND CRESSIDA.
TWO GENTLEMEN OF VERONA, THE.
TWELFTH NIGHT.

Classics of Art.

Edited by Dr. J. H. W. LAING.
With numerous Illustrations. Wide Royal 8vo. Gilt top.

THE ART OF THE GREEKS. By H. B. Walters. 12s. 6d. net.
FLORENTINE SCULPTORS OF THE RENAISSANCE. Wilhelm Bode, Ph.D. Translated by Jessie Haynes. 12s. 6d. net.
*GEORGE ROMNEY. By Arthur B. Chamberlain. 12s. 6d. net.
GHIRLANDAIO. Gerald S. Davies. *Second Edition.* 10s. 6d.

MICHELANGELO. By Gerald S. Davies. 12s. 6d. net.
RUBENS. By Edward Dillon, M.A. 25s. net.
RAPHAEL. By A. P. Oppé. 12s. 6d. net.
*TITIAN. By Charles Ricketts. 12s. 6d. net.
*TURNER'S SKETCHES AND DRAWINGS. By A. J. Finberg. 12s. 6d. net.
VELAZQUEZ. By A. de Beruete. 10s. 6d. net.

The "Complete" Series.
Fully Illustrated. Demy 8vo.

THE COMPLETE COOK. By Lilian Whitling. 7s. 6d. net.
THE COMPLETE CRICKETER. By Albert E. Knight. 7s. 6d. net.
THE COMPLETE FOXHUNTER. By Charles Richardson. 12s. 6d. net. *Second Edition.*
THE COMPLETE GOLFER. By Harry Vardon. 10s. 6d. net. *Tenth Edition.*
THE COMPLETE HOCKEY-PLAYER. By Eustace E. White. 5s. net. *Second Edition.*
THE COMPLETE LAWN TENNIS PLAYER. By A. Wallace Myers. 10s. 6d. net. *Second Edition.*

THE COMPLETE MOTORIST. By Filson Young. 12s. 6d. net. *New Edition (Seventh).*
THE COMPLETE MOUNTAINEER. By G. D. Abraham. 15s. net. *Second Edition.*
THE COMPLETE OARSMAN. By R. C. Lehmann, M.P. 10s. 6d. net.
THE COMPLETE PHOTOGRAPHER. By R. Child Bayley. 10s. 6d. net. *Fourth Edition.*
THE COMPLETE RUGBY FOOTBALLER, ON THE NEW ZEALAND SYSTEM. By D. Gallaher and W. J. Stead. 10s. 6d. net. *Second Edition.*
THE COMPLETE SHOT. By G. T. Teasdale Buckell. 12s. 6d. net. *Third Edition.*

The Connoisseur's Library.
With numerous Illustrations. Wide Royal 8vo. Gilt top. 25s. net.

ENGLISH FURNITURE. By F. S. Robinson. *Second Edition.*
ENGLISH COLOURED BOOKS. By Martin Hardie.
EUROPEAN ENAMELS. By Henry H. Cunynghame, C.B.
GLASS. By Edward Dillon.
GOLDSMITHS' AND SILVERSMITHS' WORK. By Nelson Dawson. *Second Edition.*

*ILLUMINATED MANUSCRIPTS. By J. A. Herbert.
IVORIES. By A. Maskell.
JEWELLERY. By H. Clifford Smith. *Second Edition.*
MEZZOTINTS. By Cyril Davenport.
MINIATURES. By Dudley Heath.
PORCELAIN. By Edward Dillon.
SEALS. By Walter de Gray Birch.

GENERAL LITERATURE 17

Handbooks of English Church History.
Edited by J. H. BURN, B.D. *Crown 8vo. 2s. 6d. net.*

THE FOUNDATIONS OF THE ENGLISH CHURCH. By J. H. Maude.
THE SAXON CHURCH AND THE NORMAN CONQUEST. By C. T. Cruttwell.
THE MEDIÆVAL CHURCH AND THE PAPACY. By A. C. Jennings.

THE REFORMATION PERIOD. By Henry Gee.
THE STRUGGLE WITH PURITANISM. By Bruce Blaxland.
THE CHURCH OF ENGLAND IN THE EIGHTEENTH CENTURY. By Alfred Plummer.

The Illustrated Pocket Library of Plain and Coloured Books.
Fcap. 8vo. 3s. 6d. net each volume.

WITH COLOURED ILLUSTRATIONS.

OLD COLOURED BOOKS. By George Paston. 2s. net.
THE LIFE AND DEATH OF JOHN MYTTON, ESQ. By Nimrod. *Fifth Edition.*
THE LIFE OF A SPORTSMAN. By Nimrod.
HANDLEY CROSS. By R. S. Surtees. *Third Edition.*
MR. SPONGE'S SPORTING TOUR. By R. S. Surtees.
JORROCKS' JAUNTS AND JOLLITIES. By R. S. Surtees. *Third Edition.*
ASK MAMMA. By R. S. Surtees.
THE ANALYSIS OF THE HUNTING FIELD. By R. S. Surtees.
THE TOUR OF DR. SYNTAX IN SEARCH OF THE PICTURESQUE. By William Combe.
THE TOUR OF DR. SYNTAX IN SEARCH OF CONSOLATION. By William Combe.
THE THIRD TOUR OF DR. SYNTAX IN SEARCH OF A WIFE. By William Combe.
THE HISTORY OF JOHNNY QUAE GENUS. By the Author of 'The Three Tours.'
THE ENGLISH DANCE OF DEATH, from the Designs of T. Rowlandson, with Metrical Illustrations by the Author of 'Doctor Syntax.' *Two Volumes.*

THE DANCE OF LIFE: A Poem. By the Author of 'Dr. Syntax.'
LIFE IN LONDON. By Pierce Egan.
REAL LIFE IN LONDON. By an Amateur (Pierce Egan). *Two Volumes.*
THE LIFE OF AN ACTOR. By Pierce Egan.
THE VICAR OF WAKEFIELD. By Oliver Goldsmith.
THE MILITARY ADVENTURES OF JOHNNY NEWCOME. By an Officer.
THE NATIONAL SPORTS OF GREAT BRITAIN. With Descriptions and 50 Coloured Plates by Henry Alken.
THE ADVENTURES OF A POST CAPTAIN. By a Naval Officer.
GAMONIA. By Lawrence Rawstone, Esq.
AN ACADEMY FOR GROWN HORSEMEN. By Geoffrey Gambado, Esq.
REAL LIFE IN IRELAND. By a Real Paddy.
THE ADVENTURES OF JOHNNY NEWCOME IN THE NAVY. By Alfred Burton.
THE OLD ENGLISH SQUIRE. By John Careless, Esq.
THE ENGLISH SPY. By Bernard Blackmantle. *Two Volumes. 7s. net.*

WITH PLAIN ILLUSTRATIONS.

THE GRAVE: A Poem. By Robert Blair.
ILLUSTRATIONS OF THE BOOK OF JOB. Invented and engraved by William Blake.
WINDSOR CASTLE. By W. Harrison Ainsworth.
THE TOWER OF LONDON. By W. Harrison Ainsworth.

FRANK FAIRLEGH. By F. E. Smedley.
HANDY ANDY. By Samuel Lover.
THE COMPLEAT ANGLER. By Izaak Walton and Charles Cotton.
THE PICKWICK PAPERS. By Charles Dickens.

Leaders of Religion.

Edited by H. C. BEECHING, M.A., Canon of Westminster. *With Portraits.*

Crown 8vo. 2s. net.

CARDINAL NEWMAN. By R. H. Hutton.
JOHN WESLEY. By J. H. Overton, M.A.
BISHOP WILBERFORCE. By G. W. Daniell, M.A.
CARDINAL MANNING. By A. W. Hutton, M.A.
CHARLES SIMEON. By H. C. G. Moule, D.D.
JOHN KNOX. By F. MacCunn. *Second Edition.*
JOHN HOWE. By R. F. Horton, D.D.
THOMAS KEN. By F. A. Clarke, M.A.
GEORGE FOX, THE QUAKER. By T. Hodgkin, D.C.L. *Third Edition.*

JOHN KEBLE. By Walter Lock, D.D.
THOMAS CHALMERS. By Mrs. Oliphant.
LANCELOT ANDREWES. By R. L. Ottley, D.D. *Second Edition.*
AUGUSTINE OF CANTERBURY. By E. L. Cutts, D.D.
WILLIAM LAUD. By W. H. Hutton, M.A. *Third Edition.*
JOHN DONNE. By Augustus Jessop, D.D.
THOMAS CRANMER. By A. J. Mason, D.D.
BISHOP LATIMER. By R. M. Carlyle and A. J. Carlyle, M.A.
BISHOP BUTLER. By W. A. Spooner, M.A.

The Library of Devotion.

With Introductions and (where necessary) Notes.

Small Pott 8vo, gilt top, cloth, 2s. ; leather, 2s. 6d. net.

THE CONFESSIONS OF ST. AUGUSTINE. *Seventh Edition.*
THE IMITATION OF CHRIST. *Sixth Edition.*
THE CHRISTIAN YEAR. *Fourth Edition.*
LYRA INNOCENTIUM. *Second Edition.*
THE TEMPLE. *Second Edition.*
A BOOK OF DEVOTIONS. *Second Edition.*
A SERIOUS CALL TO A DEVOUT AND HOLY LIFE. *Fourth Edition.*
A GUIDE TO ETERNITY.
THE INNER WAY. *Second Edition.*
ON THE LOVE OF GOD.
THE PSALMS OF DAVID.
LYRA APOSTOLICA.
THE SONG OF SONGS.
THE THOUGHTS OF PASCAL. *Second Edition.*
A MANUAL OF CONSOLATION FROM THE SAINTS AND FATHERS.
DEVOTIONS FROM THE APOCRYPHA.
THE SPIRITUAL COMBAT.
THE DEVOTIONS OF ST. ANSELM.
BISHOP WILSON'S SACRA PRIVATA.

GRACE ABOUNDING TO THE CHIEF OF SINNERS.
LYRA SACRA: A Book of Sacred Verse. *Second Edition.*
A DAY BOOK FROM THE SAINTS AND FATHERS.
A LITTLE BOOK OF HEAVENLY WISDOM. A Selection from the English Mystics.
LIGHT, LIFE, and LOVE. A Selection from the German Mystics.
AN INTRODUCTION TO THE DEVOUT LIFE.
THE LITTLE FLOWERS OF THE GLORIOUS MESSER ST. FRANCIS AND OF HIS FRIARS.
DEATH AND IMMORTALITY.
THE SPIRITUAL GUIDE.
DEVOTIONS FOR EVERY DAY IN THE WEEK AND THE GREAT FESTIVALS.
PRECES PRIVATAE.
HORAE MYSTICAE: A Day Book from the Writings of Mystics of Many Nations.

Little Books on Art.

With many Illustrations. Demy 16mo. Gilt top. 2s. 6d. net.

Each volume consists of about 200 pages, and contains from 30 to 40 Illustrations, including a Frontispiece in Photogravure.

ALBRECHT DÜRER. J. Allen.
ARTS OF JAPAN, THE. E. Dillon.
BOOKPLATES. E. Almack.
BOTTICELLI. Mary L. Bloomer.
BURNE-JONES. F. de Lisle.
*CHRISTIAN SYMBOLISM. Mrs. H. Jenner.
CHRIST IN ART. Mrs. H. Jenner.
CLAUDE. E. Dillon.
CONSTABLE. H. W. Tompkins.
COROT. A. Pollard and E. Birnstingl.
ENAMELS. Mrs. N. Dawson.
FREDERIC LEIGHTON. A. Corkran.
GEORGE ROMNEY. G. Paston.
GREEK ART. H. B. Walters.
GREUZE AND BOUCHER. E. F. Pollard.

HOLBEIN. Mrs. G. Fortescue.
ILLUMINATED MANUSCRIPTS. J. W. Bradley
JEWELLERY. C. Davenport.
JOHN HOPPNER. H. P. K. Skipton.
SIR JOSHUA REYNOLDS. J. Sime.
MILLET. N. Peacock.
MINIATURES. C. Davenport.
OUR LADY IN ART. Mrs. H. Jenner.
RAPHAEL. A. R. Dryhurst. *Second Edition.*
REMBRANDT. Mrs. E. A. Sharp.
TURNER. F. Tyrrell-Gill.
VANDYCK. M. G. Smallwood.
VELASQUEZ. W. Wilberforce and A. R. Gilbert.
WATTS. R. E. D. Sketchley.

The Little Galleries.

Demy 16mo. 2s. 6d. net.

Each volume contains 20 plates in Photogravure, together with a short outline of the life and work of the master to whom the book is devoted.

A LITTLE GALLERY OF REYNOLDS.
A LITTLE GALLERY OF ROMNEY.
A LITTLE GALLERY OF HOPPNER.

A LITTLE GALLERY OF MILLAIS.
A LITTLE GALLERY OF ENGLISH POETS.

The Little Guides.

With many Illustrations by E. H. NEW and other artists, and from photographs.

Small Pott 8vo, gilt top, cloth, 2s. 6d. net; leather, 3s. 6d. net.

The main features of these Guides are (1) a handy and charming form; (2) illustrations from photographs and by well-known artists; (3) good plans and maps; (4) an adequate but compact presentation of everything that is interesting in the natural features, history, archaeology, and architecture of the town or district treated.

CAMBRIDGE AND ITS COLLEGES. A. H. Thompson. *Second Edition.*
ENGLISH LAKES, THE. F. G. Brabant.
ISLE OF WIGHT, THE. G. Clinch.
MALVERN COUNTRY, THE. B. C. A. Windle.
NORTH WALES. A. T. Story.
OXFORD AND ITS COLLEGES. J. Wells. *Ninth Edition.*

SHAKESPEARE'S COUNTRY. B. C. A. Windle. *Third Edition.*
ST. PAUL'S CATHEDRAL. G. Clinch.
WESTMINSTER ABBEY. G. E. Troutbeck. *Second Edition.*

BUCKINGHAMSHIRE. E. S. Roscoe.
CHESHIRE. W. M. Gallichan.

THE LITTLE GUIDES—continued.

CORNWALL. A. L. Salmon.
DERBYSHIRE. J. C. Cox.
DEVON. S. Baring-Gould.
DORSET. F. R. Heath. Second Edition.
ESSEX. J. C. Cox.
HAMPSHIRE. J. C. Cox.
HERTFORDSHIRE. H. W. Tompkins.
KENT. G. Clinch.
KERRY. C. P. Crane.
MIDDLESEX. J. B. Firth.
MONMOUTHSHIRE. G. W. Wade and J. H. Wade.
NORFOLK. W. A. Dutt. Second Edition, Revised.
NORTHAMPTONSHIRE. W. Dry.
*NORTHUMBERLAND. J. E. Morris.
NOTTINGHAMSHIRE. L. Guilford.
OXFORDSHIRE. F. G. Brabant.
SOMERSET. G. W. and J. H. Wade.
*STAFFORDSHIRE. C. E. Masefield.
SUFFOLK. W. A. Dutt.
SURREY. F. A. H. Lambert.
SUSSEX. F. G. Brabant. Second Edition.
*WILTSHIRE. F. R. Heath.
YORKSHIRE, THE EAST RIDING. J. E. Morris.
YORKSHIRE, THE NORTH RIDING. J. E. Morris.

BRITTANY. S. Baring-Gould.
NORMANDY. C. Scudamore.
ROME. C. G. Ellaby.
SICILY. F. H. Jackson.

The Little Library.

With Introductions, Notes, and Photogravure Frontispieces.

Small Pott 8vo. Gilt top. Each Volume, cloth, 1s. 6d. net; leather, 2s. 6d. net.

Anon. A LITTLE BOOK OF ENGLISH LYRICS. *Second Edition.*

Austen (Jane). PRIDE AND PREJUDICE. *Two Volumes.*
NORTHANGER ABBEY.

Bacon (Francis). THE ESSAYS OF LORD BACON.

Barham (R. H.). THE INGOLDSBY LEGENDS. *Two Volumes.*

Barnet (Mrs. P. A.). A LITTLE BOOK OF ENGLISH PROSE.

Beckford (William). THE HISTORY OF THE CALIPH VATHEK.

Blake (William). SELECTIONS FROM WILLIAM BLAKE.

Borrow (George). LAVENGRO. *Two Volumes.*
THE ROMANY RYE.

Browning (Robert). SELECTIONS FROM THE EARLY POEMS OF ROBERT BROWNING.

Canning (George). SELECTIONS FROM THE ANTI-JACOBIN: with GEORGE CANNING's additional Poems.

Cowley (Abraham). THE ESSAYS OF ABRAHAM COWLEY.

Crabbe (George). SELECTIONS FROM GEORGE CRABBE.

Craik (Mrs.). JOHN HALIFAX, GENTLEMAN. *Two Volumes.*

Crashaw (Richard). THE ENGLISH POEMS OF RICHARD CRASHAW.

Dante (Alighieri). THE INFERNO OF DANTE. Translated by H. F. CARY.
THE PURGATORIO OF DANTE. Translated by H. F. CARY.
THE PARADISO OF DANTE. Translated by H. F. CARY.

Darley (George). SELECTIONS FROM THE POEMS OF GEORGE DARLEY.

Deane (A. C.). A LITTLE BOOK OF LIGHT VERSE.

Dickens (Charles). CHRISTMAS BOOKS. *Two Volumes.*

Ferrier (Susan). MARRIAGE. *Two Volumes.*
THE INHERITANCE. *Two Volumes.*

Gaskell (Mrs.). CRANFORD.

Hawthorne (Nathaniel). THE SCARLET LETTER.

Henderson (T. F.). A LITTLE BOOK OF SCOTTISH VERSE.

Keats (John). POEMS.

Kinglake (A. W.). EOTHEN. *Second Edition.*

Lamb (Charles). ELIA, AND THE LAST ESSAYS OF ELIA.

Locker (F.). LONDON LYRICS.

Longfellow (H. W.). SELECTIONS FROM LONGFELLOW.

Marvell (Andrew). THE POEMS OF ANDREW MARVELL.
Milton (John). THE MINOR POEMS OF JOHN MILTON.
Moir (D. M.). MANSIE WAUCH.
Nichols (J. B. B.). A LITTLE BOOK OF ENGLISH SONNETS.
Rochefoucauld (La). THE MAXIMS OF LA ROCHEFOUCAULD.
Smith (Horace and James). REJECTED ADDRESSES.
Sterne (Laurence). A SENTIMENTAL JOURNEY.
Tennyson (Alfred, Lord). THE EARLY POEMS OF ALFRED, LORD TENNYSON.
IN MEMORIAM.
THE PRINCESS.

MAUD.
Thackeray (W. M.). VANITY FAIR. *Three Volumes.*
PENDENNIS. *Three Volumes.*
ESMOND.
CHRISTMAS BOOKS.
Vaughan (Henry). THE POEMS OF HENRY VAUGHAN.
Walton (Izaak). THE COMPLEAT ANGLER.
Waterhouse (Elizabeth). A LITTLE BOOK OF LIFE AND DEATH. *Thirteenth Edition.*
Wordsworth (W.). SELECTIONS FROM WORDSWORTH.
Wordsworth (W.) and Coleridge (S. T.) LYRICAL BALLADS.

The Little Quarto Shakespeare.

Edited by W. J. CRAIG. With Introductions and Notes.

Pott 16mo. In 40 Volumes. Gilt top. Leather, price 1s. net each volume. Mahogany Revolving Book Case. 10s. net.

Miniature Library.

Gilt top.

EUPHRANOR: A Dialogue on Youth. By Edward FitzGerald. *Demy 32mo. Leather, 2s. net.*
THE LIFE OF EDWARD, LORD HERBERT OF CHERBURY. Written by himself. *Demy 32mo. Leather, 2s. net.*

POLONIUS: or Wise Saws and Modern Instances. By Edward FitzGerald. *Demy 32mo. Leather, 2s. net.*
THE RUBÁIYÁT OF OMAR KHAYYÁM. By Edward FitzGerald. *Fourth Edition. Leather, 1s. net.*

The New Library of Medicine.

Edited by C. W. SALEEBY, M.D., F.R.S.Edin. *Demy 8vo.*

CARE OF THE BODY, THE. By F. Cavanagh. *Second Edition. 7s. 6d. net.*
CHILDREN OF THE NATION, THE. By the Right Hon. Sir John Gorst. *Second Edition. 7s. 6d. net.*
CONTROL OF A SCOURGE, THE: or, How Cancer is Curable. By Chas. P. Childe. *7s. 6d. net.*
DISEASES OF OCCUPATION. By Sir Thomas Oliver. *10s. 6d. net.*
DRINK PROBLEM, THE, in its Medico-Sociological Aspects. Edited by T. N. Kelynack. *7s. 6d. net.*
DRUGS AND THE DRUG HABIT. By H. Sainsbury.

FUNCTIONAL NERVE DISEASES. By A. T. Schofield. *7s. 6d. net.*
HEREDITY, THE LAWS OF. By Archdall Reid. *21s. net.*
HYGIENE OF MIND, THE. By T. S. Clouston. *Fifth Edition. 7s. 6d. net.*
INFANT MORTALITY. By George Newman. *7s. 6d. net.*
PREVENTION OF TUBERCULOSIS (CONSUMPTION), THE. By Arthur Newsholme. *10s. 6d. net.*
AIR AND HEALTH. By Ronald C. Macfie. *7s. 6d. net. Second Edition.*

The New Library of Music.

Edited by ERNEST NEWMAN. *Illustrated. Demy 8vo. 7s. 6d. net.*

HUGO WOLF. By Ernest Newman. Illustrated.

HANDEL. By R. A. Streatfeild. Illustrated. *Second Edition.*

Oxford Biographies.

Illustrated. Fcap. 8vo. Gilt top. Each volume, cloth, 2s. 6d. net; leather, 3s. 6d. net.

DANTE ALIGHIERI. By Paget Toynbee, M.A., D. Litt. *Third Edition.*
GIROLAMO SAVONAROLA. By E. L. S. Horsburgh, M.A. *Second Edition.*
JOHN HOWARD. By E. C. S. Gibson, D.D., Bishop of Gloucester.
ALFRED TENNYSON. By A. C. Benson, M.A. *Second Edition.*
SIR WALTER RALEIGH. By I. A Taylor.
ERASMUS. By E. F. H. Capey.

THE YOUNG PRETENDER. By C. S. Terry.
ROBERT BURNS. By T. F. Henderson.
CHATHAM. By A. S. M'Dowall.
FRANCIS OF ASSISI. By Anna M. Stoddart.
CANNING. By W. Alison Phillips.
BEACONSFIELD. By Walter Sichel.
JOHANN WOLFGANG GOETHE. By H. G. Atkins.
FRANÇOIS FENELON. By Viscount St. Cyres.

Romantic History.

Edited by MARTIN HUME, M.A. *Illustrated. Demy 8vo.*

A series of attractive volumes in which the periods and personalities selected are such as afford romantic human interest, in addition to their historical importance.

THE FIRST GOVERNESS OF THE NETHERLANDS, MARGARET OF AUSTRIA. Eleanor E. Tremayne. 10s. 6d. net.
TWO ENGLISH QUEENS AND PHILIP. Martin Hume, M.A. 15s. net.
THE NINE DAYS' QUEEN. Richard Davey. With a Preface by Martin Hume, M.A. 10s. 6d. net.

Handbooks of Theology.

THE DOCTRINE OF THE INCARNATION. By R. L. Ottley, D.D. *Fourth Edition revised.* Demy 8vo. 12s. 6d.
A HISTORY OF EARLY CHRISTIAN DOCTRINE. By J. F. Bethune-Baker, M.A. Demy 8vo. 10s. 6d.
AN INTRODUCTION TO THE HISTORY OF RELIGION. By F. B. Jevons. M.A. Litt. D. *Fourth Edition.* Demy 8vo. 10s. 6d.

AN INTRODUCTION TO THE HISTORY OF THE CREEDS. By A. E. Burn, D.D. Demy 8vo. 10s. 6d.
THE PHILOSOPHY OF RELIGION IN ENGLAND AND AMERICA. By Alfred Caldecott, D.D. Demy 8vo. 10s. 6d.
THE XXXIX. ARTICLES OF THE CHURCH OF ENGLAND. Edited by E. C. S. Gibson, D.D. *Sixth Edition.* Demy 8vo. 12s. 6d.

FICTION

The Westminster Commentaries.

General Editor, WALTER LOCK, D.D., Warden of Keble College.

Dean Ireland's Professor of Exegesis in the University of Oxford.

THE ACTS OF THE APOSTLES. Edited by R. B. Rackham, M.A. *Demy 8vo. Fourth Edition.* 10s. 6d.

THE FIRST EPISTLE OF PAUL THE APOSTLE TO THE CORINTHIANS. Edited by H. L. Goudge, M.A. *Second Ed. Demy 8vo.* 6s.

THE BOOK OF EXODUS. Edited by A. H. M'Neile, B.D. With a Map and 3 Plans. *Demy 8vo.* 10s. 6d.

THE BOOK OF EZEKIEL. Edited by H. A. Redpath, M.A., D.Litt. *Demy 8vo.* 10s. 6d.

THE BOOK OF GENESIS. Edited with Introduction and Notes by S. R. Driver, D.D. *Eighth Edition. Demy 8vo.* 10s. 6d.

ADDITIONS AND CORRECTIONS IN THE SEVENTH EDITION OF THE BOOK OF GENESIS. By S. R. Driver, D.D. *Demy 8vo.* 1s.

THE BOOK OF JOB. Edited by E. C. S. Gibson, D.D. *Second Edition. Demy 8vo.* 6s.

THE EPISTLE OF ST. JAMES. Edited with Introduction and Notes by R. J. Knowling, D.D. *Second Edition. Demy 8vo.* 6s.

PART III.—A SELECTION OF WORKS OF FICTION

Albanesi (E. Maria). SUSANNAH AND ONE OTHER. *Fourth Edition. Cr. 8vo.* 6s.
LOVE AND LOUISA. *Second Edition. Cr. 8vo.* 6s.
THE BROWN EYES OF MARY. *Third Edition. Cr. 8vo.* 6s.
I KNOW A MAIDEN. *Third Edition. Cr. 8vo.* 6s.
THE INVINCIBLE AMELIA; OR, THE POLITE ADVENTURESS. *Third Edition. Cr. 8vo.* 3s. 6d.
*THE GLAD HEART. *Second Edition. Cr. 8vo.* 6s.

Allerton (Mark). SUCH AND SUCH THINGS. *Cr. 8vo.* 6s.

Annesley (Maude). THIS DAY'S MADNESS. *Second Edition. Cr. 8vo.* 6s.

Bagot (Richard). A ROMAN MYSTERY. *Third Edition. Cr. 8vo.* 6s.
THE PASSPORT. *Fourth Edition. Cr. 8vo.* 6s.
TEMPTATION. *Fifth Edition. Cr. 8vo.* 6s.
ANTHONY CUTHBERT. *Fourth Edition. Cr. 8vo.* 6s.
LOVE'S PROXY. *Cr. 8vo.* 6s.
DONNA DIANA. *Second Edition. Cr. 8vo.* 6s.
CASTING OF NETS. *Twelfth Edition. Cr. 8vo.* 6s.

Bailey (H. C.). STORM AND TREASURE. *Second Edition. Cr. 8vo.* 6s.

Ball (Oona H.) (Barbara Burke). THEIR OXFORD YEAR. Illustrated. *Cr. 8vo.* 6s.

BARBARA GOES TO OXFORD. Illustrated. *Third Edition. Cr. 8vo.* 6s.
Baring-Gould (S.). ARMINELL. *Fifth Edition. Cr. 8vo.* 6s.
IN THE ROAR OF THE SEA. *Seventh Edition. Cr. 8vo.* 6s.
MARGERY OF QUETHER. *Third Edition. Cr. 8vo.* 6s.
THE QUEEN OF LOVE. *Fifth Edition. Cr. 8vo.* 6s.
JACQUETTA. *Third Edition. Cr. 8vo.* 6s.
KITTY ALONE. *Fifth Edition. Cr. 8vo.* 6s.
NOÉMI. Illustrated. *Fourth Edition. Cr. 8vo.* 6s.
THE BROOM-SQUIRE. Illustrated. *Fifth Edition. Cr. 8vo.* 6s.
DARTMOOR IDYLLS. *Cr. 8vo.* 6s.
GUAVAS THE TINNER. Illustrated. *Second Edition. Cr. 8vo.* 6s.
BLADYS OF THE STEWPONEY. Illustrated. *Second Edition. Cr. 8vo.* 6s.
PABO THE PRIEST. *Cr. 8vo.* 6s.
WINEFRED. Illustrated. *Second Edition. Cr. 8vo.* 6s.
ROYAL GEORGIE. Illustrated. *Cr. 8vo.* 6s.
CHRIS OF ALL SORTS. *Cr. 8vo.* 6s.
IN DEWISLAND. *Second Edition. Cr. 8vo.* 6s.
THE FROBISHERS. *Cr. 8vo.* 6s.
DOMITIA. Illustrated. *Second Edition. Cr. 8vo.* 6s.
MRS. CURGENVEN OF CURGENVEN. *Cr. 8vo.* 6s.

Barr (Robert). IN THE MIDST OF ALARMS. *Third Edition. Cr. 8vo.* 6s.
THE COUNTESS TEKLA. *Fifth Edition. Cr. 8vo.* 6s.

THE MUTABLE MANY. *Third Edition.* Cr. 8vo. 6s.

Begbie (Harold). THE CURIOUS AND DIVERTING ADVENTURES OF SIR JOHN SPARROW; or, THE PROGRESS OF AN OPEN MIND. *Second Edition.* Cr. 8vo. 6s.

Belloc (H.). EMMANUEL BURDEN, MERCHANT. Illustrated. *Second Edition.* Cr. 8vo. 6s.

A CHANGE IN THE CABINET. *Third Edition.* Cr. 8vo. 6s.

Benson (E. F.). DODO: A DETAIL OF THE DAY. *Sixteenth Edition.* Cr. 8vo. 6s.

Birmingham (George A.). THE BAD TIMES. *Second Edition.* Cr. 8vo. 6s.
SPANISH GOLD. *Fifth Edition.* Cr. 8vo. 6s.
THE SEARCH PARTY. *Fourth Edition.* Cr. 8vo. 6s.

Bowen (Marjorie). I WILL MAINTAIN. *Fourth Edition.* Cr. 8vo. 6s.

Bretherton (Ralph Harold). AN HONEST MAN. *Second Edition.* Cr. 8vo. 6s.

Capes (Bernard). WHY DID HE DO IT? *Third Edition.* Cr. 8vo. 6s.

Castle (Agnes and Egerton). FLOWER O' THE ORANGE, and Other Tales. *Third Edition.* Cr. 8vo. 6s.

Clifford (Mrs. W. K.). THE GETTING WELL OF DOROTHY. Illustrated. *Second Edition.* Cr. 8vo. 3s. 6d.

Conrad (Joseph). THE SECRET AGENT: A Simple Tale. *Fourth Ed.* Cr. 8vo. 6s.
A SET OF SIX. *Fourth Edition.* Cr. 8vo. 6s.

Corelli (Marie). A ROMANCE OF TWO WORLDS. *Thirtieth Ed.* Cr. 8vo. 6s.
VENDETTA. *Twenty-Eighth Edition.* Cr. 8vo. 6s.
THELMA. *Fortieth Ed.* Cr. 8vo. 6s.
ARDATH: THE STORY OF A DEAD SELF. *Nineteenth Edition.* Cr. 8vo. 6s.
THE SOUL OF LILITH. *Sixteenth Edition.* Cr. 8vo. 6s.
WORMWOOD. *Seventeenth Ed.* Cr. 8vo. 6s.
BARABBAS: A DREAM OF THE WORLD'S TRAGEDY. *Forty-Fourth Edition.* Cr. 8vo. 6s.
THE SORROWS OF SATAN. *Fifty-Sixth Edition.* Cr. 8vo. 6s.
THE MASTER CHRISTIAN. *Twelfth Edition.* 177th Thousand. Cr. 8vo. 6s.
TEMPORAL POWER: A STUDY IN SUPREMACY. *Second Edition.* 150th Thousand. Cr. 8vo. 6s.
GOD'S GOOD MAN: A SIMPLE LOVE STORY. *Fourteenth Edition.* 152nd Thousand. Cr. 8vo. 6s.
HOLY ORDERS: THE TRAGEDY OF A QUIET LIFE. *Second Edition.* 120th Thousand. Crown 8vo. 6s.
THE MIGHTY ATOM. *Twenty-eighth Edition.* Cr. 8vo. 6s.

BOY: a Sketch. *Eleventh Edition.* Cr. 8vo. 6s.
CAMEOS. *Thirteenth Edition.* Cr. 8vo. 6s.

Cotes (Mrs. Everard). See Duncan (Sara Jeannette).

Crockett (S. R.). LOCHINVAR. Illustrated. *Third Edition.* Cr. 8vo. 6s.
THE STANDARD BEARER. *Second Edition.* Cr. 8vo. 6s.

Croker (Mrs. B. M.). THE OLD CANTONMENT. Cr. 8vo. 6s.
JOHANNA. *Second Edition.* Cr. 8vo. 6s.
THE HAPPY VALLEY. *Fourth Edition.* Cr. 8vo. 6s.
A NINE DAYS' WONDER. *Third Edition.* Cr. 8vo. 6s.
PEGGY OF THE BARTONS. *Seventh Edition.* Cr. 8vo. 6s.
ANGEL. *Fifth Edition.* Cr. 8vo. 6s.
A STATE SECRET. *Third Edition.* Cr. 8vo. 3s. 6d.
KATHERINE THE ARROGANT. *Sixth Edition.* Cr. 8vo. 6s.

Cuthell (Edith E.). ONLY A GUARDROOM DOG. Illustrated. Cr. 8vo. 3s. 6d.

Dawson (Warrington). THE SCAR. *Second Edition.* Cr. 8vo. 6s.
THE SCOURGE. Cr. 8vo. 6s.

Douglas (Theo.). COUSIN HUGH. *Second Edition.* Cr. 8vo. 6s.

Doyle (A. Conan). ROUND THE RED LAMP. *Eleventh Edition.* Cr. 8vo. 6s.

Duncan (Sara Jeannette) (Mrs. Everard Cotes).
A VOYAGE OF CONSOLATION. Illustrated. *Third Edition.* Cr. 8vo. 6s.
COUSIN CINDERELLA. *Second Edition.* Cr. 8vo. 6s.
THE BURNT OFFERING. *Second Edition.* Cr. 8vo. 6s.

*Elliott (Robert). THE IMMORTAL CHARLATAN. Crown 8vo. 6s.

Fenn (G. Manville). SYD BELTON: or, The Boy who would not go to Sea. Illustrated. *Second Ed.* Cr. 8vo. 3s. 6d.

Findlater (J. H.). THE GREEN GRAVES OF BALGOWRIE. *Fifth Edition.* Cr. 8vo. 6s.
THE LADDER TO THE STARS. *Second Edition.* Cr. 8vo. 6s.

Findlater (Mary). A NARROW WAY. *Third Edition.* Cr. 8vo. 6s.
OVER THE HILLS. *Second Edition.* Cr. 8vo. 6s.
THE ROSE OF JOY. *Third Edition.* Cr. 8vo. 6s.
A BLIND BIRD'S NEST. Illustrated. *Second Edition.* Cr. 8vo. 6s.

Francis (M. E.). (Mrs. Francis Blundell). STEPPING WESTWARD. *Second Edition.* Cr. 8vo. 6s.

MARGERY O' THE MILL. *Third Edition*. *Cr. 8vo*. 6s.
HARDY-ON-THE-HILL. *Third Edition*. *Cr. 8vo*. 6s.
GALATEA OF THE WHEATFIELD. *Second Edition*. *Cr. 8vo*. 6s.

Fraser (Mrs. Hugh). THE SLAKING OF THE SWORD. *Second Edition*. *Cr. 8vo*. 6s.

GIANNELLA. *Second Edition*. *Cr. 8vo*. 6s.
IN THE SHADOW OF THE LORD. *Third Edition*. *Cr. 8vo*. 6s.

Fry (B. and C. B.). A MOTHER'S SON. *Fifth Edition*. *Cr. 8vo*. 6s.

Gerard (Louise). THE GOLDEN CENTIPEDE. *Third Edition*. *Cr. 8vo*. 6s.

Gibbs (Philip). THE SPIRIT OF REVOLT. *Second Edition*. *Cr. 8vo*. 6s.

Gissing (George). THE CROWN OF LIFE. *Cr. 8vo*. 6s.

Glendon (George). THE EMPEROR OF THE AIR. Illustrated. *Cr. 8vo*. 6s.

Hamilton (Cosmo). MRS. SKEFFINGTON. *Second Edition*. *Cr. 8vo*. 6s.

Harraden (Beatrice). IN VARYING MOODS. *Fourteenth Edition*. *Cr. 8vo*. 6s.
THE SCHOLAR'S DAUGHTER. *Fourth Edition*. *Cr. 8vo*. 6s.
HILDA STRAFFORD and THE REMITTANCE MAN. *Twelfth Ed*. *Cr. 8vo*. 6s.
INTERPLAY. *Fifth Edition*. *Cr. 8vo*. 6s.

Hichens (Robert). THE PROPHET OF BERKELEY SQUARE. *Second Edition*. *Cr. 8vo*. 6s.
TONGUES OF CONSCIENCE. *Third Edition*. *Cr. 8vo*. 6s.
FELIX. *Seventh Edition*. *Cr. 8vo*. 6s.
THE WOMAN WITH THE FAN. *Eighth Edition*. *Cr. 8vo*. 6s.
BYEWAYS. *Cr. 8vo*. 6s.
THE GARDEN OF ALLAH. *Nineteenth Edition*. *Cr. 8vo*. 6s.
THE BLACK SPANIEL. *Cr. 8vo*. 6s.
THE CALL OF THE BLOOD. *Seventh Edition*. *Cr. 8vo*. 6s.
BARBARY SHEEP. *Second Edition*. *Cr. 8vo*. 6s.

Hilliers (Ashton). THE MASTER-GIRL. Illustrated. *Second Edition*. *Cr. 8vo*. 6s.

Hope (Anthony). THE GOD IN THE CAR. *Eleventh Edition*. *Cr. 8vo*. 6s.
A CHANGE OF AIR. *Sixth Edition*. *Cr. 8vo*. 6s.
A MAN OF MARK. *Sixth Ed*. *Cr. 8vo*. 6s.
THE CHRONICLES OF COUNT ANTONIO. *Sixth Edition*. *Cr. 8vo*. 6s.
PHROSO. Illustrated. *Eighth Edition*. *Cr. 8vo*. 6s.
SIMON DALE. Illustrated. *Eighth Edition*. *Cr. 8vo*. 6s.
THE KING'S MIRROR. *Fifth Edition*. *Cr. 8vo*. 6s.

QUISANTE. *Fourth Edition*. *Cr. 8vo*. 6s.
THE DOLLY DIALOGUES. *Cr. 8vo*. 6s.
A SERVANT OF THE PUBLIC. Illustrated. *Fourth Edition*. *Cr. 8vo*. 6s.
TALES OF TWO PEOPLE. *Third Edition*. *Cr. 8vo*. 6s.
THE GREAT MISS DRIVER. *Fourth Edition*. *Cr. 8vo*. 6s.

Hueffer (Ford Maddox). AN ENGLISH GIRL: A ROMANCE. *Second Edition*. *Cr. 8vo*. 6s.
MR. APOLLO: A JUST POSSIBLE STORY. *Second Edition*. *Cr. 8vo*. 6s.

Hutten (Baroness von). THE HALO. *Fifth Edition*. *Cr. 8vo*. 6s.

Hyne (C. J. Cutcliffe). MR. HORROCKS, PURSER. *Fifth Edition*. *Cr. 8vo*. 6s.
PRINCE RUPERT, THE BUCCANEER. Illustrated. *Third Edition*. *Cr. 8vo*. 6s.

Jacobs (W. W.). MANY CARGOES. *Thirty-first Edition*. *Cr. 8vo*. 3s. 6d.
SEA URCHINS. *Sixteenth Edition*. *Cr. 8vo*. 3s. 6d.
A MASTER OF CRAFT. Illustrated. *Ninth Edition*. *Cr. 8vo*. 3s. 6d.
LIGHT FREIGHTS. Illustrated. *Eighth Edition*. *Cr. 8vo*. 3s. 6d.
THE SKIPPER'S WOOING. *Ninth Edition*. *Cr. 8vo*. 3s. 6d.
AT SUNWICH PORT. Illustrated. *Tenth Edition*. *Cr. 8vo*. 3s. 6d.
DIALSTONE LANE. Illustrated. *Seventh Edition*. *Cr. 8vo*. 3s. 6d.
ODD CRAFT. Illustrated. *Fourth Edition*. *Cr. 8vo*. 3s. 6d.
THE LADY OF THE BARGE. Illustrated. *Eighth Edition*. *Cr. 8vo*. 3s. 6d.
SALTHAVEN. Illustrated. *Second Edition*. *Cr. 8vo*. 3s. 6d.
SAILORS' KNOTS. Illustrated. *Fifth Edition*. *Cr. 8vo*. 3s. 6d.

James (Henry). THE SOFT SIDE. *Second Edition*. *Cr. 8vo*. 6s.
THE BETTER SORT. *Cr. 8vo*. 6s.
THE GOLDEN BOWL. *Third Edition*. *Cr. 8vo*. 6s.

Le Queux (William). THE HUNCHBACK OF WESTMINSTER. *Third Edition*. *Cr. 8vo*. 6s.
THE CLOSED BOOK. *Third Edition*. *Cr. 8vo*. 6s.
THE VALLEY OF THE SHADOW. Illustrated. *Third Edition*. *Cr. 8vo*. 6s.
BEHIND THE THRONE. *Third Edition*. *Cr. 8vo*. 6s.
THE CROOKED WAY. *Second Edition*. *Cr. 8vo*. 6s.

Lindsey (William). THE SEVERED MANTLE. *Cr. 8vo*. 6s.

London (Jack). WHITE FANG. *Seventh Edition*. *Cr. 8vo*. 6s.

Lubbock (Basil). DEEP SEA WARRIORS. Illustrated. *Third Edition. Cr. 8vo. 6s.*

Lucas (St John). THE FIRST ROUND. *Cr. 8vo. 6s.*

Lyall (Edna). DERRICK VAUGHAN, NOVELIST. *44th Thousand. Cr. 8vo. 3s. 6d.*

Maartens (Maarten). THE NEW RELIGION: A MODERN NOVEL. *Third Edition. Cr. 8vo. 6s.*
BROTHERS ALL; MORE STORIES OF DUTCH PEASANT LIFE. *Third Edition. Cr. 8vo. 6s.*
THE PRICE OF LIS DORIS. *Second Edition. Cr. 8vo. 6s.*

M'Carthy (Justin H.). THE DUKE'S MOTTO. *Fourth Edition. Cr. 8vo. 6s.*

Macnaughtan (S.). THE FORTUNE OF CHRISTINA M'NAB. *Fifth Edition. Cr. 8vo. 6s.*

Malet (Lucas). COLONEL ENDERBY'S WIFE. *Fourth Edition. Cr. 8vo. 6s.*
A COUNSEL OF PERFECTION. *Second Edition. Cr. 8vo. 6s.*
THE WAGES OF SIN. *Sixteenth Edition. Cr. 8vo. 6s.*
THE CARISSIMA. *Fifth Ed. Cr. 8vo. 6s.*
THE GATELESS BARRIER. *Fifth Edition. Cr. 8vo. 6s.*
THE HISTORY OF SIR RICHARD CALMADY. *Seventh Edition. Cr. 8vo. 6s.*

Mann (Mrs. M. E.). THE PARISH NURSE. *Fourth Edition. Cr. 8vo. 6s.*
A SHEAF OF CORN. *Second Edition. Cr. 8vo. 6s.*
THE HEART-SMITER. *Second Edition. Cr. 8vo. 6s.*
AVENGING CHILDREN. *Second Edition. Cr. 8vo. 6s.*

Marsh (Richard). THE COWARD BEHIND THE CURTAIN. *Cr. 8vo. 6s.*
THE SURPRISING HUSBAND. *Second Edition. Cr. 8vo. 6s.*
A ROYAL INDISCRETION. *Second Edition. Cr. 8vo. 6s.*
LIVE MEN'S SHOES. *Second Edition. Cr. 8vo. 6s.*

Marshall (Archibald). MANY JUNES. *Second Edition. Cr. 8vo. 6s.*
THE SQUIRE'S DAUGHTER. *Third Edition. Cr. 8vo. 6s.*

Mason (A. E. W.). CLEMENTINA. Illustrated. *Third Edition. Cr. 8vo. 6s.*

Maud (Constance). A DAUGHTER OF FRANCE. *Second Edition. Cr. 8vo. 6s.*

Maxwell (W. B.). VIVIEN. *Ninth Edition. Cr. 8vo. 6s.*
THE RAGGED MESSENGER. *Third Edition. Cr. 8vo. 6s.*
FABULOUS FANCIES. *Cr. 8vo. 6s.*

THE GUARDED FLAME. *Seventh Edition. Cr. 8vo. 6s.*
ODD LENGTHS. *Second Ed. Cr. 8vo. 6s.*
HILL RISE. *Fourth Edition. Cr. 8vo. 6s.*
THE COUNTESS OF MAYBURY: BETWEEN YOU AND I. *Fourth Edition. Cr. 8vo. 6s.*

Meade (L. T.). DRIFT. *Second Edition. Cr. 8vo. 6s.*
RESURGAM. *Second Edition. Cr. 8vo. 6s.*
VICTORY. *Cr. 8vo. 6s.*
A GIRL OF THE PEOPLE. Illustrated. *Fourth Edition. Cr. 8vo. 3s. 6d.*
HEPSY GIPSY. Illustrated. *Cr. 8vo. 2s. 6d.*
THE HONOURABLE MISS: A STORY OF AN OLD-FASHIONED TOWN. Illustrated. *Second Edition. Cr. 8vo. 3s. 6d.*

Mitford (Bertram). THE SIGN OF THE SPIDER. Illustrated. *Seventh Edition. Cr. 8vo. 3s. 6d.*

Molesworth (Mrs.). THE RED GRANGE. Illustrated. *Second Edition. Cr. 8vo. 3s. 6d.*

Montague (C. E.). A HIND LET LOOSE. *Third Edition. Cr. 8vo. 6s.*

Montgomery (K. L.). COLONEL KATE. *Second Edition. Cr. 8vo. 6s.*

Morrison (Arthur). TALES OF MEAN STREETS. *Seventh Edition. Cr. 8vo. 6s.*
A CHILD OF THE JAGO. *Fifth Edition. Cr. 8vo. 6s.*
THE HOLE IN THE WALL. *Fourth Edition. Cr. 8vo. 6s.*
DIVERS VANITIES. *Cr. 8vo. 6s.*

Nesbit (E.), (Mrs. H. Bland). THE RED HOUSE. Illustrated. *Fourth Edition. Cr. 8vo. 6s.*

Noble (Edward). LORDS OF THE SEA. *Third Edition. Cr. 8vo. 6s.*

Ollivant (Alfred). OWD BOB, THE GREY DOG OF KENMUIR. With a Frontispiece. *Eleventh Ed. Cr. 8vo. 6s.*

Oppenheim (E. Phillips). MASTER OF MEN. *Fourth Edition. Cr. 8vo. 6s.*

Oxenham (John). A WEAVER OF WEBS. Illustrated. *Fourth Ed. Cr. 8vo. 6s.*
THE GATE OF THE DESERT. *Fourth Edition. Cr. 8vo. 6s.*
PROFIT AND LOSS. *Fourth Edition. Cr. 8vo. 6s.*
THE LONG ROAD. *Fourth Edition. Cr. 8vo. 6s.*
THE SONG OF HYACINTH, AND OTHER STORIES. *Second Edition. Cr. 8vo. 6s.*
MY LADY OF SHADOWS. *Fourth Edition. Cr. 8vo. 6s.*

Pain (Barry). THE EXILES OF FALOO. *Crown 8vo. 6s.*

Parker (Gilbert). PIERRE AND HIS PEOPLE. *Sixth Edition. Cr. 8vo. 6s.*

FICTION

MRS. FALCHION. *Fifth Edition. Cr. 8vo. 6s.*
THE TRANSLATION OF A SAVAGE. *Third Edition. Cr. 8vo. 6s.*
THE TRAIL OF THE SWORD. Illustrated. *Tenth Edition. Cr. 8vo. 6s.*
WHEN VALMOND CAME TO PONTIAC: The Story of a Lost Napoleon. *Sixth Edition. Cr. 8vo. 6s.*
AN ADVENTURER OF THE NORTH. The Last Adventures of 'Pretty Pierre.' *Fourth Edition. Cr. 8vo. 6s.*
THE SEATS OF THE MIGHTY. Illustrated. *Sixteenth Edition. Cr. 8vo. 6s.*
THE BATTLE OF THE STRONG: a Romance of Two Kingdoms. Illustrated. *Sixth Edition. Cr. 8vo. 6s.*
THE POMP OF THE LAVILETTES. *Third Edition. Cr. 8vo. 3s. 6d.*
NORTHERN LIGHTS. *Fourth Edition. Cr. 8vo. 6s.*

Pasture (Mrs. Henry de la). THE TYRANT. *Fourth Edition. Cr. 8vo. 6s.*

Patterson (J. E.). WATCHERS BY THE SHORE. *Third Edition. Cr. 8vo. 6s.*

Pemberton (Max). THE FOOTSTEPS OF A THRONE. Illustrated. *Fourth Edition. Cr. 8vo. 6s.*
I CROWN THEE KING. Illustrated. *Cr. 8vo. 6s.*
LOVE THE HARVESTER: A STORY OF THE SHIRES. Illustrated. *Third Edition. Cr. 8vo. 3s. 6d.*
THE MYSTERY OF THE GREEN HEART. *Second Edition. Cr. 8vo. 6s.*

Phillpotts (Eden). LYING PROPHETS. *Third Edition. Cr. 8vo. 6s.*
CHILDREN OF THE MIST. *Fifth Edition. Cr. 8vo. 6s.*
THE HUMAN BOY. With a Frontispiece. *Seventh Edition. Cr. 8vo. 6s.*
SONS OF THE MORNING. *Second Edition. Cr. 8vo. 6s.*
THE RIVER. *Third Edition. Cr. 8vo. 6s.*
THE AMERICAN PRISONER. *Fourth Edition. Cr. 8vo. 6s.*
THE SECRET WOMAN. *Fourth Edition. Cr. 8vo. 6s.*
KNOCK AT A VENTURE. *Third Edition. Cr. 8vo. 6s.*
THE PORTREEVE. *Fourth Edition. Cr. 8vo. 6s.*
THE POACHER'S WIFE. *Second Edition. Cr. 8vo. 6s.*
THE STRIKING HOURS. *Second Edition. Cr. 8vo. 6s.*
THE FOLK AFIELD. *Crown 8vo. 6s.*

Pickthall (Marmaduke). SAID THE FISHERMAN. *Seventh Edition. Cr. 8vo. 6s.*

'Q' (A. T. Quiller Couch). THE WHITE WOLF. *Second Edition. Cr. 8vo. 6s.*
THE MAYOR OF TROY. *Fourth Edition. Cr. 8vo. 6s.*
MERRY-GARDEN AND OTHER STORIES. *Cr. 8vo. 6s.*

MAJOR VIGOUREUX. *Third Edition. Cr. 8vo. 6s.*

Querido (Israel). TOIL OF MEN. Translated by F. S. ARNOLD. *Cr. 8vo. 6s.*

Rawson (Maud Stepney). THE ENCHANTED GARDEN. *Fourth Edition. Cr. 8vo. 6s.*
THE EASY GO LUCKIES: OR, ONE WAY OF LIVING. *Second Edition. Cr. 8vo. 6s.*
HAPPINESS. *Second Edition. Cr. 8vo. 6s.*

Rhys (Grace). THE BRIDE. *Second Edition. Cr. 8vo. 6s.*

Ridge (W. Pett). ERB. *Second Edition. Cr. 8vo. 6s.*
A SON OF THE STATE. *Second Edition. Cr. 8vo. 3s. 6d.*
A BREAKER OF LAWS. *Cr. 8vo. 3s. 6d.*
MRS. GALER'S BUSINESS. Illustrated. *Second Edition. Cr. 8vo. 6s.*
THE WICKHAMSES. *Fourth Edition. Cr. 8vo. 6s.*
NAME OF GARLAND. *Third Edition. Cr. 8vo. 6s.*
SPLENDID BROTHER. *Fourth Edition. Cr. 8vo. 6s.*

Ritchie (Mrs. David G.). MAN AND THE CASSOCK. *Second Edition. Cr. 8vo. 6s.*

Roberts (C. G. D.). THE HEART OF THE ANCIENT WOOD. *Cr. 8vo. 3s. 6d.*

Robins (Elizabeth). THE CONVERT. *Third Edition. Cr. 8vo. 6s.*

Rosenkrantz (Baron Palle). THE MAGISTRATE'S OWN CASE. *Cr. 8vo. 6s.*

Russell (W. Clark). MY DANISH SWEETHEART. Illustrated. *Fifth Edition. Cr. 8vo. 6s.*
HIS ISLAND PRINCESS. Illustrated. *Second Edition. Cr. 8vo. 6s.*
ABANDONED. *Second Edition. Cr. 8vo. 6s.*
MASTER ROCKAFELLAR'S VOYAGE. Illustrated. *Fourth Edition. Cr. 8vo. 3s. 6d.*

Sandys (Sydney). JACK CARSTAIRS OF THE POWER HOUSE. Illustrated. *Second Edition. Cr. 8vo. 6s.*

Sergeant (Adeline). THE PASSION OF PAUL MARILLIER. *Cr. 8vo. 6s.*

*Shakespear (Olivia). UNCLE HILARY. *Cr. 8vo. 6s.*

Sidgwick (Mrs. Alfred). THE KINSMAN. Illustrated. *Third Edition. Cr. 8vo. 6s.*
THE SEVERINS. *Fourth Edition. Cr. 8vo. 6s.*

Stewart (Newton V.). A SON OF THE EMPEROR: BEING PASSAGES FROM THE LIFE OF ENZIO, KING OF SARDINIA AND CORSICA. *Cr. 8vo. 6s.*

Swayne (Martin Lutrell). THE BISHOP AND THE LADY. *Second Edition. Cr. 8vo. 6s.*

Thurston (E. Temple). MIRAGE. *Fourth Edition. Cr. 8vo. 6s.*

Underhill (Evelyn). THE COLUMN OF DUST. *Cr. 8vo. 6s.*

Vorst (Marie Van). THE SENTIMENTAL ADVENTURES OF JIMMY BULSTRODE. *Cr. 8vo. 6s.*
IN AMBUSH. *Second Edition. Cr. 8vo. 6s.*

Waineman (Paul). THE WIFE OF NICHOLAS FLEMING. *Cr. 8vo. 6s.*

Watson (H. B. Marriott). TWISTED EGLANTINE. Illustrated. *Third Edition. Cr. 8vo. 6s.*
THE HIGH TOBY. *Third Edition. Cr. 8vo. 6s.*
A MIDSUMMER DAY'S DREAM. *Third Edition. Cr. 8vo. 6s.*
THE CASTLE BY THE SEA. *Third Edition. Cr. 8vo. 6s.*
THE PRIVATEERS. Illustrated. *Second Edition. Cr. 8vo. 6s.*
A POPPY SHOW: BEING DIVERS AND DIVERSE TALES. *Cr. 8vo. 6s.*
THE FLOWER OF THE HEART. *Third Edition. Cr. 8vo. 6s.*

Webling (Peggy). THE STORY OF VIRGINIA PERFECT. *Third Edition. Cr. 8vo. 6s.*
*THE SPIRIT OF MIRTH. *Cr. 8vo. 6s.*

Wells (H. G.). THE SEA LADY. *Cr. 8vo. 6s.* Also *Medium 8vo. 6d.*

Weyman (Stanley). UNDER THE RED ROBE. Illustrated. *Twenty-Second Edition. Cr. 8vo. 6s.*

Whitby (Beatrice). THE RESULT OF AN ACCIDENT. *Second Edition. Cr. 8vo. 6s.*

White (Edmund). THE HEART OF HINDUSTAN. *Cr. 8vo. 6s.*

White (Percy). LOVE AND THE WISE MEN. *Third Edition. Cr. 8vo. 6s.*

Williamson (Mrs. C. N.). THE ADVENTURE OF PRINCESS SYLVIA. *Second Edition. Cr. 8vo. 6s.*
THE WOMAN WHO DARED. *Cr. 8vo. 6s.*
THE SEA COULD TELL. *Second Edition. Cr. 8vo. 6s.*
THE CASTLE OF THE SHADOWS. *Third Edition. Cr. 8vo. 6s.*
PAPA. *Cr. 8vo. 6s.*

Williamson (C. N. and A. M.). THE LIGHTNING CONDUCTOR: The Strange Adventures of a Motor Car. Illustrated. *Seventeenth Edition. Cr. 8vo. 6s.* Also *Cr. 8vo. 1s. net.*
THE PRINCESS PASSES: A Romance of a Motor. Illustrated. *Ninth Edition. Cr. 8vo. 6s.*
MY FRIEND THE CHAUFFEUR. Illustrated. *Tenth Edition. Cr. 8vo. 6s.*
LADY BETTY ACROSS THE WATER. *Tenth Edition. Cr. 8vo. 6s.*
THE CAR OF DESTINY AND ITS ERRAND IN SPAIN. Illustrated. *Fourth Edition. Cr. 8vo. 6s.*
THE BOTOR CHAPERON. Illustrated. *Sixth Edition. Cr. 8vo. 6s.*
SCARLET RUNNER. Illustrated. *Third Edition. Cr. 8vo. 6s.*
SET IN SILVER. Illustrated. *Third Edition. Cr. 8vo. 6s.*
LORD LOVELAND DISCOVERS AMERICA. *Second Edition. Cr. 8vo. 6s.*

Wyllarde (Dolf). THE PATHWAY OF THE PIONEER (Nous Autres). *Fourth Edition. Cr. 8vo. 6s.*

Books for Boys and Girls.

Illustrated. Crown 8vo. 3s. 6d.

THE GETTING WELL OF DOROTHY. By Mrs. W. K. Clifford. *Second Edition.*
ONLY A GUARD-ROOM DOG. By Edith E. Cuthell.
MASTER ROCKAFELLAR'S VOYAGE. By W. Clark Russell. *Fourth Edition.*
SYD BELTON: Or, the Boy who would not go to Sea. By G. Manville Fenn. *Second Edition.*
THE RED GRANGE. By Mrs. Molesworth. *Second Edition.*

A GIRL OF THE PEOPLE. By L. T. Meade. *Fourth Edition.*
HEPSY GIPSY. By L. T. Meade. *2s. 6d.*
THE HONOURABLE MISS. By L. T. Meade. *Second Edition.*
THERE WAS ONCE A PRINCE. By Mrs. M. E. Mann.
WHEN ARNOLD COMES HOME. By Mrs. M. E. Mann.

FICTION

The Novels of Alexandre Dumas.

Medium 8vo. Price 6d. Double Volumes, 1s.

ACTÉ.
THE ADVENTURES OF CAPTAIN PAMPHILE.
AMAURY.
THE BIRD OF FATE.
THE BLACK TULIP.
THE CASTLE OF EPPSTEIN.
CATHERINE BLUM.
CÉCILE.
THE CHATELET.
THE CHEVALIER D'HARMENTAL. (Double volume.)
CHICOT THE JESTER.
THE COMTE DE MONTGOMERY.
CONSCIENCE.
THE CONVICT'S SON.
THE CORSICAN BROTHERS; and OTHO THE ARCHER.
CROP-EARED JACQUOT.
DOM GORENFLOT.
THE FATAL COMBAT.
THE FENCING MASTER.
FERNANDE.
GABRIEL LAMBERT.
GEORGES.
THE GREAT MASSACRE.
HENRI DE NAVARRE.
HÉLÈNE DE CHAVERNY.

THE HOROSCOPE.
LOUISE DE LA VALLIÈRE. (Double volume.)
THE MAN IN THE IRON MASK. (Double volume.)
MAÎTRE ADAM.
THE MOUTH OF HELL.
NANON. (Double volume.)
OLYMPIA.
PAULINE; PASCAL BRUNO; and BONTEKOE.
PÈRE LA RUINE.
THE PRINCE OF THIEVES.
THE REMINISCENCES OF ANTONY.
ROBIN HOOD.
SAMUEL GELB.
THE SNOWBALL AND THE SULTANETTA.
SYLVANDIRE.
THE TAKING OF CALAIS.
TALES OF THE SUPERNATURAL.
TALES OF STRANGE ADVENTURE.
TALES OF TERROR.
THE THREE MUSKETEERS. (Double volume.)
THE TRAGEDY OF NANTES.
TWENTY YEARS AFTER. (Double volume.)
THE WILD-DUCK SHOOTER.
THE WOLF-LEADER.

Methuen's Sixpenny Books.

Medium 8vo.

Albanesi (E. Maria). LOVE AND LOUISA.
I KNOW A MAIDEN.
Anstey (F.). A BAYARD OF BENGAL.
Austen (J.). PRIDE AND PREJUDICE.
Bagot (Richard). A ROMAN MYSTERY.
CASTING OF NETS.
DONNA DIANA.
Balfour (Andrew). BY STROKE OF SWORD.

Baring-Gould (S.). FURZE BLOOM.
CHEAP JACK ZITA.
KITTY ALONE.
URITH.
THE BROOM SQUIRE.
IN THE ROAR OF THE SEA.
NOÉMI.
A BOOK OF FAIRY TALES. Illustrated.
LITTLE TU'PENNY.
WINEFRED.
THE FROBISHERS.
THE QUEEN OF LOVE.

ARMINELL.
BLADYS OF THE STEWPONEY.

Barr (Robert). JENNIE BAXTER.
IN THE MIDST OF ALARMS.
THE COUNTESS TEKLA.
THE MUTABLE MANY.

Benson (E. F.). DODO.
THE VINTAGE.

Brontë (Charlotte). SHIRLEY.

Brownell (C. L.). THE HEART OF JAPAN.

Burton (J. Bloundelle). ACROSS THE SALT SEAS.

Caffyn (Mrs.). ANNE MAULEVERER.

Capes (Bernard). THE LAKE OF WINE.

Clifford (Mrs. W. K.). A FLASH OF SUMMER.
MRS. KEITH'S CRIME.

Corbett (Julian). A BUSINESS IN GREAT WATERS.

Croker (Mrs. B. M.). ANGEL.
A STATE SECRET.
'PEGGY OF THE BARTONS.
JOHANNA.

Dante (Alighieri). THE DIVINE COMEDY (Cary).

Doyle (A. Conan). ROUND THE RED LAMP.

Duncan (Sara Jeannette). A VOYAGE OF CONSOLATION.
THOSE DELIGHTFUL AMERICANS.

Eliot (George). THE MILL ON THE FLOSS.

Findlater (Jane H.). THE GREEN GRAVES OF BALGOWRIE.

Gallon (Tom). RICKERBY'S FOLLY.

Gaskell (Mrs.). CRANFORD.
MARY BARTON.
NORTH AND SOUTH.

Gerard (Dorothea). HOLY MATRIMONY.
THE CONQUEST OF LONDON.
MADE OF MONEY.

Gissing (G.). THE TOWN TRAVELLER.
THE CROWN OF LIFE.

Glanville (Ernest). THE INCA'S TREASURE.
THE KLOOF BRIDE.

Gleig (Charles). BUNTER'S CRUISE.

Grimm (The Brothers). GRIMM'S FAIRY TALES.

Hope (Anthony). A MAN OF MARK.
A CHANGE OF AIR.
THE CHRONICLES OF COUNT ANTONIO.
PHROSO.
THE DOLLY DIALOGUES.

Hornung (E. W.). DEAD MEN TELL NO TALES.

Ingraham (J. H.). THE THRONE OF DAVID.

Le Queux (W.). THE HUNCHBACK OF WESTMINSTER.

Levett-Yeats (S. K.). THE TRAITOR'S WAY.
ORRAIN.

Linton (E. Lynn). THE TRUE HISTORY OF JOSHUA DAVIDSON.

Lyall (Edna). DERRICK VAUGHAN.

Malet (Lucas). THE CARISSIMA.
A COUNSEL OF PERFECTION.

Mann (Mrs. M. E.). MRS. PETER HOWARD.
A LOST ESTATE.
THE CEDAR STAR.
ONE ANOTHER'S BURDENS.
THE PATTEN EXPERIMENT.
A WINTER'S TALE.

Marchmont (A. W.). MISER HOADLEY'S SECRET.
A MOMENT'S ERROR.

Marryat (Captain). PETER SIMPLE.
JACOB FAITHFUL.

March (Richard). A METAMORPHOSIS.
THE TWICKENHAM PEERAGE.
THE GODDESS.
THE JOSS.

Mason (A. E. W.). CLEMENTINA.

Mathers (Helen). HONEY.
GRIFF OF GRIFFITHSCOURT.
SAM'S SWEETHEART.
THE FERRYMAN.

Meade (Mrs. L. T.). DRIFT.

Miller (Esther). LIVING LIES.

Mitford (Bertram). THE SIGN OF THE SPIDER.

Montresor (F. F.). THE ALIEN.

FICTION

Morrison (Arthur). THE HOLE IN THE WALL.

Nesbit (E.). THE RED HOUSE.

Morris (W. E.). HIS GRACE.
GILES INGILBY.
THE CREDIT OF THE COUNTY.
LORD LEONARD THE LUCKLESS.
MATTHEW AUSTEN.
CLARISSA FURIOSA.

Oliphant (Mrs.). THE LADY'S WALK.
SIR ROBERT'S FORTUNE.
THE PRODIGALS.
THE TWO MARYS.

Oppenheim (E. P.). MASTER OF MEN.

Parker (Gilbert). THE POMP OF THE LAVILETTES.
WHEN VALMOND CAME TO PONTIAC.
THE TRAIL OF THE SWORD.

Pemberton (Max). THE FOOTSTEPS OF A THRONE.
I CROWN THEE KING.

Phillpotts (Eden). THE HUMAN BOY.
CHILDREN OF THE MIST.
THE POACHER'S WIFE.
THE RIVER.

'Q' (A. T. Quiller Couch). THE WHITE WOLF.

Ridge (W. Pett). A SON OF THE STATE.
LOST PROPERTY.
GEORGE and THE GENERAL.

ERB.

Russell (W. Clark). ABANDONED.
A MARRIAGE AT SEA.
MY DANISH SWEETHEART.
HIS ISLAND PRINCESS.

Sergeant (Adeline). THE MASTER OF BEECHWOOD.
BALBARA'S MONEY.
THE YELLOW DIAMOND.
THE LOVE THAT OVERCAME.

Sidgwick (Mrs. Alfred). THE KINSMAN.

Surtees (R. S.). HANDLEY CROSS.
MR. SPONGE'S SPORTING TOUR.
ASK MAMMA.

Walford (Mrs. L. B.). MR. SMITH.
COUSINS.
THE BABY'S GRANDMOTHER.
TROUBLESOME DAUGHTERS.

Wallace (General Lew). BEN-HUR.
THE FAIR GOD.

Watson (H. B. Marriott). THE ADVENTURERS.
*CAPTAIN FORTUNE.

Weekes (A. B.). PRISONERS OF WAR.

Wells (H. G.). THE SEA LADY.

White (Percy). A PASSIONATE PILGRIM.

Lightning Source UK Ltd.
Milton Keynes UK
UKHW010005160219
337399UK00011B/902/P